CARETAKER OF THE DEAD

The American Funeral Director

Caretaker of the Dead

THE AMERICAN FUNERAL DIRECTOR

By Vanderlyn R. Pine

IRVINGTON PUBLISHERS, INC., New York

Halsted Press Division of
JOHN WILEY & SONS
NEW YORK   LONDON   TORONTO   SYDNEY

Copyright © 1975 by Irvington Publishers, Inc.

Distributed by Halsted Press Division of
John Wiley & Sons, New York.

Library of Congress Cataloging in Publication Data

Pine, Vanderlyn R
  Caretaker of the dead.

  Bibliography: p.
  Includes index.
  1. Funeral rites and ceremonies—United States
2. Undertakers and undertaking—United States. I. Title
GT3203.P56   393.1'023   75-8687
ISBN 0-470-68992-7

Printed in the United States of America

Contents

Acknowledgments

The original preparation of this book was greatly facilitated by the support of a National Institutes of Health Fellowship, No. 1 F01 MH 3812401A1, from the National Institute of Mental Health.

In addition, I have been fortunate in having been assisted in the writing of this book by many people. I would like to express my deep appreciation to all of them. There are a few individuals who deserve special thanks, and it is to them that the following remarks are addressed.

I would like to thank sociologists Robert Bierstedt, James A. Davis, Irwin Goffman, Herbert Menzel, and Derek Phillips. Their assistance has been considerable because of specific comments on earlier drafts. They provided the essential food for thought for many aspects which only they and I will recognize or fully appreciate. The final version received invaluable suggestions, recommendations, and comments from Robert Fulton, Edgar Jackson, and Robert C. Slater. To all of them, I am very grateful.

Of course, without the aid, cooperation, and understanding of a number of funeral directors, especially the staffs of the Community Funeral Home and Cosmopolitan Funeral Home, all of my thanks would be not only unnecessary but impossible. To most of them, I promised anonymity and can offer only my sincere gratitude. I would like to thank the officers of the National Funeral Directors Association for their cooperation in carrying out some of the research. I owe a debt of special appreciation to Howard C. Raether, Executive Director of NFDA. His astute observations and perceptive comments about funerals and funeral directors provided me with an invaluable perspective of American funeral directing.

I have had the extreme good fortune of having an extraordinarily capable secretarial assistant. A special thank you goes to Kathy Deitrich Williams, who has hacked her way through so many versions of this book that she knows much of it by heart. In addition, she provided useful substantive insights, helpful comments, and moral support.

My special appreciation goes to my longtime friend, colleague and wife, Patricia P. Pine, for her specific and helpful suggestions on this and earlier drafts; to my mother, Marion R. Pine, for her editorial commentary on earlier versions and careful editing of the final draft; and to my colleague Kenneth T. Skelton, for his editorial criticism and suggestions on an earlier version. A note of thanks goes to Peggy Pine, whose patience and understanding through earlier versions of this book are gratefully acknowledged. Finally, I would like to thank my three sons, Gordon, Brian, and Daniel, who, only at the very end, asked, "When are you going to finish your book?"

CARETAKER OF THE DEAD

The American Funeral Director

Introduction:
The Study of Death

There are a number of personal and professional interests which guided me in the selection of a study on the subject of death. Members of my family have been funeral directors for the last five generations, operating a funeral home in the same community for more than 75 years. As a result, my interest in death-related behavior stems from an accumulation of experiences spanning not just my own, but several lifetimes. How to treat such experiences has been problematic for a number of sociologists. For instance, Max Weber's experiences in the Prussian Army's bureaucracy considerably influenced his work; Robert Park was never able to separate himself from the journalist that he was before becoming a sociologist; Howard Becker, the sociologist, is also Howard Becker, the jazz musician.[1] Thus, I realize that many of my notions are subjective assessments concerning the behavior I am attempting to clarify; however, I consider such subjective thought to be the basis for a pertinent brand of sociology.

The mere living of experiences, however, is not enough to qualify one's endeavors as analytical sociology. Furthermore, even though such experiences are an important element of all social research, seldom are they explicated as such. One attempt to do so is Phillip Hammond's *Sociologists At Work*, in which ten sociologists portray their own research activities as they were experienced during several specific investigations. Their essays provide research chronicles of their investigations, describing in considerable detail the ways in which they actually thought, felt, and acted during the process of their research. My discussion of the research process of this study is an effort to provide such a chronicle and to give an accurate description of why and how this study came about.

My exposure to funeral directing began as a child. One of the things I most consistently was expected to remember was to "behave" because I was a direct reflection upon the funeral home in the community, and it is important to have a "good image." Often, my nicknames were "Digger" or "Pine Box," and I have heard, "You'll be the last one to let me down," and, "People are just dying to ride in your car," more times than I can or wish to count. As a child I had a firm conviction that I would never be a funeral director. I do not remember having any particular aversion to death, but I definitely did not want to be a funeral director.

I changed my mind during my sophomore year at Dartmouth College and told my parents that I would like to join in the operation of the family funeral home after completing college. Three days later, my father died. After his death, I left college to "take over" the funeral home. I was an absolute neophyte in the field. I had only the superficial impressions that had been gathered as a child with no interest in funeral service. Never had I spoken to my father about the operation of the funeral home or about his attitudes toward death and funerals.

After a year of embalming school, I went to work as an apprentice for a very large funeral firm in New York City. In a few months I completed the state requirements for licensing and returned to our funeral home and became a "full-fledged" funeral director. As a new young funeral director (home to "run the funeral home"), I became involved in many community activities. For instance, I was active in such organizations as the Lions and Rotary Clubs, participated in such drives as the County Heart Fund and the Community Chest, was on the governing board of a large Protestant church, and acted as the master of ceremonies at a number of community shindigs. During these years I sporadically took college courses, always with the hope that someday I would return to school. After about ten years, several circumstances combined to enable me to do so, and I reentered Dartmouth as a full-time student.

My initial interest in funerary behavior, which had arisen because of my background and life experiences, was concerned primarily with both theoretical and practical implications of some rather common matters. For example, I was interested in cross cultural funeral practices largely because, based on everyday observations, I believed that there are certain essential similarities in them.[2] Also, my everyday experiences led me to believe that reactions to death are to a great extent dependent upon something like the "human net worth" of the dead person and his bereaved family as much as they are upon such psychological factors as guilt feelings and repression. Furthermore, it seemed to me that such net worth was somehow connected to social status and the community evaluation of individuals. Such sociological phenomena interested me as topics for consideration; however, the ways in which to examine them are by no means a simple matter. Thus, I was confronted not with the problem of knowing what I wanted to study but of knowing how to do so.

At about this stage of the game, I discovered empirical sociology via several people whose efforts and interests were quite diverse. The first was Edmund Meyers, who helped me prepare an attitude questionnaire which was sent to a sample of funeral directors. The second was Ronald Maris, in whose course I carried out an analysis of some suicide data. In both efforts I attempted to incorporate some "honest-to-goodness sociology" as well as to try to get at what seemed to be relevant and important matters from my having been a funeral director.

Next, I was introduced to multivariate analysis by Robert Sokol. In a course in social stratification, I examined funeral home records for a five-year period and carried out an analysis of funeral expenditure and social status. Later, I decided to go a bit further and examine the data in a more extensive study. This cost-of-dying project became a thesis in which I did a more detailed analysis of high and low funeral expenditure, attempting to be as objective as possible.

After receiving a Bachelor of Arts degree, I entered New York University for graduate study. In a course with Herbert Menzel, I prepared a theoretical paper on institutionalized communication about death.[3] This paper gave rise to a survey research project investigating the communication processes about dying and death. Also during the year, Derek Phillips and I prepared a paper about the relationship between funeral expenditure and social status.[4]

Returning to Dartmouth as a special graduate student, I became a research and teaching assistant for James A. Davis. During that Fall, a strange set of events combined to expose me to a different form of social research. There was a major airplane crash just outside of Hanover, N.H. The local funeral director asked if I would help him because "thirty-two people have been killed and I can't do everything by myself." I spent a week working with him as a funeral director. I was able to investigate many facets of the aftermath that would have been inaccessible to other social researchers. As a result of this participant observation and under the guidance of Bernard E. Segal, I prepared a paper that later became my Master's thesis.[5]

At the end of that year, I received a National Institute of Health, Public Health Service Pre-Doctoral Research Fellowship and returned to New York University to complete my doctoral requirements. Derek Phillips agreed to be my advisor for the fellowship period as well as for my dissertation, and we began to have many long talks about this research. For several years, I had been gathering as much information about death-related behavior as possible, including both my own work and that of other investigators.

For many years, death has been a popular research subject and the theme of numerous scholarly works for disciplines such as anthropology, history, medicine, psychiatry, psychology, and religion.[6] Until recently, the study of death has been neglected from the sociological viewpoint; however, there is a growing body of literature emphasizing an increasing interest in death from this perspective.[7]

Among the recent sociological studies there are four major approaches. First, Fox (1959), Glaser and Strauss (1965), Kubler-Ross (1969), Fulton and Fulton (1971), Simmons, Fulton, and Fulton (1972), Brim, Freeman, Levine, and Scotch (1970), and Pine (1972b and c, 1973) are concerned with the process of dying as a social phenomenon, focusing on the social and psychological problems of dying people. These studies assess death from the viewpoint of the dying person, family, friends, doctors, nurses, and others.

Second, Kephart (1950), Fulton (1961), Salomone (1967), Sudnow (1967b), and Pine (1969e) focus their attention on the functionaries of death, such as clergy, physicians, nurses, morgue attendants, and funeral directors. This approach examines such things as the role of the funeral director, the role conflict between clergy and funeral directors, and the public's orientation toward funerals and attitudes toward the funeral director.

Third, Parsons (1963), Fulton (1963 and 1967), Fulton and Fulton (1971), Simmons, Fulton, and Fulton (1972), Gorer (1965), Blauner (1966), Pine and Phillips (1970), and Pine (1972a) write about reactions to the occurrence of death. These studies include examinations of the impact of death in society, the handling of death, and the cost of dying. As Parsons (1963, p. 65) explains, such studies are valuable because a society's mortuary customs and practices are very obvious phenomena which merit attention for the light they may throw on many of the basic problems and values of that society.

Fourth, Bowman (1959), Harmer (1963), Mitford (1963), Morgan (1973), and others have written sociological and semisociological material criticizing funeral service practitioners and various aspects of the American funeral. Their work focuses on what they claim is the "commercialization" of funeral practices, funeral directors' efforts to "disguise" death through such things as restoration, the setting of the funeral home, the use of argot, the form of present-day funeral practices, and similar matters.

Despite these studies, Sudnow (1967, p. 3) points out that his work alone attempts to describe how death actually is handled in an everyday setting. Among other things, he found that access to and observation of death-related behavior is very difficult. Along similar lines, Kephart (1950, p. 637) argues that empirical evidence of actual mortuary customs may be obtained by investigating funeral directors; but he, too, emphasizes that access is a major problem.

These works produced numerous findings, two of which now became important guides for my research.

First, the relevant behavior of funeral directors is easily observable because their practice is limited primarily to the funeral home. Notably, funeral directors seldom go out of their funeral establishments to provide services. This is unlike medicine in which there are physicians who make house calls or law in which there are attorneys who go to courts.

Second, there is evidence of ambivalence toward funeral directors and confusion concerning their occupational and social status. This raises questions about what gives rise to such feelings.

I decided to examine the behavior of funeral directors in their everyday activities in hopes of clarifying not just their occupational patterns but to answer the questions about ambivalence and confusion. At this time and with the advice of Eliot Freidson, I began a case study research project of two diverse funeral homes. I arranged to carry out part of the study at a fairly large funeral home with an obviously complex organizational structure. At the same time, I made a similar plan with a somewhat smaller funeral home with a decidedly simple organizational structure.

The exact methods I used were developed over time, did not emerge well-formulated in the research until it was practically completed, and included multiple operations.* Moreover, they constantly underwent modifications and took on new orientations. There were two sources of continuous influence, my background as a funeral director and my contact with the sociologists whom I have mentioned. It was through the interaction of these two sources that ideas developed into research vehicles and then back to ideas again.

Among the multiple methods which I finally employed are: autobiographical material, participant observation, interviews with bereaved families and with funeral directors, and extensive field observations in and around a number of funeral homes.

In order to develop autobiographical material, I made detailed notes of "random" recollections. These bits of information were collected any time something came to mind regarding funeral-related behavior. Thus, I "looked back" in time and reexamined events and activities that had occurred in the past. Even though these have been reconstructed many times over in the mind's eye,[9] it is still possible to get an idea of what was going on at the time and record it as a bit of information.[10]

Another important part of the research methods was unobtrusive participant observation.[11] I personally played the role of moderately participating observer in both funeral homes.[12] As such, I carried out certain requested activities in order not to be rejected from my observation post, but I was careful not to be classed as a complete participant by the funeral directors. That is, I moved in the presence of funeral personnel conscious of my observer role.

As observations continued, I hope that my presence exerted less and less effect on their behavior. In one sense, this is an unrealistic expectation, for it is absurd to assume that the presence of any human being does not modify behavior to some extent. Even so, I believe that by developing characteristics similar to the "woodwork," my presence did not seriously bias the observations.

To augment the use of autobiographical material and participant observation, I also conducted interviews.[13] I informally interviewed about 50 funeral directors in the course of my research in both funeral homes. In addition, I carried out more detailed interviews with about 25 others.

Another kind of interviewing involved about 200 interviews with those recently bereaved. In this regard, I considered whoever arranged for funerals as the unit of observation, and I interviewed these recently bereaved survivors while they were making funeral arrangements.[14]

At both firms, I spent many hours on all shifts, talking, observing, interviewing, and participating in the activities of the funeral directors. I kept an extensive diary and notes throughout the research process. In an effort to reduce the bias of my observations and to increase the validity and generality of my findings, and because gaining access was no problem, I carried out additional observations at two other funeral firms.[15] The first has characteristics very similar to the simply organized funeral home. The second is a funeral home located in a large city quite similar to the complexly organized funeral home.

The data retrieval process for field observations is always a difficult matter.[16] In order to make use of such observations, I developed a series of index and filing systems which gave rise to several sets of distributions of activities, events, and observations that were subsequently used in a descriptive fashion.

It is important that the descriptive materials were my own choice;

however, my intentions throughout were to use those observations which occurred most commonly so as to make my descriptions as accurate as possible. Such data have proven problematic for a number of sociologists. This leads to what I believe to be an important aspect of all sociological research. Whatever their characteristics, data are continuously modified by the human mind. What on the one hand may seem to be hard data well-gathered and coded by one researcher may quite possibly be seen by another researcher as something less than concrete. As a matter of fact, two people viewing the same phenomenon may see it in two completely different fashions. Thus, it is important to point out that my use of these data is based on my own notions of what is important, rather than upon some higher source of guidance.[17]

While I was preparing working papers to help clarify my location in the research process, something happened that considerably altered my efforts. I spent several days at the annual meeting of the National Funeral Directors Association. This gave me a chance to make observations of people out of their funeral homes. I became aware that there were major differences between those with a bureaucratic orientation and those with a personal service orientation. This revelation should not have come as any great surprise for several reasons. Derek Phillips and I had talked extensively about the ways in which an organization influences the individuals within it, especially in terms of how the individual performs as an actor on the stage of that organization. Furthermore, the personal service model dominates the philosophy and orientation of funeral directors, and it is an essential element of their education and training. Most of the occupational literature indicates that funeral directing's most important job is that of providing professional services at the time of death.

Even though this notion of personal service exists, the bureaucratic model is the organizational characteristic in certain funeral home operations. My research post in the two funeral homes enabled me to examine funeral directing from the two perspectives: One organized solely around the providing of professional personal services, and the other organized around the providing of bureaucratic services. Thus, I became concerned with determining the ways in which funeral directors perform as service practitioners and with the influence of the type of organization peculiar to the funeral home in which they work.

The awareness of the differences between bureaucrats and professionals only clarified the focus of the study; however, it did not foster the analysis without more conceptual development. The main problems were to decide what aspects of funeral behavior I should examine. Once this decision had been made, I had to devise a means of analysis. As the research continued and I talked to more funeral directors, I became aware that most of them assess their occupation in terms of rather specific models. This led to the development of the concept of occupational models.

At this time, I had to hazard a definition of occupational models, realizing full well that it would be useful only as a guide to the research and that it might not be the best one for other purposes. I understand an occupational model to be that constellation of beliefs, notions, and concepts which everyday actors construct regarding the various occupations with which they are familiar in their own society.

After developing my conception of the two occupational models and the disruptive potential between them, it was necessary to delineate how funeral directors perform in understandable terms. At this point, I decided to utilize some of the concepts developed by Erving Goffman (1959) regarding the performing characteristics of individuals acting in the presence of others.

This book provides detailed case studies of the everyday behavior of American funeral directors and the actual mortuary customs and practices which comprise the American way of death. It analyzes some of the problematic aspects of the occupation of funeral directing by examining the differences between the typical conceptions of personal service occupations and of bureaucratic occupations. This study gives a glimpse of the influence that such differences may have for people in jobs with possible multiple orientations and definitions; and thus, it is also pertinent to other fields such as law, medicine, nursing, and social service,

The idea of "typical conceptions" exists on the practical, everyday level. All people construct models of social phenomena and continuously use them to orient personal actions and behavior in a given situation. We help define a situation through the possession of common-sense conceptions of personally held models. The individual defines these models for himself; however, since they are formed because of social forces, they tend to be consistent within any given society. Even so, each individual makes his own subjective interpretation of the situation utilizing the models he possesses at a given time.

There are distinctions between "personal servers" and "bureaucrats" which are more or less obvious when we enter the presence of either. Thus, on the everyday level, we have little difficulty recognizing the differences between the two when we confront them. It makes sense that in order to classify such occupations, we use everyday typical models of personal service occupations compared to bureaucratic occupations.

It is the difference between the models of personal service versus bureaucracy and the perception of everyday occupational behavior which delineated the research problem. My objective became the analytical examination of the relationship between the typical conceptions for servants and bureaucrats on the basis of my investigation of the everyday behavior of funeral directors.

Both theoretical and practical interests raise the following research questions. What common techniques do funeral directors use to sustain and control impressions concerning their occupational activities? What common contingencies are associated with the use of these techniques? How are these techniques affected by the organization of the service practice? What influence on impression sustenance and control does it make whether the funeral director is a solo service practitioner or a member of a bureaucratically organized practice? How do funeral directors perceive their occupation? How do they perceive themselves as individual practitioners within that occupation? This book was written in an attempt to answer these questions.

The method of analysis has been a process of continuous conceptual development, including personal insights, sudden revelations, a concern with the past, and an overfamiliarity with the subject matter. Throughout, I have attempted to be true to the data. Several funeral directors as well as a few people not connected with funeral service have read portions of the book and have had reactions which lead me to believe that the study is essentially valid. As a check on whether or not the data are generalizable, I have had conversations with numerous funeral directors, and I believe that the study is largely accurate. My conviction about how valid and generalizable this study is may be a result of the fact that the selection of which findings to report was mine, and I selected those which were most believable to me.

Notes

1. A useful question to ask sociologists is what their "maiden occupation" may have been, for it is likely that many of their sociological enterprises stem directly from such previous experiences.

2. This interest led to my paper "Comparative Funeral Practices," *Practical Anthropology* (March-April, 1969), pp. 49-62. Notably, funeral practices do possess similiarities; however, the functionaries who implement them differ from society to society.

3. This led to my paper "Institutionalized Communication About Dying and Death," *Journal of Thanatology* (forthcoming 1975).

4. Vanderlyn R. Pine and Derek L. Phillips, "The Cost of Dying: A Sociological Analysis of Funeral Expenditure," *Social Problems* (Winter, 1970), pp. 405-17.

5. This also led to my paper "Grief Work and Dirty Work: The Aftermath of an Aircrash," given at the annual meeting of the Eastern Sociological Society. New York, April 18, 1970 and in *Omega*, 5 (Winter, 1974).

6. Among the representative works in these fields are Emile Durkheim, *Suicide*, New York: The Free Press, 1966; Herman Feifel (ed.), *The Meaning of*

Death. New York: McGraw-Hill, 1959; Raymond Firth, *Elements of Social Organization.* Boston: Beacon Press, 1964; Jack Goody, *Death, Property and the Ancestors.* Stanford: Stanford University Press, 1962; Earl A. Grollman, *Concerning Death: A Practical Guide for the Living.* Boston: Beacon Press, 1974; Robert Habenstein and William Lamers, *Funeral Customs the World Over.* Milwaukee: Bulfin Printers, 1960; Habenstein and Lamers, *The History of American Funeral Directing.* Milwaukee: Bulfin Printers, 1955; David Hendin, *Death As A Fact Of Life.* New York: W. W. Norton & Company, Inc., 1973; Robert Hertz, *Death and the Right Hand.* Glencoe: The Free Press, 1960; Paul Irion, *The Funeral and the Mourners.* New York: Abingdon Press, 1954; Edgar M. Jackson, *Understanding Grief.* New York: Abingdon Press, 1957; Robert Kastenbaum and Ruth Aisenberg, *The Psychology of Death.* New York: Springer Publishing Company, Inc., 1972; Elizabeth Kubler-Ross, *On Death and Dying.* London: The Macmillan Company, 1969; Robert Jay Lifton, *Home From The War.* New York: Simon and Schuster, 1973; Bronislaw Malinowski, *Magic, Science and Religion.* Garden City, New York: Doubleday and Company, 1948; Colin Murray Parkes, *Bereavement: Studies of Grief in Adult Life.* New York: International Universities Press, Inc., 1972; Arnold Van Gennep, *The Rites of Passage.* Chicago: University of Chicago Press, 1960; Avery D. Weisman, *On Dying and Denying: A Psychiatric Study of Terminality.* New York: Behavioral Publications, Inc., 1972.

7. For three theoretical treatments from this perspective see William Faunce and Robert Fulton, "The Sociology of Death: A Neglected Area of Research," *Social Forces,* 36 (March, 1958), pp. 205-209; Robert Fulton, *Death and Identity.* New York: John Wiley and Sons, Inc., 1965; and Vanderlyn R. Pine, "The Sociology of Death," *The American Funeral Director,* 92 (June, 1969), pp. 29-30, 44.

8. For a full treatment of this concept see Eugene J. Webb, et. al., *Unobtrusive Measures: Nonreactive Research in the Social Sciences.* Chicago: Rand McNally & Co., 1966.

9. For a discussion of this process see George H. Mead, *Mind, Self and Society from the Standpoint of a Social Behaviorist.* Chicago: University of Chicago Press, 1934.

10. Taken individually, such bits of information are nothing more than episodic reflections about personal assessments of observed behavior. By amassing a large number of such bits, I developed a filing system of episodic experiences. Interestingly, a distribution of common and uncommon events has emerged, and I suspect that if arduously carried out, this technique might result in a distribution with "normal" characteristics. At this time my point is not to develop a statistical approach to subjective material, but rather to indicate the way in which I went about the process of recalling what it was like to be a funeral director. For a similar discussion about such an approach see Howard S. Becker, "Problems of Inference and Proof in Participant Observation," *American Sociological Review,* 23 (1958), pp. 656-66.

11. Participant observation proved useful in studying the institutional treatment of dying patients. See Renee Fox, *Experiment Perilous.* Glencoe: The Free Press, 1959; Barney Glaser and Anselm Strauss, *Awareness of Dying.* Chicago: Aldine

Publishing Co., 1965; Elisabeth Kubler-Ross, *On Death and Dying*. London: The Macmillan Company, 1969; and David Sudnow, *Passing On*. New York: Prentice-Hall, 1967. After death has occurred, however, the observation of survivors becomes somewhat more difficult. Namely, the bereaved generally leave the confines of the hospital and go about making funeral arrangements in a variety of places, most of which are not easily accessible to sociologists.

12. For a discussion about such techniques see Raymond Gold, "Roles in Sociological Field Observations," *Social Forces*, **36** (1958), pp. 217-23.

13. Interviews were the bases of previous studies by Robert Fulton, *A Compilation of Studies of Attitudes Toward Death, Funerals and Funeral Directors*. Minneapolis: Privately printed, 1971; and Geoffrey Gorer, *Death, Grief and Mourning*. New York: Doubleday, Inc., 1965, both of whom assess reactions and attitudes toward funerals among various publics. William Kephart in "Status After Death," *American Sociological Review*, **15** (October, 1950), pp. 635-43, used interviews to learn about common funerary practices and patterns of funeral behavior from funeral directors.

14. An interview schedule was designed so as not to create added burdens for the bereaved. It contained a series of questions about dying and death, as well as the standard statistical questions commonly used in completing funeral arrangements.

15. Many problems exist for investigators doing this sort of supplementary research. For a fairly complete reader about this and related concerns see George J. McCall and J.L. Simmons, *Issues in Participant Observation*. Reading, Mass.: Addison-Wesley Publishing Co., Inc., 1969.

16. During the course of the research, I wrote thousands of pages of material about the funeral homes and their characteristics and about their operational differences.

17. For a treatment of this and related problems see Weber's discussion in A.M. Henderson and Talcott Parsons, *Max Weber: The Theory of Social and Economic Organization*. New York: The Free Press, 1966, pp. 94-98.

Chapter 1

The Care of the Dead: an Historical Portrait

L ittle is known about the origin of the care of the dead except that it appears to have come about very early in man's history. An anthropological investigation in Iraq reports apparent funeral practices of the Neanderthal man.[1] This discovery dates man's concern about caring for the dead to at least 60,000 years ago. We need not go back so far in our past to discuss the care of the dead, for we have well documented reports from numerous early civilizations.[2]

Ancient Times

Ancient Egyptian society had an intricate system of care for the dead which was carried out by an elaborate, extensive division of labor.[3] Undertaking and embalming specialists cared for the dead and carried out many of the funeral arrangements. A well-defined division of labor emerged for the care of the dead and their surviving relatives; however, its primary concern was the dead. It is generally claimed that the Egyptians preserved the dead by embalming because of their belief that after death the soul left the body to travel through "time" and eventually came back to reinhabit the dead body. Thus, for the Egyptians, the emergence of embalming reflected a belief in life after death; however, it is not at all clear which came first, the practice or the belief. In any case, the care of the dead was provided in an essentially bureaucratic fashion.

The preparations of the ancient Greek dead were made by the family, and although embalming was not practiced, perfumes and spices were used to mask the odor of putrefying flesh.[4] Friends and relatives provided flowers for the dead, and special clothing marked the mourning of the bereaved. The Greeks viewed the dead body largely to ensure that death actually had occurred and that the body had not been molested. Later in Greek history, cremation was practiced because of the belief that flames set the soul free. Throughout their history, the Greeks dealt with death in a personal way, with certain experienced family members and friends acting as funeral experts.

The ancient Romans practiced both burial and cremation at various times; in either case, the body lay in state for viewing by the public.[5] The wealthy were cared for by a professional undertaker or *libitinarius*. This specialist was the direct ancestor of the modern funeral director, and in the large cities his work was essentially bureaucratic.[6] The *libitinarius* took care of anointing or embalming, supplied professional mourners and mourning clothes, arranged for services aimed at relieving the grief of the bereaved, and arranged for the details of the funeral procession. The practices of the ancient Romans have had a direct impact on the funeral practices of the contemporary Western world, especially our notions of splendor, pomp, and ceremony. The care of the dead was the direct responsibility of an expert server who carried out the many facets of his work as a service occupation practitioner. Habenstein and Lamers sum up the impact of the Romans as follows:

> Roman influence upon modern funeral practices is to be regarded in the last instance not so much for the *content* of those death beliefs which might have been transmitted to the Western world, but for the *occupational models* useful to mass societies exhibiting an urban way of life. Most important from the point of view of this study is the secular functionary, the Roman undertaker, who as arranger, manager and director of funeral affairs, as well as supplier of mortuary paraphernalia, sets a pattern of occupational behavior meaningful to the funeral director of mid-twentieth century. Additionally, the administrative measures of the Romans have stood as a source of suggestion to modern societies in which a body of mortuary law has been felt necessary to insure adequate public protection in the matter of the disposal of the dead.[7]

The early Hebrews believed that man was composed of two elements, flesh and breath, and that upon death the flesh returned to dust while the breath persisted.[8] To the Hebrews, cremation was considered an indignity to the body, and burial either with or without a coffin was practiced throughout their history. Hebrew funeral practices included the washing and perfuming of the dead, and, for hygienic reasons, burial on the evening of the day of death. These tasks were carried out by experienced members of the family, and the level of experience was determined largely by the number of times such people provided this care. After the dead were prepared, professional mourners helped carry out the funeral. Funerary details and the care of the dead were largely the responsibility and duty of the deceased's family, and expertise was determined primarily by personal experience.

Early Christian burial practices were unpretentious.[9] Friends and relatives commonly viewed the dead and practiced the long-standing Jewish custom of watching or "waking" the dead which had arisen largely from the fear of burying someone alive. An important belief among the early Christians was that death does not end all human relationships, but merely represents a transition from one type of relationship to another.

In about the fourth century A.D., the organized church established feast days to commemorate publicly and solemnly the death anniversaries of the martyrs. From this time on the Christian funeral developed into a set of actions organized as part of the wider operation of the developing urban society. Although most of the funeral functions of the early Christians were carried out by relatives of the dead, they were generally done under the direction of the clergy. The clergy's supervision was often a bureaucratically oriented service; however, it was not provided primarily for a fee. The early priests were careful to give the appearance of personal involvement to help effect an air of concern. There was a merging of personal service in a bureaucratic setting. This led to the development of minor, bureaucratically organized functionaries to tend to some of the specific needs of caring for the dead. Even though it has been suggested that such functionaries were the forerunners of the modern funeral director, the evidence indicates that this distinction belongs to the *libitinarii* and their assistants of ancient Rome.[10]

The Middle Ages

As time passed the Christian Church emerged from persecution and became increasingly institutionalized. The simple burial customs of the early Christians gave way to an imposing dignity that expressed the feeling of the importance of the Church and its members. As society dispersed and grew, and urban life began to exert more influence on specific segments of the population, local funeral customs evolved that did not necessarily conform to those practiced when Christianity was a small sect in the vicinity of the Mediterranean Sea.

During the Middle Ages the Christian version of embalming included removing some body organs, washing the body with water, alcohol, and pleasant smelling oils, chemically drying and preserving the flesh, wrapping the body in layers of cloth sealed with tar or oak sap, and mummifying in a way similar to the Egyptians. These tasks were performed by specialists who acted solely as embalmers. Apparently, there was relatively little bureaucratic handling of formal arrangements, and most funerary services were kin-provided and essentially personal in nature.

Leonardo da Vinci developed a system of venous injection for preservation of the dead body to enable him to draw anatomical plates. His method served as an inspiration to the early medical embalmers whose practices later gave rise to many modern embalming procedures.[11] By the end of the seventeenth century, embalming was used by medical anatomists primarily to preserve the dead for anatomical dissection and exploration. While medical practitioners were improving embalming techniques, chemists were developing preservative fluids which made arterial and venous injection more than a mere exercise. Thus, embalming developed as a medical specialty long before and with little connection to funeral practices as we know them.

By the end of the seventeenth century the English undertaker was recognized as a tradesman, even though his was neither a well-defined nor highly specialized trade. As his work became more intricate and additional tasks were shuffled into his hands, for some in urban centers undertaking became a regular service occupation. In the eighteenth century there emerged in small towns part-time undertakers whose full-time occupations were such things as livery stable owner, carpenter, and cabinet maker.[12]

At about this time the English funeral developed into a full-fledged performance. Mutes, mourners, and livery men were gathered and directed in an effort to provide a "proper setting" for an atmosphere of heavy gloom and despair. Thus, the role of the English undertaker became even more diversified and all-encompassing, with a more complex set of practices. In urban centers the work began to take on a bureaucratic nature.

Early America

Funeral behavior in colonial America generally included church funeral services, with brief prayers said at graveside ceremonies. Early New Englanders seemed to accept death as natural and inevitable and saw no reason to disguise cemeteries, since "the grave was as familiar as the cradle."[13] Funeral ceremonies were essentially simple, and the mourners actively participated by accompanying the coffin to the grave and filling the grave with dirt. The mourning process took on an extensive social character, and rings, scarves, gloves, purses, and needlework products were given away as tributes to the dead.[14] The communal atmosphere emphasized the personal service aspects of the work.

American undertaking evolved by gradually adding to itself specific funeral tasks previously carried out largely by other occupational groups or by the family. For instance, certain members of the community became expert at the "laying out" of the dead after a number of such experiences. Some seemed to feel an informal responsibility to offer their knowledge and services to others in the community, and by the end of the eighteenth century the laying out of the dead in larger cities had become a specialty, with certain of the attendant bureaucratic elements, such as impersonal service in funeral firms handling many funerals.[15]

During the nineteenth century the American undertaker became something other than a jack-of-all-trades. He brought together the functions which formerly were scattered among and performed by several trades into a single and unified occupation. An important reason for his rise to prominence was the church's unwillingness or inability to maintain authority over all aspects of the burial process. Furthermore, largely because of urbanization and changes in the social order, families were increasingly unlikely to do such things themselves.

Nineteenth-century American funerals were intensely gloomy and distressing for the bereaved.[16] As a result, there emerged a desire to provide a "beautiful" setting in which to experience loss, grief, and bereavement during the funeral. In cities, undertakers were called immediately upon someone's death. Generally, they came to the home and directed the funeral in the presence of and with the cooperation of the deceased's family. Embalming often was carried out in the home, and there were early attempts to "restore" the faces of the dead with liquid tints that had been developed by the embalming chemical fluid companies.

One of the main reasons for the growth in popularity of embalming stemmed from the Civil War, when large numbers of soldiers died far from home. Since most families wanted their dead brought to their own burial grounds for final services, medical embalmers emerged on and around the battlefields of the Civil War. At the conclusion of the war the assassination of President Abraham Lincoln brought about new public awareness of embalming. The funeral procession with Lincoln's body on display extended from Washington, D.C., to Springfield, Illinois. As it progressed through many portions of the Northeast and Midwest, people along its path became aware that it was possible to keep and view the dead for long periods of time. Although buried in 1865, Lincoln's body was so well embalmed that as late as 1899 it was viewed and was proclaimed to be in a perfect state of preservation. For such reasons, embalming became a more important aspect of the American way of death.

At the end of the nineteenth century states began to pass licensing legislation to regulate the practice of embalming. State boards of health began to be concerned about such things as burial and cremation permits, and the filing of death certificates increasingly became required by state law. Thus, in addition to the technological, occupational, and social changes through which undertaking and embalming passed, the nineteenth century brought about legislative pressures which contributed to the growth of undertaking as an occupational specialty group.

During this era, funeral services normally were conducted in the deceased's home. The undertaker would bring all the supplies and paraphernalia and set them up in the living room or parlor. A defined period of mourning restricted social activity for the bereaved surviving relatives. A basket of flowers was hung on the front door, replacing a crepe badge which had been an earlier mark of mourning.

Religious services usually were held at the home or in the church; in either case, the funeral concluded with a procession to the cemetery. An important new aspect of the undertaker's job developed at this time. Someone had to remove all signs of the funeral from the home while it was vacant for the funeral procession. Thus, when it returned from the cemetery the family had no further tasks. The undertaker bore that burden.

Because of the need for paraphernalia and other funeral equipment, funeral establishments began to appear in urban areas, and in small towns undertakers began to use their stores' back room, their barn, or their living room to provide facilities for those families to whom the home no longer was appropriate for the laying out of the dead. Usually, undertakers used a specific (large) room in which to lay out the dead and in which the bereaved could greet callers. This room replaced the parlor formerly used in the home of the deceased; thus, the undertaker's establishment came to be called a "funeral parlor." In this homelike setting, the undertaker supplied the casket, carriages, mourning materials, memorial cards, flowers, chairs, robes, pillows, and crucifixes, and he generally was responsible for the direction of the funeral services.

The notion of the "funeral director" arose in the late nineteenth century, with several factors contributing to the development of this new occupation. First, occupational mobility and the decline of the extended family led to the development of smaller houses and other living units. This change gave rise to a need for a building large enough to house big families gathered for mourning. Funeral parlors were built or existing houses modified to take into account the new needs of the bereaved and the caretakers of the dead.

Second, as embalming became more sophisticated, the equipment to carry out this task became increasingly difficult to take into private homes. Embalming became a procedure in the laboratory or "preparation room" of the newly developed buildings housing the funeral director's equipment and supplies.

Third, transportation problems increased the difficulty of gathering the mourners for the funeral ceremonies at a church. Moreover, since the church did not encourage the development of special rooms for the care of the dead, funeral directors found an additional reason to develop facilities to house such activities.

A combination of the need for a large parlor, a special laboratory, and a chapel-like facility evolved into what has become the present-day funeral home. This provided additional impetus for a specialist to carry out the new specialized tasks in such a setting. The funeral director came to look upon himself as being useful to society rather than as merely a provider of merchandise and equipment. This feeling seems to have led to the development of notions of administrative and managerial skills and the practices of funeral counseling as well as directing. It contributed to the occupational orientation as the provider of services, that is, as a professional personal service practitioner.[17]

These trends in America's care of the dead have led to contemporary American patterns. Before we examine the contemporary scene, however, it is important to emphasize the uniqueness of the American funeral director. Let us turn to a brief description of the care of the dead in three other technologically developed societies. The patterns of these three continue to emphasize that both personal service and bureaucratic organization are guiding models in societies other than America.

Abroad Today[18]

In England the care of the dead has been an occupational activity for a long time. The care of the dead in England depends on two factors which are basically distinct yet to some extent interrelated. First, the economic status of a bereaved family influences funeral customs. For instance, economic differences help determine the choice of a funeral firm for handling final disposition. The possibilities range from the small combination business, *e.g.*, a carpenter shop with a sideline undertaking business, to the large exclusively undertaking funeral firm. To a great extent, the cost of a funeral service is determined by this choice.

Second, funeral practices are influenced by regional differences. In the south of England the service ends simply at the grave. The custom in the north is for the funeral director to arrange a high tea for all the mourners after the cemetery service is concluded.

Whatever the case, the dead body is cared for at the place of death, either by a nurse, who performs the "last offices" for the living, or by a funeral director, who performs "the first offices" for the dead.[19] Embalming is optional and not required by law, and there are no government regulations concerning specific embalming procedures. The bodies that are embalmed are "treated to hold up" until the day of the funeral.[20] No attempt is made to create an appearance of life in the dead. "Somewhere between seven and ten per cent of all bodies are given temporary preservation, most of them in private homes and on the bed on which they died."[21] The practice of embalming is rapidly growing, however, with some firms now reporting embalming up to 80-90% of the dead that they handle.[22]

The English tend not to view the dead body. When they do, such viewing takes place in the home, with the body lying on the bed of death or in the casket. There is a trend toward utilizing a funeral home or "chapel of rest," and purchasing "complete" funerals, which include the casket, embalming, viewing, and other related services.[23]

There are two types of funeral home ownership. The usual "old-fashioned," family-owned business has been the main type. Historically, such firms have been unwilling to change practices, attitudes, or atmosphere. Recently, cooperative funeral establishments have been set up, and the co-ops are run by voting members who determine how they will conduct funerals. Since the formation of the co-ops, there have been some noteworthy changes in funeral practices. For example, many more funerals are held in funeral homes, embalming is practiced more regularly, and visiting and viewing by friends and relatives is encouraged.[24]

The care of the dead in England also appears to be oriented to the two occupational models. The long-established, privately owned funeral homes are essentially bureaucratic, and do not aim to provide services but rather to accomplish specific tasks. The new cooperative funeral firms are organized with greater attention given to providing personal services for bereaved families.

In Japan, the dead are cared for in two distinct fashions. On the one hand, there is rural-village Japan and on the other, urban-center Japan. Rural-village funerals are regulated largely by the village headman. He personally supervises specific community projects when someone dies, and the entire community works cooperatively to provide all of the necessary funeral equipment, services, and labor. The relatives of the deceased are notified and generally gather at the home of the deceased to help carry out the funeral rites. Distant relatives and friends make preparations for final disposition and place the dead body in a wooden coffin. Thus, the dead are cared for in a personal service fashion.

In urban-center Japan the care of the dead is largely Westernized. Funeral establishments are owned privately, municipally, or nationally, and specialists provide services, equipment, and labor necessary for conducting funerals. Distant relatives and friends of the bereaved family make most of the funerary arrangements and decisions. This custom stems from the ancient belief that the immediate mourners are too upset by death to be able to make appropriate funeral arrangements.

There is little embalming, or a large public assembly to view the dead, but the relatives do gather to see the deceased in the coffin. Only the face is visible through a small opening in the coffin lid. The face is painted white, and the head is shaven. At this time, friends and relatives call to offer condolences. Funerals are held either at the home of the deceased or at his temple.

Funeral directors function primarily as providers of funeral equipment. They deliver all the necessary paraphernalia to the place where the funeral is to be held and supply the needed transportation. The dead are cremated, and the family of the deceased returns to the crematory the day after to gather up the bones and ashes, These cremated remains are buried. This last disposition of the remains generally is accompanied by more ceremony and elaborate ritual. None of this final work is done by the funeral director.[25]

The urban-center funeral firms are organized in a bureaucratic fashion. Moreover, Japanese funeral directors resemble the early American undertakers and often do not conduct themselves in a personal service fashion. The care of the dead in Japan conforms to the model of personal service in the rural-village setting and to the bureaucratic model in the urban-center setting.

In Russia, the care of the dead has been influenced by several factors. After the Russian Revolution of 1917, government regulations reduced the care of the dead to immediate, unceremonial disposal of the body. "However, a return to a more formal and ceremonious funeral [was] reported some fifteen years later."[26] There is evidence that this trend has continued, and death now seems to be approached somewhat more on the basis of individual desires.

Today, the Soviet government grants money to bereaved families to be used for funeral expenses. There are state funeral stores which have all the necessary equipment and paraphernalia. These stores have fixed prices for funeral merchandise and equipment such as caskets, hearses, and other supplies.[27]

Relatives of the deceased help make the arrangements and provide almost all of the labor themselves. "A do-it-yourself funeral" is the result.[28] Embalming is optional and is done by medically trained specialists. Viewing the dead is common at either the home of the deceased, the hospital where the death occurs, or a neighborhood club. Generally, within forty-eight hours a funeral service is held. Such services are either civil or religious and often include participation by fellow workers.[29]

The funerary choices available to the bereaved family appear to be increasing, and the governmental agencies are loosening their hold over funeral rites. Habenstein and Lamers (1960: 438) remark,

> There is evidence in sufficient amounts to indicate that far from having reduced burial to a matter of simple disposal of a meaningless dead body the Soviets have come to a position, perhaps grudgingly, where most of the con-

ventions—as defined by Western European standards—will be met at least minimally by the government agency. Or if not by it, by other groups including family, relatives, fellow workers, and religious denominations.

In sum, the care of the dead in Russia is handled in a bureaucratic fashion by the governmental funeral agencies. However, occupational associations, friends, and relatives of the deceased cooperate to stage a funeral in a much more personal fashion. Thus, in Russia the contemporary practices fit both the personal service and the bureaucratic models.

In England, Japan, and Russia, the care of the dead is carried out both by personal servers and by bureaucrats. In summary, in the three societies examined, there is no single dominant form of organization for the care of the dead.

Contemporary America

There are approximately 22,000 funeral establishments in the United States and approximately 50,000 people licensed to practice funeral directing. Until the past thirty to fifty years death occurred at home in familiar surroundings in the presence of kin or close friends, and funerals were community events. Times have changed, however. Each year proportionately more people die in institutions instead of their own homes, and almost all of the dead are cared for by funeral directors in funeral homes.[30] For present-day Americans, one of the common features of death is the employment of a funeral director.

The heterogeneity of the United States is reflected by differing funeral practices. Funeral customs in the United States vary because of geographic region, ethnic background, religious affiliation, and economic and social class.[31] Religious and ethnic groups tend to maintain unique traditional funeral practices, thus adding to regional, economic, and social variations. There are differing state laws and regulations which to some extent govern funeral practices. For the present, commonly reported practices will be described; however, these may not be completely accurate for a particular area of the country or a specific group of people.

Depending on where, how, and when death occurs, it is common to notify a physician or the police. Then, the cause of death is medically certified, either by a physician, a coroner, or a medical examiner. Finally, the family of the deceased chooses a funeral director.[32] Generally, the choice is ethnically oriented, but, at times, may reflect social class, status, and geographic differences.[33]

The dead body usually is removed from the place of death by the funeral director and taken to a funeral home. There, it is customary to embalm or otherwise sanitize through disinfection.[34] Embalming includes dressing the body and "restoring it" (applying cosmetics) in an attempt to render the deceased lifelike and socially presentable for a public appearance.

The immediate family of the deceased generally makes the necessary arrangements for the funeral. For example, the place, time, and type of funeral service, the place of burial or cremation, and the type of casket, are a few of the choices that must be made. These and other elements of the funeral are interrelated and seem to be based on social class, ethnic, and religious attitudes.

Viewing the dead body is widespread in the United States and occurs in all social class levels. Usually, it is done during specified hours at the funeral home; but it may take place at the home of the deceased, or occasionally at the church where the service is to be held. During the viewing, friends, and relatives spend time with the bereaved family.[35] Religious and ethnic differences appear to be the bases for varying attitudes about the length of viewing and the attendant mourning customs. American viewing customs constitute a period of visitation for the immediate survivors, their kin, and their friends.

Most funerals in the Unites States include a religious service. At times there may be a service by a fraternal or other organization, and occasionally there is no service. The religious services are held either in the funeral home, the home of the deceased, or the church.[36] With few exceptions, there is little active participation, other than attendance, by family or friends at the funeral. This is a uniquely American custom, and in many parts of the world the family actually carries out these final acts.

Generally, at the cemetery there are religious committal rites. After the committal, it is common for the family to leave the cemetery with the casket still above ground. After the departure of the mourners, the funeral director supervises the lowering of the casket into the grave. As with other parts of the funeral, there is seldom active group participation at the cemetery except for the reciting of widely known prayers.

Earth burial is the most common means of final disposition, chosen for over 92 per cent of the deaths annually. Cremation is chosen for less than 5 per cent of the deaths annually. Usually, cremations are handled like burials, with the exception that the procession to the crematory is often smaller and occasionally includes just the hearse.

Funeral expenditure is divided among the funeral director, crematory or cemetery, clergyman, and florist. The largest portion generally goes to the funeral director. His charges usually include the casket selected by the bereaved family, his professional services, use of the necessary equipment and facilities, motor equipment, and other related items.[37] This is unlike many societies in which funeral expenditure goes to other sources, such as religious or social groups or governmental agencies.[38]

An historical portrait of the care of the dead, emphasizing some of the social crosscurrents that gave rise to the occupation of funeral directing, helps clarify the occupation of funeral directing and the emergence of the funeral director as an occupational specialist in present-day society. It is useful to have such a perspective before dealing with some of the problems of the funeral director and the dilemmas of the occupation.

Notes

1. For a discussion of this report see Walter Sullivan, "The Neanderthal Man Liked Flowers," *New York Times* (June 13, 1968), pp. 1 and 43.

2. The following discussion is based to a great extent on Robert W. Habenstein and William M. Lamers, *The History of American Funeral Directing*. Milwaukee: Bulfin Printers, 1955.

3. *Ibid.*, pp. 1-22.   11. *Ibid.*, pp. 158-65.
4. *Ibid.*, pp. 26-31.   12. *Ibid.*, pp. 172-77.
5. *Ibid.*, pp. 36-50.   13. *Ibid.*, p. 200.
6. *Ibid.*, p. 40.   14. *Ibid.*, p. 203.
7. *Ibid.*, pp. 45-46.   15. *Ibid.*, p. 235.
8. *Ibid.*, pp. 52-57.   16. *Ibid.*, p. 391.
9. *Ibid.*, pp. 61-84.   17. *Ibid.*, p. 436.
10. *Ibid.*, p. 76.

18. The following discussion is based to a great extent on Robert W. Habenstein and William M. Lamers, *Funeral Customs the World Over*. Milwaukee: Bulfin Printers, 1960, pp. 41-62, 427-40, and 553-74.

19. *Ibid.*, p. 555.

20. *Ibid.*, p. 560.

21. *Ibid.*, p. 560.

22. George Jennings, "Funeral Service is Making Rapid Progress in Great Britain," *The American Funeral Director*, 87, No. 2 (1964), p. 40.

23. *Ibid.*, pp. 39 and 40.

24. *Ibid.*, pp. 39-42. Such practices are seen as being beneficial by many scholars who note that it is customary for the English to attempt to withhold any display of grief. Social expectations call for rapid emotional adjustment and a quick return to active living by the bereaved. For a full discussion see Geoffrey Gorer, *Death, Grief and Mourning*. New York: Doubleday & Co., Inc., 1965.

25. Funeral costs depend on the charges made by the funeral firms, the priests, the crematory, the cemetery, and the florist. For a full discussion see Koji Mori, "The Increased Cost of Dying in Japan," *The American Funeral Director*, 87, No. 9 (1964), pp. 35 and 36.

26. Habenstein and Lamers, *Funeral Customs the World Over*, p. 433 (brackets supplied).

27. John Manning, "Soviet Funeral Service," *The American Funeral Director*, 89, No. 1 (1966), p. 30.

28. *Ibid.*, p. 29.

29. *Ibid.*, p. 31.

30. Robert Fulton, "Death and the Self," *Journal of Religion and Health*, 3 (July, 1964), p. 364.

31. For a more complete documentation of this circumstance see Habenstein and Lamers, *Funeral Customs the World Over*, pp. 729-54.

32. American funeral directors provide specialized facilities, functions, and services, and the activities surrounding the funerals may or may not be accomplished by different individuals. That is, a funeral director may or may not also be an embalmer, arranger, or other funerary person with a specific title. For the present purposes, a funeral director is understood to be any and all of the above specialists.

33. For a fuller discussion see Habenstein and Lamers, *Funeral Customs the World Over*; also see Vanderlyn R. Pine, "Comparative Funeral Practices," *Practical Anthropology*, **16** (March-April, 1969), pp. 49-62.

34. There are a few religions which do not allow embalming, but even in these cases, it is common that some disinfection is carried out. It is noteworthy that the law does not require embalming, but because of the usual delay until final disposition, most funeral directors insist on protecting themselves by disinfectionary precautions. Embalming in the United States long has been practiced and, as noted earlier, is based largely on the lack of kinship propinquity and the need to preserve the body until the family gathers, sometimes from great distances.

35. Expressions of sympathy may include material donations to the bereaved family, the common symbolic offering of flowers, donations to a charity "in memory of" the dead person, etc. Economic group support by gifts of money is common to certain ethnic groups. For instance, Italian families and friends often give cash to the family of the deceased, and at times such collections reach one thousand dollars and more. For certain religions, perpetual masses or other spiritual contributions are often purchased for the deceased and the family by other relatives and friends.

36. There are certain religious denominations which require church funerals; otherwise, the location of the funeral is up to the bereaved family.

37. For a discussion of funeral expenditure, see Vanderlyn R. Pine and Derek Phillips, "The Cost of Dying: A Sociological Analysis of Funeral Expenditure," *Social Problems* (Winter, 1970), pp. 405-17.

38. See Pine, "Comparative Funeral Practices," *op. cit.*

Chapter 2
Professionalism
and the Funeral Director

The major concern of this study is to determine if there are important differences between funeral directors with a bureaucratic orientation and those with a personal service orientation. Three assumptions underlie this interest. First, the organization of a particular occupation influences the individual's practice of that occupation. Second, the orientation, education, and training of funeral directors are based on the philosophy of professionalism. Third, the occupational ethos of funeral service is that the funeral director's most important job is that of providing professional services at the time of death.

Throughout Chapter 1, reference was made to two diverse orientations to caring for the dead: One is the personal service orientation and the other is the bureaucratic orientation. Since these two orientations have fairly well understood meanings, they were not defined specifically. To clarify some of the unique problems of the American funeral director, it is important to delineate them more clearly. This chapter discusses the sociologically relevant aspects of the two orientations and presents problems which beset the funeral director in particular.

A Theoretical Assessment of Occupational Models

Most people assess life according to specific models which are constructed for various social phenomena and used to orient actions and be-

25

havior in a given situation. It follows that people define a situation partly because they possess common-sense conceptions of personally held models.[1]

On the common-sense level, there are clear-cut distinctions which differentiate personal servers from bureaucrats. Since our present interest is in analyzing these differences, it is essential, first, to delineate the differences between the model of personal service occupations and the model of bureaucratic occupations, and, second, to examine the differential influence of each on the perception of everyday occupational behavior.

It is helpful at the outset to understand the term "occupational model." An occupational model is that constellation of beliefs, notions, and concepts which everyday actors construct regarding the various occupations with which they are familiar. The occupational models with which we are concerned are caught up in the technological complexity of American society and in the concept of professionalism. It is common to divide occupations into groups such as professional, white collar, blue collar, and so forth. One of the ways we determine whether an occupation is a profession is to compare it to the traditional historical professions, often referred to as the "free professions." Everett C. Hughes (1958: 132) describes such occupations as being those in which the professional practitioner should "stand in a fiduciary relation which he must scrupulously keep clean of interests which arise out of his relation to other clients."

In the same vein, Talcott Parsons (1949: 186) explains:

> The professional man is not thought of as engaged in the pursuit of his personal profit, but in performing services to his patients or clients, or to impersonal values like the advancement of science.

Even though people use "professional" as a general orienting term when talking about occupations, it is common to use the word in (at least) two particular ways. First, "professional" may be used to distinguish the kind of occupation a person has; physicians, dentists, attorneys, or clergy are called "professionals," while business executives, insurance salesmen, or bank employees are called "white collar workers," and auto mechanics, carpenters, or plumbers are called "blue collar workers." Second, "professional" may be used to refer to a full-time paid expert in some field; we may speak of "a professional boxer" compared to "an amateur boxer."

The present interest is in the case when "professional" refers to the sort of occupation someone has.[2] Inherent in such usage is the assumption that certain occupations possess observable characteristics which serve as evidence that they are a profession. There are several crucial distinguishing characteristices of a profession. Ernest Greenwood (1966: 9-18) specifies five attributes traditionally isolated by sociologists as common to occupations considered professions.

First, professions possess an underlying systematic body of theory and knowledge. There is a set of propositions which describe in a general way the classes of things which make up that profession's focus of interest. For this reason, the preparation for a profession must be intellectual as well as practical, and it is acquired through long training in a professional school.

Second, professions have a high degree of professional authority. The professional determines what is "good or bad" for the client; not only must the client accept that judgment, but generally the client is not believed competent to judge the quality of the decision. This is considerably different from the business notion that "the customer is always right." Of course, along with professional authority goes the understanding that great care must be taken not to exploit the client.

Third, professions have the sanction of the community. The community approves of and gives power to professionals by such things as licensing regulations. Another form of sanction is that professional privileges include confidentiality, which encourages clients to divulge secret information which is then protected in law by professional immunity. When occupations strive for professional status, they seek to acquire the above-mentioned features. Greenwood (1966: 14) explains it this way:

> Specifically the profession seeks to prove: that the performance of the occupational skill requires specialized education; that those who possess this education, in contrast to those who do not, deliver a superior service; and that the human need being served is of sufficient social importance to justify the superior performance.

Fourth, professions possess a regulative code of ethics. Generally, such a code is established to protect the community from the monopoly held by the profession. Professional codes of ethics possess both formal and informal aspects. The formal aspect is the written code to which the professional swears when admitted into the profession, and the informal aspect is that which is unwritten, but to which the professional still adheres. Not incidentally, codes of ethics are an important element in the professional associations which also attempt to regulate the activities of their members.

Fifth, professions possess what may be called a special culture. This means that every profession operates through networks of formal and informal groups. In this framework, it is common to speak of the subculture of medicine or the subculture of law. Each subculture possesses a unique set of values and norms, and uses its own signs and symbols in carrying out its professional activities. Largely through such a subculture, most professionals tend to regard their work as their life. This may be contrasted to people whose occupations are a way of making a living but which do not hold any higher value.

In addition to these five attributes, professionals possess unique means

of being rewarded financially for their work. It is intricately caught up in
the services provided and the means of charging for them. Robert Fulton
(1971: 22) provides a useful description on this issue.

> Professional service is historically "the laying on of the hands" by a person
> "wrapped in the cloak of a sacred office," such as the priest, doctor,
> professor, and lawyer. His "blessing" is the same for all. There are no dis-
> tinctions. Extreme unction administered by a priest is the same for a prince
> as for his retainer: so, too, the ministrations of the doctor or the counsel of
> the lawyer. One pays according to his ability to do so. Thus, the concept
> "noblesse oblige" refers to the duty that the superior person must observe in
> extending succor, charity, or protection to his inferior. The wealthy knows
> that the fee charged him by the doctor permits the doctor to extend his skills
> to the poor. Other employment, such as that of the laborer, plumber,
> mechanic, is quite different. It is on a *quid pro quo* basis—a time and item
> accounting is demanded and the rich man expects to pay no more for labor
> or similar services than the poor.

Beyond the above attibutes, the professions can be characterized in
terms of a general pattern. For the most part, professionals tend to be
recruited and to succeed in practice on the basis of their ability rather than
because of any ascribed characteristics. Furthermore, ideally (at least)
professionals remain detached from other social relationships with the
served, work exclusively within their area of technical competence with
objectivity and impersonality, and have the served's best interests in mind.[3]

Because professionalism is highly respected in American society, the
word "profession" tends to be used as a symbol by occupations seeking to
improve or enhance the lay public's conception of that occupation, and
funeral directing is no exception. To some extent, this appears to be
because the funeral director hopes to overcome the stigma of "doing death
work." Even though death is an everyday occurrence, in American society
it long has been a taboo subject.[4] Most people appear to be unconcerned
about death and do, indeed, have little experience with its impact. This is
contrasted with funeral directors, who are deeply concerned about death,
deal with it daily, and for whom it is the source of income.

The American funeral director is a death *professional* partly because
he hopes to improve the public's conception of his occupation and partly
because he is one of the few people in our society who actually knows what
can, should, and must be done following a death. Making his plight more
difficult is the fact that not only does he attend to funerary concerns, but
also his very existence reminds society that death strikes us all, which is a
noxious thought for many.

In addition to the unique structural and social psychological dimensions of funeral directing which help locate it as a professional occupation,
there is the nature of the work itself. Funeral directing possesses some of
the essential elements of professionalism, since a major component of the

funeral director's work involves providing personal services. To understand the connection clearly, let us now consider the personal service model in some detail.

The Personal Service Model

In the preceding section, we mentioned that it is common for an occupation which seeks to enhance its social position to aspire to professional status. An important part of this desire involves the providing of "personal service." Erving Goffman (1961: 326) describes such occupational aspiration as well as the role that personal service occupations have played in Western societies as follows:

> Every large society has expert servers, but no society has given such service more weight than has ours. Ours is a service society, so much so that even such institutions as stores come to follow this style in word if not in fact, responding to the need of both clerks and customers to feel that expert personal service is being provided even while they despair of realizing it.

The essence of that which is "professional" resides in the historical processes of human society and culture, in the basic philosophy towards those things which require services, and in the processes which surround the providing of these services in any social setting.[5] In this sense, the ideas of a culture are not the sole possession of those who devote themselves to their chosen profession, but are also shared by the lay culture which must deal with the serving occupation.

Clearly, the services given by professionals exist in a complex institutional setting. On the one hand, an individual must have a conscious awareness of himself as a member of a given profession and must possess certain ideal conceptions of his own work. On the other hand, there are differing ideal conceptions of what the work really is or should be, what are the best means to accomplish it, and what are the proper responsibilities and rewards for it. The professional must deal with the non-professional patient or client in carrying out the work, and they may possess different ideals about it.

All of the participants in such a social relationship bring to the institutional complex their own conceptions of what is wrong, what needs service, and similar personal expectations. The lay person has expectations about the profession as a whole, about what any practitioner should be like, and about the particular practitioner as an individual. Hughes (1958: 76-77 and 1971: 310) explains that lay people

> ... do not completely accept the role-definitions handed down from above, but in communication among their own kind and in interaction with the people served, treated, or handled, work out their own definition.

Ideally, personal servers should do things *for* someone rather than *to* someone. Not so ideally, if the situation changes while the server is doing something for the served, the mood can shift so that the served believes that things are being done to him or her. The danger of this kind of shifting occupational relationship exists wherever people go or are sent for help or correction. Everett C. Hughes (1958: 70 and 1971: 305), speaking on this problem says:

> . . . the school-room, the clinic, the operating room, the confessional booth, the undertaking parlor all share this characteristic. Whatever terms we eventually may use to describe social interaction at work must be such that they will allow these subtle distortions of role or function to be brought to light and related to whatever are their significant correlates in personalities or situations.

Professional personal service occupations often are distinguished as being "clean" because they are based on notions of honor, respectability, and prestige. This viewpoint implies that professions possess only positive attributes. As Hughes (1958, pp. 70-71) points out, it is more realistic to look upon such occupations as having a clean and a dirty side. Every profession has aspects on the dirty side of the coin which it hides from the public, as well as aspects on the clean side of the coin which it emphasizes to a high degree.[6]

In addition to these characteristics, most services are provided through settings that exist before servers and served ever establish their particular relationship; for example, a doctor's office need not be created anew for each person who falls sick; watch repairmen already have shops and reputations before new customers come to see them; funeral homes exist before people die. As Goffman (1961: 332) explains, this means that "It is the client who becomes the guest."

Goffman (1961: 336) goes on to explain that in its purest form the character of the service relationship has a certain common-sense logic. Namely, the service practitioner must maintain an appropriate definition of the situation and present himself as a person who provides, merely for a fee, an expert personal service to someone who is in need of it. The served person must believe that there are such practitioners who are appropriately competent and dedicated to this service to the extent that they will devote themselves to one's concerns for that fee.

Let us summarize by defining the personal service occupational model.[7] A personal service occupation is one whose practitioners provide a specialized service to a set of individuals with whom the servers have direct contact and personal communication, but to whom the servers are not otherwise connected.

Quite naturally, such an ideal is not always the case, and any service relationship may be threatened, because as Goffman (1961: 336) explains, generally there is "a kind of matrix of anxiety and doubt, even when each party to the relationship is behaving properly." Put differently, the client is concerned about the server's actual competence, his real interests, and his specific charges. Howard S. Becker (1963: 102) says that "the problems peculiar to [an occupation] . . . are a function of the occupation's position vis-a-vis other groups in the society."

Goffman (1961: 345) locates another increasingly important problem, the threat to the service relationship that a change to a bureaucratic organization brings. Before turning to this threat specifically, however, it is essential to examine the characteristics of the bureaucratic occupational model.

The Bureaucratic Model

Although funeral directing is dominated by a professional orientation and the personal service occupational model, it is composed of many diverse tasks which are amenable to bureaucratic organization. It is common in occupations with multiple facets to solve the conflict between occupational models by separating the diverse elements which comprise it. For example, in medicine, the physician provides professional services, the hospital provides facilities and equipment, the pharmacy provides medicinal merchandise, and the ambulance service provides transportation. This is not at all the case in funeral directing, for funeral homes customarily handle all the aspects of the funeral. The number of funerals conducted annually and the way in which a funeral home is organized influence how the multiple facets of funeral directing are handled, and there is a wide range of organizational complexity in the field. No matter what its organization, the bereaved and the lay public may perceive the multiple facets of the funeral home as functions of a bureaucracy.

The stereotype bureaucracy carries a negative connotation. For example, the word "bureaucracy" often conjures up thoughts of agencies and organizations which are purported (1) to be inefficient in their operation, (2) to involve considerable red tape, and (3) to be a handicap with which modern American society, of necessity, must contend. The present interest is not in the stereotype bureaucracy, however. We are interested in those aspects of bureaucratic organization which comprise an ideal type bureaucracy. As is the case with the personal service model, occupations which are bureaucratically organized fit into the division of labor on a common-sense level. For example, as technological complexity increases, the chance that a formal bureaucratic organization will develop also increases. In this setting the classic definition of an ideal type bureaucratic organization becomes analytically useful.

Max Weber provides the classic definition of bureaucratic organization from such an ideal typical perspective.[8] Even though Weber's theory is intended primarily for administrations and political organizations, the present discussion provides the theoretical framework in which it is possible to analyze the mode of organization of many present-day service occupations including certain funeral homes. Among other things, bureaucracies possess the following characteristics.[9]

First, the organization is composed of a clear-cut division of labor in which jobs are assigned because of technical competences rather than personal ones.

Second, in order to gain entrance into the organization, one must possess qualifications which are determined by such things as examinations or licensure.

Third, the division of labor is hierarchically arranged. Each level lower than the next is responsible primarily to the level directly above it and secondarily to all other levels above that one.

Fourth, locations in the hierarchy may be thought of as positions staffed by salaried experts who work at their tasks as a career or job rather than as a calling.

With these points in mind, Weber (1946: 214-15) offers the following description of an ideal type bureaucracy:

> Precision, speed, unambiguity, knowledge of the files, continuity, discretion, unity, strict subordination, reduction of friction and of material and personal costs—these are raised to the optimum point in the strictly bureaucratic administration . . . . As compared with all collegiate, honorific, and avocational forms of administration, trained bureaucracy is superior on all these points . . . . Individual performances are allocated to functionaries who have specialized training and who by constant practice learn more and more. The "objective" discharge of business primarily means a discharge of business according to *calculable rules* and "without regard for persons."

There are three additional characteristics which Weber isolated and which are important to this study. First, the bureaucratic organization is governed by general rules which are clearly delineated and easy for everyone to follow. Such rules are intended to equalize the treatment of people who require the services of the organization. Second, the incumbents of any particular bureaucratic position are not the owners of the organization. Third, the bureaucratic organization separates home and work, and its members are expected not to have connections between business and personal matters such as property and funds.

This perspective largely ignores the dysfunctional elements of bureaucratic organizations. A formal, rationally organized social structure involves clearly defined patterns of activity in which every series of actions only ideally is related functionally to the purposes of the organization. Robert K. Merton (1949: 198) puts it this way:

Actions based upon training and skills which have been successfully applied
in the past may result in inappropriate responses *under changed conditions*.
An inadequate flexibility in the application of skills, will, in a changing
milieu, result in more or less serious maladjustments.

This is in contrast to the ideal type perspective, which is concerned
almost exclusively with the attainment of a bureaucratic organization of
precision, reliability, and efficiency. The main point is that an overdevo-
tion to rules often leads to transforming them into absolutes which are no
longer productive to the purposes of the organization. Clearly, this can in-
terfere with the organization adapting to special conditions which are not
envisioned by those who drew up the general rules. Thus, the very elements
which are conducive to efficiency in general may produce inefficiency in
specific situations.[10]

Let us summarize and define the bureaucratic occupational model: its
members are organized within an extensive hierarchical division of labor,
are technically competent experts who allocate time and effort according
to rules which govern the ways in which they treat those they serve, are not
owners of the organization, and make a clear distinction between personal
and business matters.

Before examining the strains, dilemmas, and conflicts which may exist
because the personal service model and the bureaucratic model have some
seemingly incompatible characteristics, let us turn our attention to a discussion of the occupational conflicts of professionals.

The Professions and Occupational Conflict

In the historically great professional personal service occupations such
as medicine and law, the ideas, philosophies, and social processes, as well
as the providing of the service itself, have contributed to the development
of a respected occupational model. One of the major problems for the
semi, quasi, or emerging profession is that confusions, contradictions, and
dilemmas of status may plague it as it develops.[11] Moreover, as a profession changes, the public may develop inaccurate versions or conceptions of
its culture and status. Such misconceptions provide fertile ground for conflict between professionals and the people with whom they deal. Therefore,
it is possible for conflicts to arise even when occupational models are not
the major concern.

There are social conditions inherent in the structure of any formal
organization which give rise to conflict. In this sense, conflicts occur not
only between professional personal service organizations and their clients,
but also between business organizations and their customers. Thus, the
relations between the work group itself and the clients served provide a

source of conflict. It is essential to this form of conflict that there be a clear perception of behavior which does not conform to the occupational model of the individual making the judgment. When this nonconformity occurs, occupational models serve as a source of conflict.

Another problem which may give rise to conflict involves the notion of authority. In American society, it is important that the professional practitioner exercises a considerable amount of authority, in comparison to, say, the business person.[12] The professional version of authority is based largely on the technical competence of the practitioner. Thus, according to Parsons (1949: 188), one exercises authority over those who are less skilled in the matters with which one's occupation deals. However, even though competence is limited to one's field of knowledge, it affords the professional practitioner certain status and superiority outside the field.

Both Parsons (1949: 190) and Hughes (1958: 116-18) emphasize that the relationship, contractual or otherwise, between the professional and the patient or the client gives the professional the right to seek secret information which has a functionally specific connotation and which, supposedly, is utilized as a basis for providing services. Importantly, functional specificity also is essential in a bureaucratic organization, and in this sense, there is a close similarity between the professions and bureaucracies in the American social structure.

Some bureaucrats have conflicts similar to those between the overzealous business person and the customer. Merton (1940: 202) points out that the personality of the bureaucrat, which generally develops from the norms of depersonalization, may give rise to conflicts between the bureaucrat and the clients being served by the bureaucracy. Such a conflict emerges when, say, there is organizational pressure for formal and impersonal treatment and the client may hope for individual personalized consideration.

Along with the worldwide trend toward centralization, there has been an attempt to operate large administrative organizations more efficiently. Concomitant with this trend are a number of disruptive characteristics. For example, formally organized central bureaucracies may be influenced by other than formally organized forces. Philip Selznick (1966: 251-52) argues that the unanticipated consequences of a formal organization are crucial to the maintenance and stability of the anticipated goals of the organization. It is through the informal system that individual participants in a bureaucratic organization tend to develop a commitment to the organization which contributes to the perpetuation and success of the formal organization.

In this sense, it is not hard to understand why bureaucratic performance often may be thought of as being "too strict" when it comes to interpreting organizational rules. Parsons (1951: 290-91) suggests that some bureaucrats suffer from "bureaucratic ossification," that Merton's description of the bureaucratic personality might be characterized as "predominantly a passive compulsive conformist," and that selective recruitment and strict role performance lay heavy value on "playing safe" and "not sticking one's neck out."

When this is the case, the role played by those within a bureaucratic organization may represent appropriate organizational behavior but inappropriate behavior from the viewpoint of the larger social world and of the client. Furthermore, since an ongoing bureaucracy must be successful and productive, the patterns of behavior of those in the bureaucracy are likely to be ones which are known to "produce" results.[13] Clearly, such roles and behavior may conflict with the needs of those being served by the bureaucracy.

One social mechanism that allows the bureaucrat to cope with the tensions of client conflict is informal discussion with colleagues. Such discussion treats clients as outsiders, and the colleague group bands together to sustain the bureaucrat who is in a state of conflict. Peter M. Blau (1955: 109) explains that a common means of relieving the tension in most service occupations is the ridiculing of clients. In this regard, Blau (1955: 117) goes on to say that:

> . . . conversations about clients that neutralized disruptive tensions also enabled officials to treat clients less considerately *than their service ideals* demanded, [and this] was detrimental to these [clients] and to optimum . . . service. (Emphasis supplied)

Peter M. Blau and W. Richard Scott (1962: 36) explain that one of the central issues for contemporary professional service organizations is the "conflict between disciplined compliance with administrative procedures, and adherence to professional standards in the performance of duties." Blau and Scott (1962: 51) go on to define a service bureaucratic organization as one "whose primary beneficiary is the part of the public in direct contact with the organization, with whom and on whom its members work—in short, an organization whose basic function is to serve clients." This formulation has the advantage of providing a framework in which to locate service professionals such as funeral directors in bureaucratic organizations.

As Blau and Scott (1962: 60-63) point out, professional and bureaucratic orientations have essential similarities as well as differences. The conflicts created by the merger of the two orientations are resolved in different ways. Blau and Scott (1962: 64) explain:

> Some [practitioners] retain their identification with their professional group, are highly committed to their professional skills, and look for social support to professional colleagues outside the organization as well as within. Such involvement in the larger network of professional relations that cuts across

organizations may be said to indicate a "professional" orientation. Others
have less commitment to their specialized skills, come to identify with the
particular organization by which they are employed and its program and
procedures, and are more concerned with gaining the approval of administrative superiors inside the organization than that of professional
colleagues outside. These may be said to have a "bureaucratic" orientation.

Naturally, within an organization, such orientations have an impact on
professional behavior toward clients.[14] It may be that being oriented to the
profession tends to make a worker to some extent independent of the
pressures of the organization. Such a worker may be more inclined to
deviate from organizational procedures purportedly in the interest of
better professional service to one's clients.

The everyday performances of funeral directors are guided by their
orientation to the occupation. Similarly, lay people are influenced by their
orientation to the occupation of funeral directing. It is helpful, therefore,
to use the concept of occupational orientation in conjunction with that of
occupational models to analyze the funeral director's behavior.
Throughout this book, we focus on the ways in which funeral directors and
the people with whom they come in contact utilize both their occupational
models and orientations.

Occupational orientation may be defined as the way in which individual service practitioners conceive of their occupation, *qua* occupation,
regardless of how they conceive of themselves as practitioners. For our
purposes, there are two main categories of occupational orientation. First,
there is a service orientation in which the individual practitioner believes
that funeral directing is a service occupation to be performed according to
the personal service model. Second, there is a bureaucratic orientation in
which the individual practitioner believes funeral directing to be a
bureaucratic occupation to be performed according to the bureaucratic occupational model.

Since the way in which services are rendered is also modified by the
nature of the public with which a particular service practitioner must
deal,[15] let us turn our attention to some stresses and strains of funeral
directing. It certainly is one of those personal service occupations which
must deal with a specialized public, namely, bereaved people, and which
must be influenced by occupational models and orientations.

Funeral Directing and Occupational Conflicts

One of the things that makes the funeral director's role difficult is that
funerals are ceremonially repetitive but individually singular. Part of the
funeral director's job is to provide the bereaved family with an "appropriate setting and proper ceremony" to enact routine funeral activities

for a dead individual. This means that the bereaved family and the funeral director may have different conceptions of what is important and in need of attention. This is, as mentioned earlier, the case with most personal services; however, the sensitive nature of death amplifies the problems for the funeral director. Furthermore, even though each bereaved family becomes part of the specific funeral, much of their action is as an audience of the funeral director, and this only adds to the potential for conflict.

It is possible that a bereaved person may have had prior experiences with death and funerals and may be familiar with funerary activities. In general, however, such familiarity is uncommon, and it is part of the funeral director's job to familiarize people with customary funeral practices. The funeral director's activities and behavior may be seen as the repetitive and routine actions which comprise the American funeral. Inasmuch as the funeral director is able to impart a sense of ceremony to the bereaved and to society, the funeral takes on value for the bereaved in coping with death and coming to grips with the loss of the deceased.

The funeral director's role requires him to have a definition of the situation which allows him to treat each death as important and ceremonially worthwhile, even though, to society, it may not be so.[16] The bereaved for whom the funeral director works are likely to have no definition of the funeral situation, or at best an unclear one. Moreover, the bereaved's definition of what is important in the funeral may not resemble the funeral director's.[17]

Society tends to be ambivalent in its attitudes toward and acceptance of the funeral director.[18] Part of the difficulty is that his role contains elements of and is marginal to such roles as professional, businessman, administrator, and manager.[19] Because of these multiple tasks, the rights and duties of the funeral director are not well-defined, and occupational conflicts may arise because different segments of society expect him to perform or refrain from performing different tasks.

There are two types of role conflict which exist, one within the role itself and the other in interaction with other roles. First, within the role itself, some funeral directors experience intrarole strain. One source of this strain may be a sense of guilt which accompanies the desire for many funerals coupled with the feeling that this desire may be interpreted as a wish for the death of friends and others.[20] Second, is the manner in which he is perceived by the general public. Since death is a topic which tends to be avoided and disguised in the United States, there is the practice of relegating the duties and ceremonies of death to the funeral director whose job it is to treat them impersonally. W. Lloyd Warner (1959: 317) explains it this way:

> The deep hostilities and fears men have for death, unless very carefully controlled and phrased, can turn the undertaker into a scapegoat, the ritual uncleanliness of his task being identified with his role and person.

Even when he does not become a scapegoat per se, the funeral director may be viewed by some as being different from other people. He may be thought abnormal for having chosen such an occupation; he may be perceived as "unclean;" finally, he may be a source of humor, witness such radio and TV characters as Digger O'Dell, Herman Munster, and Morticia Adams.

Considering the role in interaction with others, some funeral directors also experience interrole conflict. There may be role conflict with clergy, particularly with Protestant ministers. Robert Fulton (1961: 318) reports that Roman Catholic priests view the funeral as a ceremony honoring both the memory and the body of the dead and feel relatively little conflict between their views and role and those of the funeral director. Fulton (1961: 319-20) points out that proportionately more Protestant ministers see little value in the funeral as a source of comfort to survivors and believe the funeral director should take care of physical and mechanical matters and not attempt to counsel the bereaved.

Adding to the role conflict problems with the clergy are other factors. Some fear that an emphasis on the body will result in a lack of attention to the spirit. Setting aside spiritual reasons, there are even materialistic ones, namely, some clergy feel resentment when they compare their small honorarium with the cost of the total funeral. Finally, some clergy express a "fear of taint" from the funeral director who deals with all faiths because he seems to question the greater sanctity of one rite or church over another. Fulton (1961: 322) explains it this way:

> In a word, the funeral director, by virtue of his close association with death, and by the "relative" attitude he takes toward all funerals, is, in a religious sense, "unclean."

Another problem for funeral directors is the occasional banning of funeral homes from certain community areas. Even in the absence of zoning regulations, funeral homes have been closed or forced to move when they were offensive to neighbors in residential areas.[21] Also troublesome is that this funeral home ban may extend to the funeral director himself. Leroy Bowman (1959) reports that funeral directors have been denied membership in organizations solely because of their occupation.

The contamination by death involves not only funeral directors and their establishments but also others who daily work with death. Part of the reason people view individuals in such work as different may be because they feel that they themselves could never do it and that there must be something "strange" about those who voluntarily choose to do it.[22]

Even individuals who must come in contact with dead bodies as a peripheral part of their jobs try to avoid it as much as possible. For instance, Sudnow (1967: 42-51) explains that hospital attendants avoid preparing bodies by letting the next shift discover a death. Another technique they use is the partial preparation of a body before death so that the attendants will have to touch the body after death as little as possible. Doctors and other high status hospital workers seldom touch a dead body unless it is absolutely necessary.

Quite naturally, funeral directors are defensive on the subject of aversion to them, and they often deny that such aversion exists. However, as Bowman (1959: 72) suggests, slights must be felt since some funeral directors dwell on the injustice of such reactions and decry the tendency of acquaintances to joke about their connection with the dead. Some funeral directors say that aversion to them is no longer the problem it once was. Bowman (1959: 78) reports that this change is occurring as more people appreciate the difference between the "undertaker" of the past and the "funeral director" of today.

Such a claim, however, has an important flaw. The undertaker of yesteryear generally lived in a closely knit community and his personal contacts were more likely to overcome the aversion toward him than in the urban, impersonal world of today. Furthermore, until the emergence of the funeral home, dead bodies lay at home, and families were more in contact with their own dead than were undertakers. In this setting, the undertaker could scarcely be viewed as being more "unclean" than the family members themselves.

Many techniques other professionals commonly use to cope with role strain are not too effective for the funeral director. For instance, he cannot step out of character easily, and neither can he practice role distance on the job, nor can he joke or talk in a derogatory manner in public about his clientele. Clearly, such actions could alienate potential clients and could make the funeral director appear even more "ghoulish" than some people already believe he is. Such techniques can be practiced only among other funeral directors or alone with one's immediate family; but even then, they do not seem very useful.

Funeral directors do use certain techniques to counteract the role strain which they experience, and one such technique is the use of occupational argot, using shorthand, everyday terminology for various activities and duties. This practice arises partly to blunt the reality of death and to dissociate the funeral director from some of the stigma of his job with euphemistic terms. Occupational argot also represents the funeral director's conception of what is important about his activities. The following terms are a few of those commonly used by funeral directors in their everyday activities.[23] In addition to showing how argot helps serve as a defense mechanism, these terms are presented now so that when they are mentioned describing actual behavior, they will not be unfamiliar or confusing.

The word "funeral" means any one of a number of things. One usage is to refer to a "funeral" as a "call," in which case the two words are synonymous. Thus, funeral directors may talk about "how many calls" (or "funerals") they handle during a given period of time. "Funeral" also is used to designate a specific service commemorating the death of an individual. In this sense, the word is used to indicate when or where the "funeral" is going to be. As such, it is an abbreviated form of "funeral ceremony." A third way "funeral" is used is as a prefix or combining form to indicate any connection with the occupational specialty which deals with the dead, such as to speak of the "funeral profession" or the "funeral director." The various uses of the word "funeral" mean that it serves as a catchall phrase with multiple specific meanings each of which is easily recognizable by the funeral director. Thus, he easily can classify events and activities under a meaningful heading depending upon the situation, and this helps protect the funeral director's role when dealing with the public.

Funeral directors have "calls," and they "serve" clients referred to as "families." The use of the word "call" to represent an individual's death and funeral helps locate this activity as one of the important duties and tasks of the funeral director. Thus, while a funeral home is liable to handle many calls in a year, each one is important because it represents to most funeral directors a call to work. Furthermore, the use of the word derives in part from the fact that almost all funerals are initiated by the bereaved calling upon the funeral director to provide his services rather than the funeral director going out and seeking someone in need of his services.

Although the dead person is openly acknowledged by name, in general, one is referred to as the "body." The term "body" is utilized to help impersonalize each dead person and to make that person less a human and more a thing which requires attention as part of the mechanical aspect of the funeral director's job. The two terms, then, "call" and "body," function to balance each other as the foci of attention for the funeral director. On the one hand, he is able to treat the bereaved who have called upon him in a personal fashion, and, on the other, he is able to deal with their dead member less personally as a body.

Another means by which funeral directors help counteract aversion is by joining numerous local organizations and being highly respectable. As is the case with other business and professional people, such practices also assure that the funeral director's name will immediately come to mind should a death occur.[24]

There are other techniques used by funeral directors to cope with and counteract role strain. The most important of these include identification with the established professions, an emphasis on professional tasks such as grief counseling, pride of professional craftsmanship, and a belief in the value of the funeral as an effective means of meeting the needs of those who survive someone's death. These techniques are utilized to raise the status of funeral directing, to answer the criticism of the cost of funerals, and to overcome public aversion.

Unfortunately, these same techniques often give rise to additional conflicts and strains. An important source of these additional problems is the ambiguity inherent in the funeral director's duties. Although the funeral director himself may have fairly well defined ideas regarding his duties, the people with whom he interacts sometimes do not.

Whatever the case, it is essential to delineate how funeral directors behave in the presence of others.[25] Our specific concern is with some of the common techniques funeral directors use to sustain the impression others receive of how they appear in a given situation. This concern also includes the funeral director's dramaturgical problems of presenting funerary activity to other people. To a great extent, the assessment of "proper" role behavior is based on the appearance of the funeral director discharging the role's functional requisites or by the conscientious enactment of the role's requirements.

We are interested in the techniques funeral directors employ to present themselves to others and the conditions under which these techniques tend to be used by funeral directors.[26] Since such presentation can be thought of as taking place in a theatrical setting, it is possible to describe a number of locations which are both spatial and temporal in nature, and these will be discussed in Chapter 3. At the simplest level, there are at least two categories of the presentation of self. First, a funeral director may present himself as a server, behaving according to the personal service occupational model. Second, a funeral director may present himself as a bureaucrat, behaving according to the bureaucratic occupational model.

It is clear that one aspect of the presentation of self occurs at the private level on which the funeral director interacts with other people as individuals. Another aspect occurs at the public level, which encompasses interaction with society at large. This distinction is important, for in his funeral home, the funeral director is an expert at impression management. There the funeral director conducts himself in such a way as to guide and manage the impressions of himself that he emits to any individual or set of individuals. On the public level, the problem is far different, and visible signs and symbols must accompany activities which are open to public scrutiny.

Clearly, there are a number of stresses and strains in the practice of funeral directing. Unlike many less complex occupations, funeral directing is beset by a number of unique combinations which make any treatment of it analytically complex and practically confusing and therefore of considerable sociological interest. In light of the two occupational models, the disruptive potential between them, and the unique problems of funeral directing, let us now examine the two funeral homes.

Notes

1. Explicit in this assumption is that the individual actor defines these models personally. Implicit in it is that these models are formed as a result of social forces; thus, they tend to be consistent across a given society. Even though this is the case, each individual makes subjective interpretations of a given situation, utilizing the models possessed at that time.

2. The following discussion is based largely upon the following works: Howard M. Vollmer and Donald Mills (eds.), *Professionalization*. Englewood Cliffs, N.J.: Prentice-Hall, Inc., 1966; Erwin O. Smigel, *The Wall Street Lawyer*. Bloomington: Indiana University Press, 1969, especially pp. 264-75; and Eliot Friedson, *Profession of Medicine*. New York: Dodd, Mead and Company, 1970, especially pp. 44-95.

3. This perspective fits into Parsons' (1951, p. 454) analytical framework of the pattern variables and serves to help characterize the professional pattern in American society as including achievement, universalism, functional specificity, affective neutrality, and collectivity-orientation. Realistically, as Freidson (1970: 159) points out, these characteristics are more or less true for many occupations in addition to those providing personal services; however, the distinguishing difference involves the performance of the professional.

4. For a discussion see Herman Feifel, "Death," in Norman L. Farberow, *Taboo Topics*. New York: Atherton Press, 1966, pp. 8-21.

5. This and the following discussion are based largely on the ideas about the medical culture as a prototype of profession as found in Everett C. Hughes, *Men and Their Work*. Glencoe: The Free Press, 1958, pp. 116-30.

6. Conventionally, this problem is solved by segregating work roles either spatially, by such things as the "off-limits operating room" of the hospital, and the "preparation or embalming room" of the funeral home, or according to the division of labor in which someone other than the professional performs the dirty work aspect of the task, by such people as "paraprofessionals" or "subprofessionals." This discussion is based largely on ideas set forth by Everett Hughes, which have been extensively developed by Erving Goffman in *The Presentation of Self in Everyday Life*. Garden City: Doubleday and Company, Inc., 1959.

7. In addition to the sources cited thus far, this particular definition is based to a great extent on Erving Goffman, *Asylums*. Garden City: Doubleday and Company, Inc., 1961, p. 324; and Howard S. Becker, *Outsiders*. New York: The Free Press, 1963, p. 82.

8. The extensive literature since Weber includes numerous approaches to the subject. Most of the present-day studies of bureaucracy are case studies which focus on organizational variables and characteristics. For background see H. H. Gerth and C. Wright Mills (eds.,), *From Max Weber*. New York: Oxford University Press, 1946, which treats the political and ideological implications of his theory of bureaucracy; and A. M. Hendersen and Talcott Parsons (eds.), *Max Weber: The Theory of Social and Economic Organization*. New York: The Free Press, 1964, which provides the theoretical context of bureaucracy, locating it in Weber's general theory of authority.

9. This and following discussion are based on Gerth and Mills, *op. cit.*, pp. 221-44; and Henderson and Parsons, *op. cit.*, pp. 329-41.

10. For a discussion of this problem, see Robert K. Merton, "Bureaucratic Structure and Personality," in *Social Theory and Social Structure*. New York: The Free Press, 1949 pp. 195-206. Weber was not insensitive to this problem, and he touches upon it in at least two places. First, in a brief footnote, Weber (Gerth and Mills, *op. cit.*, p. 215) points out that he does not have the space to discuss "how the bureaucratic apparatus may, and actually does, produce definite obstacles to the discharge of business in a matter suitable for the single case." Second, Weber (Gerth and Mills, *op. cit.*, p. 221) says that when an ethos of individual importance collides with the matter-of-factness of bureaucratic administrative structure, "the ethos must emotionally reject whatever reason demands."

11. Everett C. Hughes points out that an occupational model is

> never the sole possession and certainly never the exclusive creation of those who devote themselves to the [profession]. On the other hand, [the professional culture] . . . never coincides exactly with that of the lay world. (1958: 117, 1971: 398)

12. This and the following discussion borrows heavily from Talcott Parsons, "The Professions and Social Structure," in *Essays in Sociological Theory, Pure and Applied*. Glencoe, Ill.: The Free Press, 1949, pp. 185-99.

13. This and related points are made by Gouldner (1954), pp. 19-24 and 158ff. Gouldner's concern is specifically oriented to relationships between individuals working within an industrial bureaucracy. However, his findings are useful for analytical purposes.

14. Blau and Scott, *Formal Organizations: A Comparative Approach*. San Francisco: Chandler Pulishing Company, 1962, pp. 70-71, suggest that the professional visibility of the practitioner may help determine one's orientation:

> These differences in findings can be explained by suggesting that the crucial underlying factor is not so much the visibility of performance as the nature of the limits of professional opportunity. If there is little opportunity for advancement *within the profession*, regardless of the organization by which a professional is employed, a commitment to professional skills comes into conflict with aspirations for advancement . . . .
>
> If, on the other hand, there is ample opportunity for advancement in a profession, but this opportunity is much more restricted in some organizations than in others of the same type, commitment to the profession comes into conflict with loyalty to the organization and encourages a cosmopolitan orientation.

15. It is possible to distinguish between practitioners dealing with a sequence of individuals and those dealing with a sequence of audiences. See Erving Goffman, *Asylums, op. cit.*, p. 324.

16. For discussions about the decreasing importance of the death of individuals to society, see Robert Blauner, "Death and Social Structure," *Psychiatry*, **29** (November, 1966), pp. 378-94; Robert Fulton, "Death and the Self," *Journal of Religion and Health*, **3** (July, 1964).

17. In American society there often is little effort to define the funeral situation at all except to note that someone is no longer alive. Such a situation contributes to locating the role of the funeral director as an institutionally oriented, routinized, and accessible performer in the American funeral theater.

18. The concept of marginal roles is derived from the term "marginal man," which refers to a "cultural hybrid, a man living and sharing intimately in the

cultural life and transitions of two distinct peoples," Robert E. Park, "Human Migration and the Marginal Man," *American Journal of Sociology*, 33 (1928), p. 892. Also see Everett V. Stonequist, "The Problem of the Marginal Man," *American Journal of Sociology*, 40 (1935), pp. 1-12. Such an individual has the problem of choosing between different elements of his socialization. An individual cannot be marginal with respect to one well defined role. It is possible, however, for the role itself to be marginal, and as such it is imperfectly institutionalized and ambiguous. Thus, social sanctions tend to be inconsistently applied with respect to it. For a similar treatment of this problem see Vanderlyn R. Pine, "The Multi-Professional Dimensions of a Funeral Service Practice," given at the annual meeting of the *National Funeral Directors Association*, Portland, Oregon, October 9, 1969.

19. Some of the ideas in this and the following discussion are similarly stated by Marilyn Carroll, "The Funeral Director" (unpublished manuscript, Kansas City, Missouri).

20. That funeral directors often are aware that there are numerous jokes suggesting their supposed wish that their friends and acquaintances die is reported by Leroy Bowman, *The American Funeral Director*. Washington, D.C.: Public Affairs Press, 1959.

21. Kurt W. Back and Hans W. Baade, "The Social Meaning of Death and the Law," reprinted in John C. McKinney and Frank T. DeVyver, *Aging and Social Policy*. New York: Irvington Publishers, 1966, pp. 302-29. To be sure, the occasional zoning pressures that prohibit funeral homes from being built in certain residential areas also often pertain to a number of business and professional structures such as professional medical buildings, etc.

22. David Sudnow, *Passing On*. Englewood Cliffs, N.J.: Prentice-Hall, Inc., 1967, pp. 53-58, discusses some of the problems faced by hospital morgue attendants:

> John was in a rather uncomfortable situation in his movements throughout the hospital, for he was, in a manner of speaking, "trapped by his role." His chief and daily problem was going about the hospital without, wherever he went, appearing to others to be working . . . .
> John had problems such as how to engage in friendly conversation, how to get someone to sit next to him, or not move away from him, in the hospital cafeteria, how to avoid interrogation by others about "what it is like," and, generally, how to enter any form of ordinary discourse without his affiliation with dead bodies intruding as a prominent way others attended him. . . . He commented that the thing he found most uncomfortable about the job was not the work entailed by autopsies and body transportation, but the loneliness of that work.

23. Many of these terms can be found in the professional literature of funeral directing. Especially useful is the recent and excellent treatment of funeral service by Howard C. Raether (ed.), *Successful Funeral Service Practice*. Englewood Cliffs, N.J.: Prentice-Hall, Inc., 1971.

24. Along these lines, Bowman, (1959: 75) claims:

> There is reason to believe that the client requires more than the usual assurance of the moral and ethical acceptability of the funeral director in order to overcome his reluctance to join in mutual activity with him. To put it another way, the community punishes the undertaker because of its own ambivalence toward him, in something like a scapegoat mechanism. He, in turn, accepts that phase of his role, because of his need to

make friends in large numbers for business reasons, and also because his "impeccable character" has become a mark of status in the undertaking group.

25. The following discussion is largely based on Goffman's *The Presentation of Self in Everyday Life, op. cit.*

26. We can think of the presentation of self as a complex of intertwined public and private role behaviors, the performance of which depends on spatial and temporal perceptions of and orientations to everyday life. Goffman (1959: 22), describes "performance" as "all the activity of an individual which occurs during a period marked by his continuous presence before a particular set of observers and which has some influence on the observers."

Chapter 3

Setting and Organization of the Funeral Homes

Even though it is a personal service occupation, funeral directing seldom exists without an organization of some kind, and funeral directors customarily work in one specific funeral home. The funeral director operates not just out of a building with appropriate facilities and equipment but also in an organized work setting within a particular type of firm organization.

The term "firm organization" refers to the division of labor of the funeral home and is divided into two categories. First, a simple organization involves either a solo practitioner or a few individuals who work together to carry out all aspects of funeral directing. Second, a complex organization is an hierarchically arranged, highly differentiated staff of employees which works at certain well defined, clear-cut tasks with distinct responsibilities and duties.[1] Given these two categories, it follows that a simple organization conforms to some aspects of the personal service occuptional model, while a complex organization conforms to some aspects of the bureaucratic occupational model.

The data reported in this chapter were gathered from several sources, including field observations, examination of tables of organization, corporate charters, business histories, and the responses to a large-scale national survey.[2] These sources were utilized to determine the typical features of American funeral homes, two of which were selected to represent the usual forms of organization for service versus bureaucratic funeral homes. In addition to the sources utilized in the present research, previous reports indicate that both firms are organized essentially similar to the population of counterparts in many locations across the country.[3]

Funeral Homes Throughout the United States

Funeral customs and orientations to funeral directing are diverse. So also are the forms of organization found in funeral homes throughout the United States. Before examining the two specific funeral homes which are the central foci of this book, let us consider the general situation of funeral directing on a nationwide basis.

Each year, slightly under (but soon expected to exceed) 2,000,000 people die in the United States. The vast majority of funerals for these deaths are conducted by approximately 22,000 funeral homes across the country. Simple arithmetic suggests that each funeral home conducts an average of about 90 funerals per year. Such an average, however, oversimplifies the situation and distorts the picture of the "typical" funeral home, for there is considerable diversity in the pattern of funerals conducted annually.

Table 1

The Average Number of Funerals Conducted Annually

	MEAN RANGE Number of Funerals* (Arithmetic Average)	MEDIAN Number of Funerals** (Position Average)	Number of Funeral Homes Reporting
United States	104-123	85	8,227
New England	82- 89	83	665
Middle Atlantic	88-102	75	1,740
South Atlantic	136-158	100	842
East North Central	88-103	48	2,029
West North Central	81- 93	46	1,168
East South Central	123-141	104	446
West South Central	140-165	115	551
Mountain	137-168	105	282
Pacific	190-221	152	504

*One way to measure the "typical size" funeral home is to utilize the arithmetic *mean* (the average) number of funerals conducted annually. The mean number of funerals conducted is the total number of funerals reported divided by the total number of firms reporting. The "Mean Range" shows the lower and upper limits between which the exact arithmetic mean falls. A range is reported because the questionnaire calls for respondents to indicate the *approximate* number of funerals their firm conducted during the past year by checking the appropriate *interval* (range) in which this number falls, i.e., "More than ? but Less Than ?."

**Because extremely large firms tend to "pull up" the mean, it is useful also to examine the *median* number of funerals conducted annually to measure the "typical size" funeral home. The median number of funerals conducted is the middle number of funerals reported when the firms reporting are ranked from low to high. In other words, the number of firms conducting less funerals than the median is equal to the number of firms conducting more funerals than the median. Thus, there are the same number of funeral homes which report conducting less funerals

The source for Tables 1-10 is: Vanderlyn R. Pine, *Findings Of the Professional Census*. Milwaukee: The National Funeral Directors Association, the complete report of which may be found in the appendices.

Table 2

The Percentage of Funeral Directors Reporting the Number of Complete Adult Funerals Conducted Annually by Their Firms

NUMBER OF FUNERALS CONDUCTED

	1-50	51-75	76-100	101-150	151-200	201-300	301-600	601+	N
United States	23%	21%	18%	17%	9%	7%	5%	2%	8,227
New England	18	27	18	19	10	7	1	0	665
Middle Atlantic	28	23	18	15	8	4	3	1	1,740
South Atlantic	14	15	21	20	10	8	8	4	842
East North Central	30	22	17	14	7	6	3	1	2,029
West North Central	30	24	19	14	5	4	3	1	1,168
East South Central	11	18	19	23	12	9	6	2	446
East South Central	14	17	14	20	13	11	7	4	551
Mountain	10	16	20	23	11	10	6	4	282
Pacific	5	8	15	21	18	16	10	7	504

Table 3

The Percentage of Funeral Directors Reporting That Their Firms Serve Various Size Communities

	Under 2,500	2,501-25,000	25,000-100,000	100,000-1 million or more	Mean Community Population	N
United States	10%	50%	24%	16%	11,250	8,227
New England	2	39	41	18	8,400	665
Middle Atlantic	7	48	28	17	16,000	1,740
South Atlantic	7	51	25	17	9,200	842
East North Central	14	50	20	16	11,500	2,029
West North Central	19	59	13	9	11,250	1,168
East South Central	5	60	25	10	11,500	446
West South Central	9	52	23	16	16,750	551
Mountain	5	57	23	15	13,750	282
Pacific	2	38	32	28	22,750	504

Tables 1 and 2 summarize three measures of typicality which help emphasize the complexity of the situation. Table 1 indicates the mean and the median number of adult funerals conducted in 1970. This table is useful because it indicates the wide range that exists in terms of the average number of adult funerals conducted in the various census divisions. To further clarify the diversity of the number of funerals conducted annually, Table 2 shows the percentage of funeral homes reporting the number of adult funerals conducted in 1970. It is clear that the simple arithmetic of dividing the total number of deaths by the total number of funeral homes does not allow an assessment of the operational variation among funeral homes.

Another kind of diversity in terms of the operation of a funeral home is the size of the community or market area which the firm serves. Table 3 indicates the extent to which funeral homes are distributed in communities of differing size. It is notable that 60% of the funeral homes report serving communities or market areas of 25,000 people or less. The divisional differences are considerable, ranging from a low of 40% in the Pacific division to a high of 78% in the West North Central division. The national picture alone is an inadequate indicator of the variation, this time in terms of the percentages of funeral directors within each census division which serve various size communities.

Table 4

The Percentage of Funeral Directors Reporting The Number of Other Firms Which Serve Their Community or Market Area

	0	1	2-3	4 or more	N
United States	25%	22%	21%	32%	8,227
New England	14	12	20	54	665
Middle Atlantic	15	18	20	47	1,740
South Atlantic	21	24	28	27	842
East North Central	28	23	19	30	2,029
West North Central	40	28	17	15	1,168
East South Central	23	28	28	21	446
West South Central	35	22	23	20	551
Mountain	36	25	21	18	282
Pacific	23	22	26	19	504

A good indication of the extent to which the number of funerals conducted annually and the population of the community or market area served operate simultaneously is the number of funeral homes in a given market area. Table 4 shows the percentage of firms which report how many other funeral homes serve their communities. One-quarter (25%) of the firms report that no other funeral home serves their particular community. This situation means that no matter how many deaths occur in such a community, the vast majority are handled by a single funeral home. As is clear in the table, the divisional variation is considerable. The number of other funeral homes in a given area is a good indication that in divisions in which more other firms serve a given community, there is greater colleague contact but, at the same time, greater competition.

The length of time a funeral home has been in existence is another matter which merits consideration. Table 5 indicates the average year when funeral homes were founded and the percentage of firms established in various ranges of years. Obviously, funeral homes are well established, and there is considerable ongoing community service in funeral directing in American society. This gives the field a unique dimension in a society in which stability is the exception rather than the rule.

Table 5
The Percentage of Funeral Directors Reporting
The Year Their Firms Were Founded

	Before 1900	1900-1919	1920-1939	1940-1970	Mean Year When Founded	N
United States	22%	22%	31%	25%	1919	8,227
New England	31	21	27	21	1915	665
Middle Atlantic	26	18	27	29	1918	1,740
South Atlantic	21	19	27	33	1923	842
East North Central	25	21	32	22	1916	2,029
West North Central	22	26	32	20	1920	1,168
East South Central	18	20	34	28	1922	446
West South Central	13	19	41	27	1923	551
Mountain	10	31	33	26	1925	282
Pacific	16	27	31	26	1919	504

The preceding discussion touches on some of the demographic and structural characteristics in which funeral homes exist across the country. In addition to these, there are (at least) three underlying factors which help account for the proportionately large number of firms. One factor which influences the number of firms is the somewhat amorphous concept of local power and community control. In a very real sense, funeral directors are influenced to a great extent by the local power structure and are controlled largely by the norms of their particular community. This is because of community awareness which develops through active participation in numerous local organizations. This suggests that to go elsewhere or to call in an "outsider" would place funeral arrangers at a disadvantage at a time of great stress. Furthermore, a local funeral director often is assumed to have knowledge of intimate family information or personal secrets.

Even though to select a funeral home at a distance would provide greater anonymity, it would reduce the ease with which the funeral director and the arranger could work together in planning, arranging, and conducting the funeral. Furthermore, while it might be feasible economically to drive many miles for discount or bargain shopping, when death occurs, people seldom wish to assume the additional burden of lengthy travel. Since people in most cities are highly mobile and may have little "sense of community," there often is not much chance for developing the feelings described above. It should be noted, however, that even in large cities, there are many funeral directors who serve localized areas such as urban villages. These firms may serve a large market area which also is served by many other funeral homes, but they may handle a relatively small number of funerals each year, most of which come from some specific group or subsection of a community.

The second factor underlying the number of funeral homes across the country is the existence of group-centrism. The general attitude of group-centrism exists when a specific group of people believes their own group to be superior to all others. Most familiar of this attitude is that of ethnocentrism, in which the members of a nationality or ethnic group consider their group to be "the best." Tables 6A, 6B, and 6C report the divisional breakdowns according to religion and Table 7 according to nationality.

The adherence to group-centric service is not unlike other occupations in which members of an ethnic or religious group seek most of their goods and services from people of the same group. The personal nature of death influences this tendency even more, and in many communities it is common for people to seek the services of a funeral director according to his ethnic or religious membership. As a result, there are more funeral homes per community in those areas in which a greater proportion of funeral homes serve a specific nationality.[4]

The operation of a funeral home cannot be gauged simply by examining the demographic characteristics for the community or the clientele alone. This leads to the third factor underlying the number of funeral homes, namely, the existence of the service ethos. This ethos has a very real bearing on the situation, for according to the occupational model, services are best provided on a one-to-one basis. Many communities and the funeral directors which serve them have found that this can be done successfully by funeral directors who can devote a maximum amount of time to the families they serve because they serve relatively few families. This does not necessarily fit the bureaucratic model, according to which one funeral director might serve efficiently (but impersonally) considerably more families.

Table 6
The Percentage of Funeral Directors Reporting
A. The Proportion of Protestant
Funerals Conducted by Their Firms

	Almost None	Few	Some	Most	Almost All	N
United States	4%	4%	17%	37%	38%	8,227
New England	12	14	27	31	16	665
Middle Atlantic	7	7	26	35	25	1,740
South Atlantic	1	1	7	30	61	842
East North Central	3	3	18	39	37	2,029
West North Central	1	2	13	42	42	1,168
East South Central	1	0	4	22	73	446
West South Central	1	2	9	32	56	551
Mountain	8	4	17	52	19	282
Pacific	1	1	16	61	21	504

B. The Proportion of Catholic
Funerals Conducted by Their Firms

	Almost None	Few	Some	Most	Almost All	N
United States	19%	24%	38%	13%	6%	8,227
New England	9	13	32	27	19	665
Middle Atlantic	12	19	37	21	11	1,740
South Atlantic	38	26	31	4	1	842
East North Central	17	26	42	11	4	2,029
West North Central	19	31	39	8	3	1,168
East South Central	47	28	22	2	1	446
West South Central	27	33	29	8	3	551
Mountain	13	24	54	6	3	282
Pacific	5	21	63	9	2	504

C. The Proportion of Jewish
Funerals Conducted by Their Firms

	Almost None	Few	Some	Most	Almost All	N
United States	89%	7%	2%	1%	1%	8,227
New England	89	8	1	1	1	665
Middle Atlantic	87	8	3	1	1	1,740
South Atlantic	83	11	4	1	1	842
East North Central	93	4	2	0	1	2,029
West North Central	95	4	1	0	0	1,168
East South Central	88	8	3	0	1	446
West South Central	87	9	3	1	1	551
Mountain	90	5	4	1	0	282
Pacific	86	9	4	0	1	504

Table 7
The Percentage of Funeral Directors Reporting
Whether or Not Their Firms Serve
A Specific Nationality

	Yes	No	N
United States	13%	87%	8,227
New England	34	66	665
Middle Atlantic	18	82	1,740
South Atlantic	5	95	842
East North Central	13	87	2,029
West North Central	14	86	1,168
East South Central	4	96	446
West South Central	7	93	551
Mountain	4	96	282
Pacific	7	93	504

We also must examine internal features, such as the number of employees and the form of ownership of the funeral home. Table 8 reports the divisional breakdown according to the number of licensed personnel employed full time. Table 9 indicates the extent to which funeral home ownership varies according to division. Common sense suggests that firms with very few employees or which are individual proprietorships are not as likely to be amenable to bureaucratic organization as are firms with many employees and/or extensive partnerships or private or public corporations.

Table 8
The Percentage of Funeral Directors Reporting
The Number of Licensed Personnel
Employed by Their Firms

	0	1	2-3	4 or more	N
United States	5%	55%	31%	9%	8,227
New England	5	60	29	6	665
Middle Atlantic	3	62	28	7	1,740
South Atlantic	7	47	32	14	842
East North Central	2	57	32	9	2,029
West North Central	6	59	31	4	1,168
East South Central	10	46	34	10	446
West South Central	6	40	36	18	551
Mountain	5	46	39	10	282
Pacific	9	57	26	10	504

As an index of firm organization, it is useful to examine the manner in which tasks are accomplished, as is shown in Table 10. Across the country, 45% of the funeral directors describe their firm's tasks as being done by or supervised by one person, 47% indicate that the tasks are shared or super-

Table 9
The Percentage of Funeral Directors Reporting
The Form of Ownership of Their Firms

	Individual Proprietorship	Partnership	Private Corporation	Public Corporation	N
United States	46%	15%	38%	1%	8,227
New England	38	8	54	0	665
Middle Atlantic	61	12	26	1	1,740
South Atlantic	34	16	48	2	842
East North Central	51	16	32	1	2,029
West North Central	50	15	34	1	1,168
East South Central	32	20	47	1	446
West South Central	31	19	48	2	551
Mountain	33	11	19	2	282
Pacific	30	15	53	2	504

Table 10
The Percentage of Funeral Directors Reporting
The Form of Organization of Their Firms

Tasks Done By

	Person	A Few People	Separate Specialists	N
United States	45%	47%	8%	8,227
New England	47	47	6	665
Middle Atlantic	55	38	7	1,740
South Atlantic	32	54	14	842
East North Central	46	48	6	2,029
West North Central	48	48	4	1,168
East South Central	34	52	14	446
West South Central	34	47	19	551
Mountain	40	46	14	282
Pacific	36	49	15	504

vised equally by a few people, and 8% indicate that the tasks are done by a few separate specialists. "Pure bureaucratization" probably is best evidenced in firms which employ completely separate specialists who are responsible to a manager. Divisional differences are sizable in terms of pure bureaucratization, ranging from a low of 4% in the West North Central states to a high of 19% in the West South Central states. Combining this finding with the concept of occupational orientation as discussed in Chapter 2, it makes sense that there may be a wide range of occupational behavior within any type of firm organization.

Bureaucratically organized funeral homes might be expected to bear impersonal, bureaucratic names; however, this is not the case. To identify such firms is not a simple matter of looking at their formal names.

Specifically, an analysis of funeral service directories reveals that over 90% of the funeral homes in the United States bear the name of an individual funeral director or his family rather than the name of, say, the community served or some local landmark.[5] For example, one might find that the Doe Funeral Home in Anytown, U.S.A., is operated by John Doe or his successors. This naming custom emphasizes the importance of the funeral director's conception of his role in a given community.

A realistic discussion of American funeral homes which utilizes fictitious names would be most accurate in selecting family names as pseudonyms for the funeral homes investigated and described. However, since the purpose of this book is to examine funeral homes with differing forms of organization, we use analytical pseudonyms for the two funeral homes observed. The tables and discussion thus far emphasize that there are distinguishing practical and analytical characteristics of funeral homes depending upon their firm organization, and we use some of the following identifiable ones in selecting pseudonyms which focus on the analytical features of funeral homes. They are: the number of adult funerals conducted annually, the number of firms serving a given community, the year the firms were founded, the religious and ethnic groups served, the number of licensed employees, the form of ownership, and the form of organization.

According to the criteria, funeral homes with a simple organization may be described as ones which serve a localized area or specific community and have characteristics which fit the personal service occupational model and orientation. The pseudonym for the firm investigated is the Community Funeral Home. According to the criteria, funeral homes with a complex organization serve large metropolitan areas and have characteristics which fit the bureaucratic occupational model and orientation. The pseudonym for the firm investigated is the Cosmopolitan Funeral Home.[6]

It is important to note that firms such as the Community Funeral Home are not necessarily restricted to operating in small American towns. As Habenstein and Lamers (1960: 709-22) point out, similar operations serve urban villages and ethnic or religious communities in most of our cities. Thus, it is not so much a function of being located in a small town as it is that the families served by such a funeral home somehow are defined in terms of the service model. Similarly, such firms as the Cosmopolitan Funeral Home may exist outside of large urban centers, especially if they serve a wide geographical area. Once again, the thing that distinguishes them is the tendency to define the funeral in terms of the bureaucratic model.[7]

These names are not intended to be pejorative, nor do they imply a value judgment about the quality of services rendered. Instead, they are meant to enhance the analytical clarity of our discussion. It is important to keep in mind that the two funeral homes discussed in this book actually bore family names which were well established in their respective communities, and never have the actual firms utilized our analytical names.

The Community Funeral Home

The Community Funeral Home is located in the northeastern United States in a town of approximately 15,000 people, less than 100 miles from a major metropolitan area. The Community Funeral Home was established in 1900, by the great-grandfather of the present owner. At the time of its establishment he also owned and operated a livery stable in the community. His son, the grandfather, joined him in the operation of the "undertaking parlor around 1910, and helped run both it and the livery stable as well as being a general highway contractor and a local politician. Eventually, the grandfather sold the livery stable and construction business and worked only as an undertaker, in addition to his political office. He was joined in business by the present owner's father in the late 1930's. At that time, they opened and operated for a number of years a furniture store in addition to the funeral home.

During the early years of the funeral parlor's operation, it was felt that the fitting conduct of an undertaker was as a dignified provider of necessary equipment and paraphernalia. As time passed, however, members of the firm began to see themselves in a service capacity and conducted their activities as such. They increasingly felt that an important aspect of their work was to be involved personally in all aspects of every funeral service.

After the grandfather's death, the father operated the funeral home alone until his death. At that time, the funeral home management was taken over by the father's wife and son, who continued to operate it. Today, the funeral home is owned and operated by the son.

The Community Funeral Home has occupied the same building in the center of the town for the past fifty years. However, the building was not built or designed for this purpose. It originally served as a carriage shed for the great-grandfather. As more space was needed in the funeral parlor, individual rooms were added, finished, and developed until there finally emerged the funeral home as it exists today.

The building is white with black shutters and wood shingles. The overall impression as one drives into the parking lot is of an old New England home. The effect is deliberate, and every detail is intended to foster this impression. The funeral home has wall-to-wall carpeting throughout. A conscious effort is made to give the appearance of warmth and welcome much as is done by local people in their own homes when guests are expected.

The office serves multiple purposes. First, it serves as the arrangement room in which the bereaved family and the funeral director discuss plans for the funeral. When used as such, efforts are made to make its appearance uncluttered and comfortable, thereby encouraging conversation. To enhance this atmosphere and to emphasize the funeral home's pride in its service background, the original licenses and diplomas of all the members of the family who have been engaged in the practice of funeral directing hang on the walls. The diplomas date from 1894 and the licenses from 1899, some of them among the first issued in the United States. Thus, the funeral home's long history and family commitment to the field are evident to everyone who enters.[8]

In this office is a specially built enclosed closet-desk which is used for the funeral home's business activities. The preparation of such things as funeral purchase records, bills, and receipts is carried out in this office. This office is also used to conduct much of the family's private business. Finally, it houses the historical records of the funeral home, which date back to 1900.

Such multiple usage presents certain problems for the funeral home. For instance, when bereaved families drop in unexpectedly to make funeral arrangements, the business office must be converted quickly to a conference office without upsetting the bereaved family. This "drop-in" situation at times arises because some of the clientele arrive at the door to announce the death of a family member. The office, then, is the operational center for every aspect of the Community Funeral Home, and its importance may be evidenced by the fact that its carpet is the most worn in the building.

The remainder of the rooms are used for funeral purposes and are decorated in combinations of wallpaper, painted walls, and wood paneling. Each of the rooms is decorated with occasional tables and comfortable upholstered chairs and couches. Careful attention is given to creating the appearance of a casually decorated, well kept private home.

There are two main rooms used for funeral services and three others which may be converted easily in the event of more than two funerals at once. Most funerals involve placing folding chairs in rows. Afterward, the funeral home is decorously put back into its usual "casual" order.

There is a room specified as the preparation room which is equipped to carry out "embalming, cosmetizing, dressing, and casketing" of the dead body.[9] For both practical and aesthetic reasons, the preparation room was designed to resemble an operating room in a modern hospital.

The preparation room is cleaned immediately following each embalming and always is immaculate. Every opportunity is taken to show interested parties through the preparation room whenever so requested. Interestingly, many such requests are received, and it is not unusual to show members of one family through each time another kinfolk arrives.

The owner believes that there should not be secrets revolving around the idea of embalming. However, people are discouraged from actually viewing the process.

Upstairs is a casket selection room in which are twenty-four caskets. The caskets are owned by the funeral home for display and sale; thus, the casket selected by a family is the one actually used for the subsequent funeral.

The funeral home uses a station wagon to remove the deceased from the place of death, and the station wagon also serves as a flower car during the procession. The funeral home also owns and maintains its own hearse. This vehicle is used exclusively by the firm and is not rented to other firms in the vicinity.

The properties adjoining the funeral home are owned and occupied by the owner's mother and the owner and his family. The homes are large, Colonial-style, nicely kept, and well-appointed, and they have been owned by the family for several generations. The entire complex of two private houses, the funeral home, and the garages occupy nearly an acre in the geographical center of the business district of the town.

The funeral home conducts slightly more than 100 funerals annually. Most of these funerals are for people from the immediate community, although on occasion, the funeral home is called upon to provide services to people in neighboring or distant communities. The staff which handles these funerals is composed of the owner, who is a licensed funeral director, one other licensed funeral director, and an assistant who is not licensed, but who has worked for the funeral home for many years.

Both of the licensed funeral directors work in concert on most of the funerals, and each is essentially capable of carrying out the necessary tasks individually. There is no clear differentiation of tasks and duties between them, and both see their prime responsibility as being the providing of important services to bereaved families. They share in jobs of maintenance, purchasing funeral merchandise and supplies, and counseling with families.

Death-related activities at the Community Funeral Home often are not of a regular nature. Handling about 100 funerals each year means that the funeral home personnel are much busier sometimes than they are at others, for the funerals are not spaced at planned intervals. At times, there is almost no work for anyone, while at other times there is more work than the entire staff can handle easily. This means that, although activities are routinized, they do not follow a specified schedule.

The Community Funeral Home exemplifies many of the organizational characteristics of the personal service occupation model. It is important to point out that its history, physical setting, firm organization, and community position are very similar to many other funeral homes in other American communities.[10]

The Cosmopolitan Funeral Home

The Cosmopolitan Funeral Home is located in the northeast in the heart of a city of over 1,000,000 people. It was established in 1920 by two cousins. The original funeral parlor was operated on the ground floor of a three story walk-up, and the cousins lived on the two floors above it. Their initial intention was to appeal primarily to the residents of the neighborhood, and for the first few years their activities were confined largely to providing personal services to a relatively well-defined neighborhood.

Transportation improvements in the city, however, brought changes to their operation. Former neighborhood residents who had moved to other sections of the city were able to get to the funeral home quickly and easily, and the number of funerals handled annually increased steadily. With the growing volume, the cousins decided to split up the partnership.

One cousin retained ownership of the building facilities and continued to operate the funeral home in essentially the same manner as it had been since its inception. His intentions were to continue to provide personal services for the families served. The limitations of the physical facility and of him as an individual necessitated keeping the practice small and confined to the neighborhood. As such, it has continued to prosper and still exists in the same location, a successful small funeral home.

The other cousin moved to a location near a metropolitan hospital. He retained a certain portion of the clientele of the former funeral home, in addition to attracting an entirely new and diversified one. From its inception the new firm attempted to attract a larger number of funerals. As a result of its growing volume, the funeral home needed to increase its number of employees. As it did so, it slowly began to develop a more complex firm organization. Through advertising, community contacts, and many civic and social activities, the funeral home continued to expand.

During the 1930's, the eldest son of the owner joined him in the operation of the firm, and the firm became incorporated. His addition to the firm meant attracting an even wider audience than before, and the firm's volume continued to grow. Accompanying this growth was the further complexity of its organization. As the years passed, the firm continued to grow, and the complexity of the firm organization increased.

As the organization became more complex, other members of the family were taken in on a stock ownership basis and given management level jobs. The actual employees working with families at the time of a funeral were decreasingly members of the original family. Today, except on rare occasions when personal friends die, all services are provided by employees rather than owners.[11]

In addition to these changes, the firm changed its policy concerning funeral vehicles and other motor equipment. They began to rent from a separate company which owned a fleet of limousines, hearses, flower cars, and service cars for general funeral purposes. The drivers of these vehicles came to be and are today union employees whose only function is to drive the vehicles. This change brought a new group of workers who were separate and distinct from the funeral operation itself.

The Cosmopolitan Funeral Home is located on the corner of a major avenue. The building is large, occupying most of one city block. There are overhanging structures above the entrance which resemble motion picture marquees and on which are emblazoned the firm's name in large black letters.

To enter the building one passes through glass doors which connect a small entry alcove and the outside to the lobby within. Most of the reception responsibilities fall to any one of several people whose special task it is to know where to send people.

There are two offices used only for arrangement purposes. These rooms are maintained in a neat, orderly fashion and are entered for brief periods by funeral directors with bereaved families. These rooms are as large as many home living rooms, and the decor is a combination of Chippendale Colonial and French Provincial. The rooms have six or seven comfortable armchairs spaced about small tables in a seemingly casual fashion.

The second floor is considerably different in appearance from the main lobby. The lobby is largely marble and wood and appears rather formal. The second floor is thickly carpeted and the walls are off-white, with what appear to be hand painted paintings hanging along them. A door marked PRIVATE leads into the manager's office, which is surprisingly small. In an ante-office cubicle there are two desks on which are piled papers, books, and assorted office materials. These desks are manned by a secretary and a bookkeeper. The ante-office leads into the manager's even smaller office. This office is never used for making funeral arrangements and is used by the manager for his administrative duties.

One of the distinctive characteristics of this office is that it does not resemble large executive or administrative offices with privacy, spaciousness, and convenient implements to transact intellectual or other kinds of "higher management" activities. Rather, it seems that it is more the center for the operational aspects of the Cosmopolitan Funeral Home. It appears that since very little funeral directing is actually done in this office, and since families are counseled within specific arrangement rooms, this space does not merit being decorated as a "haven" for a busy executive.

Adjacent to the manager's office is another very private office, which is used by the principal stockholder of the corporation. It was described as being used by the main owner "to read the daily newspaper each morning."

There are other offices which contribute to the workings of the

Cosmopolitan Funeral Home. Most important from the economic view-point is "the business and accounting office," for in it all of the statistical records, family histories, billings, purchases, sales, etc., are kept and handled. This office is staffed by three employees who are completely separate from those in the funeral service operation itself The three work as accountants and bookkeepers, statisticians and typists, and their jobs are confined to papers and books. This office is located on the main floor, behind the garage. It is never entered by anyone except those directly involved in the funeral home operation. As a matter of fact, those lowest in the organizational hierarchy seldom venture into it. Funeral directors and management level personnel do so occasionally, however, for they are involved in such things as payroll, sales, receipts, disbursements, and other financial matters.

Next, there is "the dispatch office," which is the funeral home's nerve center. One of the funeral directors described it: "Functionally, it is the most important office in the building." Like the business office, it is located on the main floor. It is a tiny, cramped room in which there are a series of connected desks, kneehole spaces, and wall shelves. It is at these desks during the morning hours that calls from bereaved families are received.

When a call is received, a series of forms is completed. One is used in the internal operation of the funeral home for the period until the funeral. One is used for the legal purpose of filing the death certificate with the Board of Health. Another is used for the bookkeeping office to record the funeral transaction and sale. All these forms are completed simultaneously by a funeral director as he talks with the family on the phone.

Adjacent to the dispatch office is another small cubicle in which are several wall charts explaining firm procedures and state laws. It is in this room, in back of a back room, that all of the owner and employee funeral director licenses and registrations are hung. This room serves as the spot for funeral directors to do other paperwork when they are not attending the three main phones.

In the basement there is a large selection room which contains about 35 caskets and other funeral merchandise. Also in the basement is the preparation room. It is a large room with two embalming tables and one dressing table, all of which may be in use simultaneously. The preparation room is never open to the public, and the problem of keeping visitors out is solved by locked doors. The reason for exclusion is because the room is seldom unoccupied and, in general, is quite cluttered.

The Cosmopolitan Funeral Home conducts over 300 funerals per year and may be characterized as having a complex firm organization. Quite naturally, at the top of the service organization is ownership. However, the owners seldom are present in any meaningful way; although when they do come on the scene, they are recognized quickly and universally avoided by most of the employees, purportedly because as one said: "They only come here occasionally, and I'm always worried that they'll ask me an embarrassing question or that they'll just notice me. It's just better not to have *them* know you." Next in line are family controlled managerial positions. These jobs often are as figureheads and have little functional use to the organization as a whole. One of the funeral directors explained: "In most instances, these men are related by marriage and have been saved from total oblivion in the work force at large by being placed in a titled position with little to do so they won't screw things up."

The next level contains the actual workaday managers, men whose concerns are centered primarily around funeral activities. These managers must answer to top level management and the owners for such things as efficiently run funerals, client satisfaction, profit or loss, and other related matters. There is only one licensed manager of the funeral home, and although he is a licensed funeral director, his responsibilities for funeral related tasks are limited to occasional counseling.

Funeral counselors are licensed funeral directors who meet with families which come to make arrangements for funerals. This job actually is the starting point of the extensive division of labor which is totally unrelated to ownership. Counselors assist families in the planning and arranging of the funeral service, help make decisions about the extent to which facilities, equipment, and merchandise will result in funeral. sales, and, in general, are concerned with the implementation of these concerns. The title "counselors" stems from the personal service model in that it is in the carrying out of such tasks as counseling that bereaved families are served by the funeral director.

According to their own description, the major task of the counselor is to "make arrangements." This job is seen by most of the employees as being an important one, for it is well understood that it is through "the making of arrangements" that funeral sales are accomplished. Thus, in addition to providing counseling services, the counselors are inextricably caught up in the process of sales and the financial arrangements for funerals.

Next in line to the counselors, although not formally designated by a specific title, are the supervisors, whose job it is to make certain that everyone lower in the hierarchy than counselor does his job. In a sense, the supervisors are in charge of personnel logistics, but they are concerned also with such things as employee satisfaction, work schedules, and similar concerns. The people who carry out these personnel supervisory tasks also are licensed funeral directors. Although it appears that they fall somewhere slightly below counselors, their own assessment of the situation is that they are at least equal to, if not more important than, the counselors. The primary difference seems to be that they are not concerned with funeral arrangements or sales, but rather with the employees of the organization.

The next level of employee is composed of the "directors." Their primary tasks involve the actual conduct and direction of funerals as well as such things as attending bereaved families during visiting hours. These people are licensed funeral directors, but they are not concerned often with such things as making arrangements with the family or supervising other personnel in any capacity. They turn to the supervisory personnel or the counselors for supervision and orders. Theoretically, but seldom in practice, they are also the supervisors of the next three categories.

Under the funeral directors in the organizational scheme at the Cosmopolitan Funeral Home are those referred to as "removal men." Removal men are licensed funeral directors whose primary responsibility is to go to the place of death (hospital, private home, or elsewhere) with the appropriate equipment and remove the dead body. These men, however, have other duties which actually occupy as much or more of their time than do removals. They do such things as pick up burial permits and death certificates and deliver them to the appropriate offices of vital statistics, help with embalming, and accompany hearse drivers to cemeteries when a funeral director's license is essential. In general, removal men bridge the gap between funeral directors and the group below them, the apprentices.

Both directors and removal men are licensed funeral directors and in addition to their regular tasks and responsibilities, perform the job of embalming. There is one man who is designated the "head embalmer," and it is his responsibility to attend to the carrying out of embalming, cosmetizing, and casketing. His is not a supervisory position, however, for he does a great deal of the embalming himself. When he is unable to handle the amount of work, he is assisted by any of the removal men or directors who are not busy at that moment. This means that a large number of people carry out the task of embalming, and it is not uncommon that one person begins and another finishes a job. The allocation of personnel to handle embalming is up to the head embalmer. Theoretically, this creates another level in the hierarchy; however, in actual practice, it is a one-man level, for embalmers actually may be found among the funeral directors and removal men.

The lowest level in the hierarchy of this extensive organization is that of the apprentices. These are unlicensed individuals who are registered with the state's Department of Health as certified trainees in the field. Their position is one of almost nonstatus rather than as a clearly defined office in the organization. Apprentices are those who do everything that is not the direct responsibility of all others in the organization. They run errands, clean up after embalmings, put up flowers, dust corners, and in general, carry out the most mundane funeral tasks imaginable. An especially well qualified or well trained apprentice may at times be involved in assisting at embalmings, but this only occurs when he has had enough schooling or has previously worked at a funeral home where he was trained.

   The present apprentice system is considerably different from the one which existed from just after World War II until the early 1960's, during which time apprentices were "a dime a dozen." For instance, in 1958, the Cosmopolitan Funeral Home employed about ten apprentices, thus, making the work of counselors, funeral directors, and removal men considerably easier, for each of them could "pass the buck" relatively lower with far greater ease. Today, largely because of unionization, the old system is defunct, and the firm employs only three apprentices.[12]

   The job of dispatcher is to handle the logistics of people and places, cemeteries, burials, caskets, clergy, and in general to know where living people and dead bodies are, where they are going to be, and at what times they are going to be there. The dispatchers are located strangely in the hierarchy at some unspecified point, and they work in a capacity which makes their location a difficult matter. They are concerned with the dispatching of personnel and equipment in regard to funeral arrangements and with communications with the world outside of the funeral home, such as cemeteries, churches, etc. The chief dispatcher takes considerable pride in his claim that he is a "funeral director," although he is not licensed as such and never practices as one.

Similarities and Differences

   There are a number of important similarities and differences between the two funeral service organizations which are the center of this study.[13] Table 11 summarizes the ways in which the two firms line up in terms of the criteria utilized in the beginning of this chapter.

Table 11
The Characteristics of the Two Funeral Homes

	Community Funeral Home	Cosmopolitan Funeral Home
Number of Funerals Conducted Annually	About 100	Over 300
Community Size or Market Area Served	15,000	Over 1,000,000
Number of Other Firms	0	Over 20
Year Founded	1900	1920
Percentage of Protestant, Roman Catholic, and Jewish Funerals		
Protestant	60%	50%
Roman Catholic	35%	35%
Jewish (and Other)	5%	15%
TOTAL	100%	100%
Nationality Served	No Specific	No Specific
Number of Licensed Personnel	2	Over 15
Form of Ownership	Proprietorship	Private Corporation
Form of Organization	Simple	Complex

Both funeral homes are long-established, essentially family owned, and each in its own way is very successful. Even though the Cosmopolitan Funeral Home is corporately chartered, in the truest sense of the word it does not function as a public corporation, for there is not diffuse ownership scattered over many people. Thus, both funeral homes are owned by family members who are descendants of the founders. In addition, it seems worthwhile to point out that the basic task of these two, and almost all funeral homes, is to provide funeral services when called upon to do so. This essential similarity of purpose is important, for it would be quite a different thing if one kind of funeral home devoted itself to research of funeral needs rather than to providing funeral services.

These similarities are also important from another perspective. Namely, the need for funeral directors to provide their services is commonly recognized by Americans in large urban areas as well as in small towns. Let us characterize these similarities simply as being the occurrence of a death, a dead body with which to contend, community norms and customs with which to deal, certain considerations regarding final disposition of the dead body, and the fact that death is the loss of an individual.

The very fact of permanent loss emphasizes that the emotional crisis of death for a bereaved person is considerable. There are numerous important factors involved because of the special nature of the events which bring people to the funeral director. The emergence of his special services stems, in part, from the social and demographic changes which make the events a different problem from what they were in the past.

As our earlier discussion about funeral practices makes clear, it is possible that all these demands could be met through means and activities which did not involve funeral directors; however, in America this is not the case. From farmlands to small towns to large cities, people commonly turn to the services of professional funeral directors when death occurs. Since this is the case, people seem to expect funeral directors to have similar concerns and interests. This is so just as it is when we fall sick and turn to a doctor to minister to our needs, expecting that most doctors are enough alike that any one of them will attempt to provide certain curative treatment.[14]

There are a number of ways in which the Community Funeral Home and the Cosmopolitan Funeral Home are vastly different. First, there is the number of funerals conducted annually, with the former conducting about 100 and the latter over 300. Such disparate volumes have fostered disparate service approaches and practices.

We contend that the service volume may be an important predisposing factor in determining the firm organization for a given operation. Our description of the two firms emphasizes that this is the case. Namely, the Community Funeral Home is characterized by a simple service organization and an undifferentiated division of labor. The Cosmopolitan Funeral

Home is characterized by a complex service organization and an extensively differentiated division of labor.

In the first funeral home, all aspects of each funeral may be and
generally are carried out by all of the members of the firm. Contrast this
with the second firm's hierarchy of employees which separately handles
tasks ranging from management to counseling to funeral directing to
making removals to doing whatever is left over. The behavior of the people involved in one practice is geared to the toality, while the behavior of
those in the other practice is geared to specific parts of the totality. It also
suggests that the Community Funeral Home personnel generally appear in
multiple roles whereas the Cosmopolitan Funeral Home personnel
generally appear in single, specified roles.

Another important difference between the two funeral firms are
policies and procedures relating to management. In the first funeral home,
management of the business operation and the handling of funeral services are carried out by the same individuals, whose concerns are not con-
strained by notions of a limited office. Although it is possible that management at the second funeral home could be allocated in a similar fashion, it
is not the case, nor is it likely that it is the case in other large funeral
organizations. This means, therefore, that for the larger operation, the
term management refers to some specific matters, whereas in the smaller
one management may refer to any one of a number of aspects of the
funeral home operation.

Another point of comparison between the two firms is the casket selection room, which is a subject of considerable interest to all funeral directors. Even though most of the other funeral merchandise tends to be in-
cidental and largely carried for convenience, the casket is an important
element in the funeral service. In this respect, the management of both
firms study charts, sales reports, inventory control cards, and all of the
usual mercantile devices to ensure a properly handled merchandise
operation.[15]

The selection rooms in both firms are large and well-lit, and they are
unobtrusively decorated. The differences between caskets generally are obvious, and the funeral directors do not depend upon some secret "hidden
value" of the merchandise. The selection room, with numerous caskets on
individual stands, is often frightening and distressing to the bereaved. The
funeral directors, however, seem to believe that it is the room that should
be least frightening and upsetting. "After all, it's filled with empty
caskets."

There is a great deal of difference between the bereaved and the funeral
director in their attitudes toward the casket selection room. For the
former, it often seems that the room represents death's real presence, while
for the latter, it is a place where he can demonstrate knowledge about
cabinet-making and the designs of caskets. Here, too, by explaining

funeral customs and the place of the casket in the funeral, the funeral director can assist the bereaved in making a selection from his available merchandise.

Even though the financial profit of both funeral firms is directly related to the sale of funeral merchandise, especially caskets, to most funeral directors, the casket has a symbolic value that transcends its mercantile one. Over the years, the casket has become an increasingly important part of the funeral service. At one point, it might have been merely a receptacle for the dead body. As Americans became more conscious of the symbolic status value of the casket and the funeral director saw an opportunity to operate more profitably by offering more expensive merchandise, the casket was elevated to a fairly important position.[16]

Table 12

Funeral Service Operating Income, Operating Expenses, And Investment Patterns by Size Category*

UNITED STATES Number of Services		0 to 99		100 to 199		200 to 299		300 or more		All Firms
OPERATING INCOME PER SERVICE										
Funeral Charges	$	1,001	$	966	$	976	$	940	$	969
Interment Receptacle Charge		192		160		146		112		151
Other Funeral Home Charges		18		18		17		16		17
ALL OPERATING INCOME	$	1,211	$	1,144	$	1,139	$	1,068	$	1,137
MERCHANDISE COSTS										
Casket Costs	$	181	$	177	$	171	$	162	$	172
Interment Receptacle Costs		102		85		75		59		79
Other Funeral Home Costs		15		11		14		15		14
ALL MERCHANDISE COSTS		298	$	273	$	260	$	236	$	265
Gross Margin		913		871		879		832		873
OPERATING EXPENSES		866		793		790		718		788
Net Margin	$	47	$	78	$	89	$	114	$	84
INVESTMENT DATA										
Accounts Receivable	$	6,151	$	9,583	$	16,755	$	19,047	$	9,444
Merchandise Inventory		13,565		29,953		56,046		91,133		29,566
Building		61,755		96,240		135,819		279,439		97,927
Funeral Service Equipment		15,440		27,470		46,386		69,661		26,935
Motor Equipment		15,061		24,607		31,981		53,920		22,892
ALL INVESTMENTS		$111,972		$187,853		$286,987		$513,200		$186,764

*The source for Table 12 is: Vanderlyn R. Pine, *Facts and Figures of the United States*, 1974 Edition. Milwaukee: National Funeral Directors Association, 1974, p. 36.

Both funeral homes calculate their operating expenses and overhead costs separately from their merchandise sales and casket costs. This means that if their service and facility charges recoup their operating expenses and overhead costs, it is in the sale of merchandise that most of their profits reside. However, there is considerable variation in the approach to selling funeral merchandise. Table 12 reports the figures for the entire United States. Divisional variations exist, but their complexity does not contribute usefully to the present analysis. Both funeral homes are somewhat higher than average on funeral services selected but somewhat lower than average on operating expenses.

The Regions of the Funeral Home

One of the similarities of the two firms is the manner in which they separate activities into specific "regions" in terms of the funeral home. Erving Goffman (1959: 106) defines "a region . . . as any place that is bounded to some degree by barriers to perception." Moreover, the impression and understanding which arises from specific behavior generally saturates the region and time span in which it occurs. Thus, any individual in a region will be able to observe the behavior of others and be guided by the definition of the situation which that behavior fosters.[17]

We refer to the place where the ceremonial aspect of the funeral occurs as the front region. It involves funeral directors in a setting visible to the bereaved and includes the public behavior, appearance, and the manner of the funeral director. We discuss the front region as involving public behavior in the funeral home.

There are aspects of the funeral which must be kept from public view because they may discredit the desired impression; for example, the embalming of the dead.[18] Such activities cannot take place in the front region and are relegated to a nonpublic location or the back region. We discuss the back region as involving nonpublic behavior in the funeral home.

The back region is the place where the impression fostered by the behavior may be contradicted with little chance of discrediting the performance. It is important that performers in the back region have a greater degree of control over their work. Goffman (1959: 112) puts it this way:

> It is here that the capacity of a performance to express something beyond itself may be painstakingly fabricated; it is here that illusions and impressions are openly constructed. Here stage props and items of personal front can be stored in a kind of compact collapsing of whole repertoires of actions and characters.

In sum, then, we consider front regions to be those public locations where particular funeral behavior takes place and back regions to be those nonpublic locations where action occurs that is related to the funeral but is not consistent with the funeral director's intended appearance.

It is useful to add a third residual region, that is, all places other than the two already mentioned. We call this residual region the "outside," which may include other people in other settings who may be behaving publicly or nonpublicly for their own sake; thus, the notion of *outside* is relevant only to a specific situation. Our discussion of the outside region for funeral directors focuses on those activities which take place out of the funeral home rather than outside of a specific funeral. This enables us to examine the ways in which funeral directors present themselves when they are not involved directly in a funeral.

Thus far, we have described funeral homes in general and compared the funeral homes investigated in particular, pointing out the similarities and differences regarding their settings, organizations, and operations. More important than the descriptive elements of this chapter, however, are the connections between the service and bureaucratic models and the organizational bases of the two diverse funeral homes.

We will return later to a more complete discussion of how organizational concerns can be related usefully to the service and bureaucratic models in terms of the funeral director's presentation of self. Before we attend to such concerns, however, let us move on to some comparative descriptions about the ways in which funeral directors present themselves. In the next three chapters we will discuss such behavior as it occurs out of the funeral home, publicly in the funeral home, and nonpublicly in the funeral home.

Notes

1. Many categories of firm organization are possible. The problem with utilizing too many, however, is that the analytical clarity of a simple comparison may be lost. If it were possible to measure accurately minute differences with, say, ordinal scales, it would be useful to have more categories.

2. There is a detailed summary of the research process in the introduction and the appendices. This includes a research chronicle, the funeral direction questionnaire, the arranger questionnaire and interview schedule, the questionnaires for two large-scale national studies of funeral directors, and their marginal findings. The material presented in the first part of this chapter (Tables 1-10) is drawn from responses to a questionnaire sent to the 13,625 members of the National Funeral Directors Association in 1971. A total of 8,227 questionnaires were returned, representing 60.4% of the total membership.

3. For comparative evidence and a fuller discussion about their typicality, see Robert W. Habenstein and William M. Lamers, *The History of American Funeral Directing*. Milwaukee: The Bulfin Printers, 1955, especially pp. 507-97.

4. A statistical analysis of eight variables (characteristics) indicates many important relationships. The complexity of these correlations is clarified considerably by a path analysis. Interested path analysts may utilize the following matrix of zero-order correlation coefficients in carrying out such an analysis.

Zero-Order Product-Moment Correlation Coefficients for the Eight Variables (Pearson's r)

	X_2	X_3	X_4	X_5	X_6	X_7	X_8
X_1	.424	-.079	.631	-.597	.354	.854	.805
X_2	....	.789	-.219	.388	-.338	.288	.054
X_3		....	-.528	..652	-.441	-.158	-.289
X_4			....	-.759	.804	.750	.890
X_5				....	-.630	-.428	-.683
X_6					....	.508	.637
X_7						....	.894

X_1 = number of adult funerals
X_2 = community size
X_3 = number of other funeral homes
X_4 = year founded
X_5 = nationality served
X_6 = number of licensed employees
X_7 = form of ownership
X_8 = form of organization

5. The analysis involved counts from the following two major lists of practicing funeral directors. *The 1972-1973 Directory* is the membership roster of the National Funeral Directors Association, and it lists 14,059 members of the Association's affiliated state associations. The 1972-1973 (21st Edition) *American Blue Book of Funeral Directors* is the major commerical directory of funeral homes, and it lists 22,100 funeral homes in the continental United States.

6. These pseudonyms also are useful in terms of the framework used to analyze "local and cosmopolitan" influence as presented by Robert K. Merton, *Social Theory and Social Structure*. New York: The Free Press, 1949, Chapter X, pp. 387-420.

7. There is an alternative type of organization possible, but to my knowledge it is relatively rare in funeral directing: this is a group practice in which a number of funeral directors utilize the same facility, yet provide all of their services individually for each funeral. Where such an organization does exist, it typically is composed of funeral directors each of whom handles less than 100 funerals a year and who actually carry out their practices as solo practitioners, although operating from a seemingly "organized" facility.

8. It is not unusual to find organizations attempting to connect themselves with existing institutions or with community history. For example, see the discussion by

Philip Selznick, *TVA and the Grass Roots*. New York: Harper Torchbooks, 1966, especially pp. 37-41 and 47.

9. These terms are used commonly by funeral directors to refer to the acts carried out to accomplish the tasks in question. For a treatment of funeral directing which deals with such terms see Howard C. Raether (ed.), *Successful Funeral Service Practice*. Englewood Cliffs, N.J.: Prentice-Hall, Inc., 1971.

10. Further documentation of this circumstance is provided by Howard C. Raether, *op. cit.*

11. The transformation to a large organization meant many changes for the firm. The growth characteristics of this large firm bear certain resemblance to large law firms as described by Erwin O. Smigel, *The Wall Street Lawyer*. Bloomington, Indiana: Indiana University Press, 1969, pp. 173-90.

12. It was very apparent that apprentice recruitment was a problem for this firm. For a different example of the recruitment process for a profession see Smigel, *op. cit.*, pp. 72-112.

13. Many similar points are made about lawyers by Smigel, *op. cit.*, pp. 171-204; for such a comparison in medicine see Eliot Freidson, *Profession of Medicine*. New York: Dodd, Mead and Company, 1970, pp. 87-157.

14. Such a need is treated from a different perspective by Freidson, *op. cit.*, pp. 278-301.

15. For a full treatment of these and similar concerns see Howard C. Raether, *op. cit.*, pp. 34-101.

16. For a more complete discussion of this in terms of funeral expenditure see Vanderlyn R. Pine and Derek L. Phillips, "The Cost of Dying: A Sociological Analysis of Funeral Expenditure," *Social Problems*, 17 (Winter, 1970), pp. 405-17.

17. For a discussion of this perspective and a background elaboration of the present treatment of "regions" see Erving Goffman, *The Presentation of Self in Everyday Life*. Garden City, New York: Doubleday and Company, Anchor Books, 1959, pp. 106-40.

18. For a discussion about just this topic see Goffman, *op. cit.*, p. 114.

Chapter 4

Behavior Out of the
Funeral Home

In the last chapter we described the setting and organization of the funeral home, emphasizing that different behavior occurs in different regions. In this chapter, we discuss the ways in which funeral directors present themselves when they are out of their funeral home. It will become clear that the distinction between nonpublic and public behavior inside of and all behavior outside of the funeral home is not nearly so clear-cut as implied in the previous discussion. It also will become increasingly evident that the type of organization in which one practices has considerable influence on one's behavior.

Community Participation

The extent to which the individuals of the two funeral homes are involved in the activities of their respective communities is considerably different. The personnel of the Community Funeral Home belong to and are active in the town's two largest churches, and both the owner and the employees have been or are important leaders of the governing bodies of the two churches. Similarly, in their civic organizations they are very active and generally are in leadership positions. The owner expressed it this way: "A constant concern of ours is that we present an appropriate and suitable image to the general public." Moreover, they do not rely on advertising campaigns to gain and maintain a reputation. Instead, they depend on their dealings with the public at the time of a funeral service as well as when they are doing other things.

Importantly, in most small cities or towns there is considerable emphasis placed on the social usefulness of organizational activities by many leading business and professional people. Funeral directors are no exception. However, because of the intense personal, emotional, and social needs of bereaved people, many funeral directors in such communities are more extensively involved than many other business and professional leaders. For these and similar reasons, the personnel of the Community Funeral Home are active in local churches and civic and business organizations.[1]

The Community Funeral Home directors believe that such activities are the best insurance for the future continuation of an active funeral home and for its progressive growth. There is a problem in their thinking, however. Many of the other leading members of these community activities also belong for the same reasons, and they, too, commonly participate in many of the same organizations. Thus, these leaders often form an elite power group which has diffuse control over several organizations, and most interaction is with each other, not the general membership. Although they may be very active in civic affairs, they do not necessarily have contact with as wide a range of people as their many memberships suggest.

Such active participation may result in political appointments or in elective political offices, which may lead to the curious result of losing clientele. For instance, the owner's grandfather gained and possessed considerable political power. In addition to political factors, one of the motivations for acquiring such power was to increase the clientele of the funeral home. Once a power holder, however, he was confronted with a paradoxical situation. His position of power antagonized certain potential clients, thereby defeating his original purpose. Nonetheless, as do many other funeral directors, he held political offices as a result of his community activities.[2]

The personnel of the Community Funeral Home attend dinners to honor people or groups such as a retiring employee of fifty years with the local power and light company, or a superintendent of highways with twenty-seven years as an employee of the town, or a championship football team. These activities are seen as extremely important, not only for their own value, but also because they are "essential contacts for the sustenance of the funeral home." On many occasions, such social obligations occur at inconvenient times and are very annoying to have to attend. The following remark typifies the attitude about such matters. "Well, that's just part of the job. As much as it's a pain in the neck to have to go to this party, I just feel that I *have* to do it. George always helped out whenever we needed it."

At such affairs, the Community Funeral Home directors often are the life of the party. On many occasions I overheard community residents mentioning their vivacity and outstanding social skills. Always, their effort is to appear friendly, cheerful, and intelligent. This means they enjoy a "fine reputation" as good party people who are "lots of fun to be with." It is important that these characteristics are quite different from those demonstrated while working in the funeral home in any capacity. Such light-hearted social behavior is a socially acceptable adaptation of characteristics which point out that funeral directors are not morbid, somber, and sad.

To some extent, the community participation and social life of the owners and the family connected managerial staff of the Cosmopolitan Funeral Home is similar to that of the Community Funeral Home except that it exists on an urban (cosmopolitan) basis rather than on a small town (community) basis. For the salaried employees of the Cosmopolitan Funeral Home, however, the situation is considerably different.

A few of the counselors belong to lodges such as the Masons, the Elks, and the Knights of Columbus. Most of them attend church regularly, and there are even a few who have positions on their church's governing board. The major difference is that all of the counselors claim that such activities are for purely social or personal reasons. They explained that they really do not need to belong to anything, but that they do so because they "enjoy" the meetings, or because their fathers belonged or their friends belong to the same lodge. They seldom complained about having to go to social affairs purely for the show or for the sake of business. Most of them described their community and social activities as revolving primarily around their closest friends. There seemed to be little effort to interact with the community at large and almost no concern whatever about the possibility of social contacts fostering or influencing business relations.

The community participation of the personnel of the Cosmopolitan Funeral Home is directly related to their position with the firm; that is, the amount of one's community activities decreases with one's position in the hierarchy of the firm. To a certain extent, the situation is the same for the personnel of the Community Funeral Home; however, even the employees of the Community Funeral Home are active in community affairs and essentially in leadership positions, although their level of activity may be lower than that of the owner himself.

Another major difference is that for all the personnel of the Community Funeral Home, community participation is believed to be a necessary and valuable aspect both of their position in the community and as a way in which to enhance and perpetuate the business. This is considerably different from the attitude found among most of the employees of the Cosmopolitan Funeral Home, who view such participation as a self-fulfilling experience.

Once again, the two contrasting modes of behavior regarding community participation exemplify the two occupational models. The activities of the personnel of the Community Funeral Home demonstrate the conviction that personal contacts make a real difference to the funeral home. This belief conforms to the model of individuals providing personal services. The Cosmopolitan Funeral Home personnel appear to believe that their community activities should be detached from their business activities, thereby conforming to the bureaucratic model, which separates business and personal matters.

Social Status and Life Style

As the preceding discussion suggests, the life style of the Community Funeral Home owner is such that it affords his family high social status. It was apparent consistently that people in the community locate them in the upper social status of the town with doctors, lawyers, educators, and other business or professional people. Their home bespeaks upper status as do their community activities.

The same forces provide considerably higher social status to the employees of the firm than one might expect given their backgrounds. These people are located by many community residents as being in the upper middle status, and, on occasion, some people locate them as upper status. To most of the people in the lower statuses, all of the funeral home personnel appear to be personal service professionals in the truest sense of the word, and this allows them, at least for this segment of the community, to be located in the upper status. It is only at the upper status level that the distinction between the owner and the employees becomes clear-cut, and it is by upper status people that the employees are located in the upper middle status.

The members of the Community Funeral Home believe that one of their most important assets is the reputation they have in the community. They see themselves as respected, well-received, locally prestigious, personal service practitioners. Based on general community comments, these assessments seem quite accurate, and it is apparent that the long history in the community provides a certain dignity and stability that transcends many undesirable aspects of the occupation. This is especially so, since almost everyone in the community knows who they are and the nature of their occupation. This higher status position is exemplified by the fact that often they have been sought after for honorific and important local positions, and all of them have served as members of various boards of directors of local civic and charitable organizations and as administrative officers in other local service clubs and organizations.

An interesting example of the influence that such community position affords may be seen by examining its effect on the long-time unlicensed employee. Now 60, he received an eighth-grade education, and for many years he has worked as a funeral assistant and jack-of-all-trades for the firm, receiving a modest salary. However, he has held a number of important local honorific positions that make him stand out from his peers of similar backgrounds. He has been the president of some local organizations and on the board of directors of others. Furthermore, comments from community residents locate him as possessing a higher social status than his background would suggest.[3] To a great extent, this is attributed to his affiliation with the funeral home.

This means that the ways in which they conduct themselves in the community and the ways in which they are treated by the members of the community is as respected, highly esteemed, and prestigious individuals. Of course, it is possible that they do not appear as such to all segments of the community, but they do to the majority. Even among the town's best educated and influential intellectuals, especially those who have known the funeral directors on some governing board or other important community function, there is considerable respect and no question about their location in the town's upper status.

The personnel of the Cosmopolitan Funeral Home span the status system from upper to somewhere in the working status. The major stockholder of this firm, with his high income, inherited wealth, and other similar attributes, enjoys being in the upper status of his city. The family-connected managerial staff falls somewhat lower and may not even have a recognizable position in the overall picture of the city itself. However, they usually possess fairly high status in their community.

The counselors may be classified as being in the upper middle status, sharing this position with many others of similar business responsibilities and duties. Some of the directors and removal men abide by a life style considerably like the middle status, although some of them behave more like members of the working status. Even though such designations are difficult to make for a large city, it seems useful to mention such things in rather broad terms, especially since most of them live outside the metropolitan center.

One way in which to view the social status of the members of the two firms is in terms of a comparison regarding with whom the individual practitioners may be aligned. The life style of the Community Funeral Home personnel is most like that of doctors, lawyers, and community business leaders. Moreover, they act like many of those individuals who provide professional personal services. It is our contention that the more closely one conforms to the service model, the more likely it is that one will be accorded high esteem and prestige in one's community and that one can enjoy higher social status.

The case of the Cosmopolitan Funeral Home emphasizes that social status for bureaucratically organized employees depends somewhat on the way in which they are oriented to their occupation and how they present themselves as such. Some of them view themselves as being in the upper middle status and as providing an important personal service as funeral directors. Thus, even though they have a bureaucratic position, their willingness to tie themselves to a service occupation often enables them to enjoy somewhat higher social status in addition to more nearly adhering to the ideals of personal service.

There are some members of the Cosmopolitan Funeral Home whose occupational orientation is such that they think of themselves as small cogs in a big machine, that is, as bureaucrats. These funeral directors consistently indicated the belief that they do not enjoy benefits on the social status continuum because of their occupation. Moreover, they view it as a hindrance and hesitate to admit their occupation to those they meet outside the funeral home.

The owner of the Community Funeral Home enjoys a wide circle of prominent friends in his own and neighboring communities. His closet friends are largely doctors, engineers, presidents of two manufacturing corporations, owners of assorted other businesses, and educators. In general, his circle of friends is made up of people whose occupations would be classified as "professionals and proprietors." Moreover, these friends are not mere acquaintances. There are reciprocal dinner engagements that occur periodically involving all or some of these people. He takes vacations with some of them, and their children play together.[4]

Also among the owner's acquaintances, although not to the same extent as those mentioned above, are a number of local political and social leaders. These friendships have arisen as a result of activities in civic, social, and religious organizations over many years in the community. It is common for the owner to meet these friends at Christmas cocktail parties, in local restaurants, and at important community events.

The employees of the Community Funeral Home count as their closest friends neighbors and acquaintances met through community activities. Among these people are grade and high school teachers, employees of a nearby college, other employees of the state who work nearby in a prison or conservation center, and white collar workers from some industries in neighboring cities.

Whatever their connection with the funeral home, therefore, the circle of friends of those involved in the Community Funeral Home includes a wide range of people from several occupations. The owner tends to align himself with professional people and business leaders, whereas the employees tend to align themselves with people in managerial or executive positions. In both cases, the friendships are initiated and sustained by both parties with full awareness of the funeral director's occupation.

The circle of friends of the personnel at the Cosmopolitan Funeral Home is much wider than that of the Community Funeral Home personnel. Our research did not afford the chance to interact extensively with the Cosmopolitan Funeral Home employees while they were out of the funeral home. However, in their interviews, they told of certain aspects of their friendship circles at home. The owner's circle of friends includes other owners, especially of very large businesses, psychiatrists, artists, patrons of the arts, and similar people in his city. The family-connected managerial staff count as their friends doctors, lawyers, dentists, and business personnel from firms in managerial positions.

According to their descriptions of their social events with their friends, both the owners and the upper level management personnel conduct themselves somewhat like the owners of the Community Funeral Home. One thing stood out in this regard: all of them indicated that their best friends were very much aware of their occupation and that they were not embarrassed by their connection with the Cosmopolitan Funeral Home.

The circle of friends of most of the counselors include business executives, owners of small businesses in their neighborhood, dentists, school teachers, and other white collar business people. Several of them told their friends that they were "funeral counselors" for a large funeral firm. If asked to explain their jobs further, they would describe them as involving working with bereaved families during the crisis of death. Some of the counselors openly admitted, however, that they told their friends that they were such things as "in an executive position for a large service organization." If further pressed, some even explained that they told their friends that they were employed by another corporation not connected with funeral service but also owned by the family owning the Cosmopolitan Funeral Home. Thus, they would claim to be located in the hierarchy of some other kind of large business.

The directors and removal men consistently described their circle of friends in terms of such things as bowling leagues, union parties, and similar activities. Many of these employees claimed that their friends knew of their occupation because they, too, were funeral directors. However, many of those whose neighbors and friends were unaware of their occupation explained that they found it easier to indicate that they were such things as "white collar workers with a large business firm." Others claimed immunity from funeral service and told their friends that their job had to do with transportation, probably referring to but not actually mentioning hearses and the movement of the dead.

The circles of friends of the apprentices were limited almost entirely to other apprentices or to family friends in their neighborhood. No real assessment is possible of the apprentice's circle of friends, however, since there were only three at the Cosmopolitan Funeral Home during the course of the investigation.

There are a great many differences between the friendship patterns and modes of behavior of the personnel of the two funeral homes. The one thing that seems to be outstanding is that the circle of friends in which the Community Funeral Home personnel exists is well aware that their friend is a funeral director. As a matter of fact, it seems important in aligning him with higher management and professional people. This may be contrasted to the many employees of the Cosmopolitan Funeral Home who admitted disclaiming any connection to the funeral field. Thus, it appears that the people connected with the former funeral home conduct themselves in a fashion which is in accord with the personal service model, and that many of the employees of the latter funeral home conduct themselves essentially in a detached fashion from their work, that is, as bureaucrats.

Home life for the personnel of the Community Funeral Home depends to a great extent upon the location of the individual's home. The two employees of the Community Funeral Home do not live near the premises; thus, their home life affords them a degree of freedom from the actual operation of the funeral home. However, both of them are on "twenty-four hours a day telephone call" in case deaths occur at other than business hours. In this way, they have somewhat more flexibility and freedom in their home lives than does the owner and his family, who live on property adjoining the funeral home.

All of the personnel are well-known to their neighbors and the rest of their community as being funeral directors. All of them also believe that their homes are used by the general public and their acquaintances to judge them not just as people, but also as professional service practitioners. Thus, they make conscious efforts to maintain high standards in their homes, always predicating such behavior on their notion that people judge them professionally by the way they live at home.

In addition to these common constraints, the owner, who lives near the funeral home, has an extra one. He is constantly prepared in case someone comes to his home regarding a funeral. Moreover, he tends not just to maintain his home in a careful fashion, he also attempts to dress and act "professionally" at all times, even in the confines of his own home. He takes such precautions as having mints or breath fresheners available in case a bereaved family comes during the cocktail hour, and even when puttering around the house, he often wears a necktie and jacket.[5]

Clearly, the constant pressure of having drop-in clients has a strong impact on other forms of behavior. The funeral director who lives in or next to his funeral home must in a very real sense always toe the mark. Such precise behavior may not present extreme problems to adults, although for some it may be difficult. However, the problems are magnified for the children of such funeral directors, for they must always maintain the proper decorum befitting a funeral director's child. This means the children are cautioned against deviant behavior for, among other things, the "sake of the funeral home." Not surprisingly, it is common that funeral directors' children tend either to walk the straight and narrow and become funeral directors themselves, or decide "to hell with all this" and leave town, or pursue a far different occupation.

Home life for members of the Cosmopolitan Funeral Home is different in many ways. First, most of the personnel live a considerable distance from the firm. The few exceptions who live close at hand do so in apartment buildings so large that their funeral home connection is meaningless. Many of the employees claimed that even their neighbors did not know their occupation. One said he told friends that he was employed "in a managerial job," because this eliminated curios and embarrassing questions about funerals and death in general. One man even claimed that his children did not know what his occupation was except that he was "a manager of a large organization in the city." A few of them were known in their neighborhoods as funeral directors employed at the Cosmopolitan Funeral Home, and on occasion they were called upon to provide services to friends and neighbors. When asked to do so, these men generally rented facilities from other firms and handled such calls as solo practitioners.

Many of the Cosmopolitan Funeral Home employees described their home life as being "typical middle-class suburban living." A high proportion of them commute daily from outlying suburbs. Some have summer homes some 100 miles from the city.

An interesting aspect of the home life of such employees emerges when one considers the ways in which they dressed to come to work. Most of the counselors came dressed in business suits, generally not black, but dark and always well-tailored and well-kept. Of the supervisory personnel, about half came dressed like the counselors, in business suits. The other half came dressed in the same way as the removal men and directors, often in sport clothes or casual attire. This casual attire was not mod dress or high style but rather like that worn by nonuniformed blue collar workers. Generally, the apprentices wore black suits so as to be prepared to serve as directors, assistants, or in other capacities demanding such clothes. All of the dispatch men dressed in black suits and often claimed that their neighbors knew of their work as "funeral directors," and they think it is appropriate to wear funeral directing clothes both to and from work and often at home.

One could characterize the difference between the home lives of the Community Funeral Home personnel and those of the Cosmopolitan Funeral Home personnel as being related to their occupation. In the latter case, there is little or no association between home life and work. Thus, employees of the Cosmopolitan Funeral Home conform to that aspect of the bureaucratic model which separates occupational and personal matters as completely as possible, and this separation has the potential of increasing the anonymity of each practitioner. In the case of the Community Funeral Home personnel, their connection with the firm helps to focus more clearly their identity both in a personal and community fashion. Once again, it is important that this identity is as a serving professional.

Funeral Directors Association Activity

There is an aspect of the funeral director's professional activities which is connected to the occupation in one sense but is separated from it in another, the activities of the funeral director in professional associations. Such association work is intricately involved in the occupation of and occupational concerns of funeral directors; however, when participating in association activities and when being concerned with association matters, they conduct themselves as if out of their funeral home. To be sure, some association work is carried out in the confines of one's office, and the advice of the various associations influences the practice of funeral directing and eventually has an impact on those for whom the funeral director works professionally. However, the essence of professional association activities involves the funeral director away from his funeral home. Thus, we discuss funeral director associations as an out of the funeral home activity.

There are several professional associations, organizations, and societies to which funeral directors belong,⁶ the largest and most influential of which is the National Funeral Directors Association (NFDA). In each state there is a Funeral Directors Association (State FDA) which belongs to NFDA, and within each state, there are sectional, county, and city Funeral Directors Associations. These associations are affiliated with their state associations, which form the federation of associations comprising NFDA.⁷

Although they are much smaller than NFDA, there are three other major national associations. First, there is the Jewish Funeral Directors of America (JFDA). Second, there is the National Funeral Directors and Morticians Association (NFDMA), which originally was called the National Negro Funeral Directors and Morticians Association and which still is comprised only of black members. Third, there is the National Selected Morticians (NSM), membership in which depends upon an invitation from the organization.

There are three major national organizations which provide services of various kinds to funeral directors. These are the Order of the Golden Rule (OGR), primarily an advertising and accounting service, the Associated Funeral Directors Service (AFDS), a service to assist funeral directors in sending and receiving dead bodies to and from distant cities, and the Federated Funeral Directors of America, primarily an accounting and collection service.

There are numerous small, specialized funeral director associations, organizations, and societies which are intended to serve particular concerns, such as advertising, collection, travel opportunities, and so forth. These associations are too numerous to name, and they appear to have relatively little influence on funeral directing in general. In addition to the associations and organizations, there is a well-known postgraduate educational institute, the National Foundation of Funeral Service. The Foundation is intended to provide education for funeral directors beyond the schooling which they receive during their training.[8]

The owner and licensed employee of the Community Funeral Home participate in their section and state funeral directors associations, NFDA, and AFDS. Some of the personnel of the Cosmopolitan Funeral Home participate in the city and state funeral directors associations and NFDA. Two of the funeral directors are active in the Order of the Golden Rule and one in the Jewish Funeral Directors of America. Several of the employees of the Cosmopolitan Funeral Home have attended the National Foundation of Funeral Service, and three of the employees have worked at firms which were members of NSM. The orientation and philosophy of NSM is to improve and enhance the "business and profession of the funeral director," primarily through an extensive business and accounting system.[9]

Since the funeral directors of both firms are actively involved in NFDA, let us consider this Association in greater detail. NFDA was founded in 1882 by a group of undertakers and embalmers who were concerned with the protection of their interests. Over the years, NFDA has grown considerably, and in 1973, it listed 14,059 members, representing over two-thirds of the funeral homes in the continental United States. Its members annually conduct over 75 per cent of all funeral services held in the United States. The underlying philosophy of NFDA is that funeral service is a profession and that all bereaved families should select the funeral of their choice on the basis of "to each his own."

The governing body of NFDA is its House of Delegates, and it meets annually in convention. This House of Delegates is comprised of representatives from each state association and the living past presidents of NFDA. When the House of Delegates is not in session, the Association's Board of Governors determines policies and programs subject to the approval of the House of Delegates.

The Board of Governors includes one representative from each of the geographical districts plus the current officers and the immediate past president. The Board's Executive Committee consists of the officers and the immediate past president. NFDA also has a number of standing committees that report to the House of Delegates.

National headquarters are in Milwaukee, Wisconsin, and Association activities are under the leadership of an Executive Director and an administrative staff. NFDA maintains a liaison with all of the agencies of the federal government which have any interest in funeral service. Such agencies generally send representatives to attend national meetings, and often they seek advice from NFDA regarding the interpretation of existing laws and regulations.

NFDA retains a General Counsel whose services are available to both the national and state associations on matters important to funeral directing. The Association also retains or secures as necessary the services of consultants in such fields as public relations, education, sociology, clergy relations, applied psychology, management, and public opinion.

NFDA services are primarily for members and affiliated groups. The services include pertinent bulletins about important national developments and current legislative, educational, and professional matters. In addition to the regular members, these are sent regularly to the various state association officers. NFDA also provides its members with a reference manual in which there is a section concerning the policies and programs of the federal government and its agencies, a section on transportation laws and rules, a section on public and clergy relations, a section on management aids, and finally, a miscellaneous section which includes information about the accredited colleges of mortuary science, the legal responsibilities in the event of an air disaster, and other information useful to funeral directors and other interested parties.

The Association also publishes a monthly professional journal, *The Director*. It is the only funeral service journal which does not depend upon advertising for its publication, and it is financed by the educational fund of the NFDA. It contains scholarly and professional articles pertinent to funeral service. For instance, there are reports on the findings of Association-sponsored national surveys studying death and attitudes toward funerals and funeral directing which have been conducted and analyzed by professional sociologists and survey researchers.

Each year, the Association conducts a series of professional conferences in which new developments in the field are presented to interested members. These conferences are attended by over 1,000 funeral directors annually. Usually, the professional conferences include sessions on funeral home management, technical and embalming concerns, and important professional activities.

The Association has conducted annual conventions and exhibits since its inception in 1882. The exhibits include funeral merchandise, embalming supplies, funeral vehicles, and sundry funerary equipment and supplies. Attendance at the convention averages about 5,000.

Membership in NFDA includes licensed funeral directors who belong to their state association. Both firms investigated belong, as do individuals in each firm. The funeral directors of the Community Funeral Home are active on the county, state, and national levels. Their activities in the organization include participation on state committees and in social events with other members, both from their state and elsewhere. They consider

NFDA to be an important funeral directing organization and try to abide by its standards and code of ethics. They follow most of the suggestions made by the Association's professional consultants regarding such things as professionalism, grief therapy, and the social psychological value of the funeral ceremony.

The members from the Cosmopolitan Funeral Home are active primarily in their city funeral directors association. Their concerns, however, are of a different nature from those just described. These Cosmopolitan Funeral Home directors tend to be interested in such things as union-management relations, contractual pension plans and retirement funds for members and employees, merchandising, marketing, and similar matters. They seem to pay considerably less heed to NFDA's "professional" suggestions and considerably more to operationally expedient concerns.

There is a recent modification in this pattern, however, and several important members of the Cosmopolitan Funeral Home have been influential in this regard. The city association has begun to recognize the value of NFDA's philosophy and increasingly is emphasizing the need for better "professional and personal services" by funeral directors. Some of the motivation for this feeling seems to revolve around the apparent decreasing public popularity of basing profits on the sale of merchandise rather than on providing services. Thus, to some extent, the change may be partly utilitarian rather than humanitarian, but its impact helps bring these funeral directors closer to the personal professional service ideal.

At NFDA meetings and conventions, even though all funeral directors are out of their funeral homes, they still are attuned to their occupation. However, their behavior typically is not the same as that which is evident in their communities. It was mentioned by funeral directors from both firms that going to Association meetings allowed them to feel as if they were "contributing to the professionalism of funeral service," as well as giving them a chance to relax away from the pressures of their funeral home.

Members of both firms indicated that they feel that out of the funeral home they can "be ourselves at these meetings." They almost always bring their wives, for the program has a portion devoted to the entertainment of women. The funeral directors also use this as an opportunity to take a tax-deductible vacation. Furthermore, they can dress casually, go to bars and night clubs, get drunk (although most remain fairly careful in this regard), and in general, have the freedom to behave completely out of character if they so choose. Because their home lives are dissociated from the establishment, those from the Cosmopolitan Funeral Home do not feel quite as liberated, but for the Community Funeral Home directors, these meetings provide "one chance to escape from the funeral home." Somehow, it seems ironic that even this escape is related to their occupation.

The funeral directors from the Community Funeral Home are involved in committee work and serve in other official capacities at such meetings and conventions. They seem to take their work seriously and count it as valuable professional activity. Furthermore, they feel that their work with the Association and their attendance at the convention is a chance to perform professionally out of their funeral home. They are interested in such things as new ideas about advertising, information about grief counseling, new products in embalming supplies, new programs of "community education," and new perspectives on such things as the value of the funeral and the social and psychological implications of modern funeral service. They also are concerned with profits, sales, management, and other matters relevant to the overall operation of their funeral home.

The representatives of the Cosmopolitan Funeral Home use the convention as a place to check out matters which are directly connected to their jobs. The counselors go to the sessions on grief therapy and funeral director-bereaved relations; the supervisory personnel are more interested in manpower oriented programs; and the embalmers pay attention to chemical displays and other matters of concern to them.

The differences of association participation between the two firms may be summarized as follows. The members of the Community Funeral Home are concerned with the overall aspects of the operation of their funeral home and those of the Cosmopolitan Funeral Home are concerned with departmentally specific aspects of their operation. Once again, the funeral directors present themselves differently depending upon their orientation to funeral directing as a service or bureaucratic occupation.

We can characterize the Community Funeral Home directors out of their funeral home as giving the impression of being personable and responsible citizens with the community's interest at heart, and as believing full well that they will be judged professionally on the basis of this behavior. The situation is different for the directors of the Cosmopolitan Funeral Home. Out of their funeral home, they behave in whatever manner they see fit with the belief that their behavior will not affect their professional *position*. In these ways, funeral directors who are out of their funeral homes have presenting characteristics that may or may not be different from those when they are inside their funeral homes. Moreover, the organization in which one practices largely determines what these will be.

Notes

1. That funeral directors are very active in community affairs is well known in the field, and it is a topic of conversation at professional meetings and elsewhere. Personal experience documents this tendency, for at one point in my career as a funeral director, I simultaneously served as a member of the board of directors of

the Lion's Club, the treasurer of the local Chamber of Commerce, the secretary of an exclusive local men's club, and was on the governing board of a large Protestant church.

2. An example of a similar situation is the case of funeral director W. C. Celantano, Mayor of New Haven, Connecticut from 1945 to 1954. For a detailed analysis see Robert W. Dahl, *Who Governs?* New Haven: Yale University Press, 1961.

3. The sorts of activities participated in by this man are similar to those described as being at "the top of the social pyramid" by Alvin Gouldner, *Patterns of Industrial Bureaucracy*. Glencoe: The Free Press, 1954, especially pp. 31-44. It is important that such community position is related to one's occupational location in many "small town" settings, even though the community is no longer rural, as is the case with the one under investigation.

4. Importantly, some of these friends indicated separately that the owner and his family are their closest friends.

5. The pressures on him are very common among funeral directors in similar settings, and I have been told by numerous such persons that this is one disliked aspect of funeral directing. Much of the following discussion may be seen in Goffman's own treatment of "backstage" behavior; however, interest in the influence of regions on one's occupation makes me change this slightly. For comparison see Erving Goffman's *The Presentation of Self in Everyday Life*. Garden City, New York: Doubleday and Company, Anchor Books, 1959, pp. 112-40.

6. For a more detailed discussion see Habenstein and Lamers, *The History of American Funeral Directing*. Milwaukee: Bulfin Printers, 1962, especially pp. 445-503 and 534-58.

7. For a detailed discussion of the histories of all the state associations see Habenstein and Lamers, *Funeral Customs the World Over*. Milwaukee: Bulfin Printers, 1960, pp. 793-925.

8. There are twenty-six schools of funeral service accredited by the American Board of Funeral Service Education, Inc., and endorsed by the Conference of Funeral Service Examining Board.

9. For a more complete discussion see Habenstein and Lamers, *The History of American Funeral Directing*, pp. 536-38.

Chapter 5

Public Behavior
in the Funeral Home

This chapter describes, discusses, and analyzes how funeral directors carry out the public aspects of their work. It is largely through the conduct of the funeral director and the carrying out of his conception of relevant funeral activities that the bereaved develop a notion of "appropriate" funeral behavior. In this way, the funeral director helps establish the context in which funerals occur much as doctors collectively help set the boundaries of illness.[1] Therefore, we focus on the funeral director's *public* behavior in the funeral home.

The First Call

Whenever the telephone rings in a funeral home, it represents a potential summons for the funeral director, for it may be a "call" that informs of a death. If it is an initial summons, it is referred to as the "first call." Someone has died and the funeral home must direct its activities to take care of that dead person and his bereaved survivors. All funeral directors try to treat their first calls calmly and patiently.

No matter what else is said, the Community Funeral Home directors make an effort to assure the family that "We will take care of all the necessary details and get things under control right away, and we will do everything we can to make the next few days easier." This assurance may be met with silence on the part of the calling family, or there may be questions or requests; at other times, statements may be made about funeral plans. The funeral director usually offers as the next bit of information:

> I'm very sorry for your troubles. For the time being, you needn't worry about anything. We'll take care of all the necessary details. However, it would be a good idea if you and your family could collect your thoughts, organize your ideas, and plan to come to the funeral home to make the funeral arrangements. At that time, we can work out your wishes for the funeral.

What the funeral director really means by this statement is that he will remove the deceased from the place of death and ready himself for the encounter with the family. This encounter is to complete making funeral arrangements, to gather the statistical information regarding the bereaved and deceased, and to provide an opportunity for the funeral director to offer to the bereaved his various services, facilities, and merchandise. It is felt that the funeral director's seeming imperturbability and professional competence is important to demonstrate at this time. By carefully weighing each word and paying close attention to what the bereaved say, the funeral directors of the Community Funeral Home generally are able to effect the impression of deep concern and knowledgeable control.

When a first call is received at the Cosmopolitan Funeral Home, it is answered by the switchboard operator, who transfers the call to one of the funeral counselors. The counselor's method of handling first calls is different from the one described above for the Community Funeral Home directors. The counselor's main concern is getting enough information so that most of the funeral arrangements can be made without waiting for the family to come into the funeral home.

Each counselor is careful to identify himself individually to affect a sense of personal service. Then, he offers some words of sympathy to foster this impression. Once these preliminaries are over, the counselor begins to ascertain every possible bit of pertinent information. By carefully measuring his words and not rushing the bereaved with questions, the counselor elicits a great deal of information in a short period of time. He fills out three sets of cards while he is talking and generally gathers all of the statistical information for the death certificate in a matter of minutes.

Both the Community Funeral Home directors and the Cosmopolitan Funeral Home counselors appear to be competent professionals carrying out an important aspect of their job when handling first calls. The difference between them is emphasis and direction. The funeral directors of the Community Funeral Home are concerned primarily with giving the appearance over the phone that they are concerned, knowledgeable, and anxious to be of assistance, but that they want to deal with the bereaved in a face-to-face personal situation at the funeral home. The Cosmopolitan Funeral Home counselors, on the other hand, use this occasion to gather information and do not waste their time with comforting efforts that have little functional value for them.

Having spoken to a number of families about such first calls, it seems that the funeral directors of both firms were successful in what they were trying to do. Some families served by the Community Funeral Home said such things as, "Once I had made the call, I felt so much at ease. They seemed to know just what they were doing," and, "You just know they care and will do the best job possible after talking with them on the phone." The remarks of the families served by the Cosmopolitan Funeral Home went typically like this: "After talking with the funeral director, I felt relieved because he obviously knew what he was talking about. He seemed to be so efficient at his work that I figured he must know what he's doing," or, "It was really a pleasure to talk with him. After dealing with those people at the hospital switchboard, I expected somebody who couldn't tell me anything. Instead, I got a man who knew exactly what was going on and why."[2]

After the first call is received by either funeral home, it sets in motion a series of activities, many of which will be described as nonpublic activities, including the removal, embalming, and laying out of the deceased. These nonpublic activities may occur all at the same time or different times from the making of funeral arrangements which involves the bereaved families and the funeral director in the funeral home. Let us turn first to this face-to-face experience.

Making Arrangements

It is customary that following the first call and sometime before, during, or after the removal of the deceased from the place of death, the funeral director and the family sit down together and plan the funeral, that is, "they make arrangements."[3] This process is an important aspect of every funeral call, and all funeral directors take particular care in assuring that their setting is appropriate and that they are psychologically prepared for such an encounter. Sometimes the notification of the death is made by people in person at the funeral home, and while there, they make the complete plans and arrangements for the funeral. In such a case the first call actually occurs at the same time as the making of arrangements, but for present purposes we treat them as two separate events.

In the Community Funeral Home those making the arrangements for the funeral gather in the office of the funeral director. The conversation often includes a discussion of general funeral customs, the specific customs that the particular family wishes to carry out, and the schedule which will be followed for the next few days of the funeral. During this period the funeral director usually ascertains all of the necessary vital statistics for filing the death certificate and burial permit.[4] Most questions are asked in a straightforward fashion and the answers recorded on a standard form provided by the state's Department of Health. Such additional items as the names of survivors and the deceased's educational background are gathered by the funeral director at this time. It is during this period that many families voluntarily discuss the dying period, how they learned of the deceased's death, and similar matters. Although the funeral directors do not make note of this extra information, it is offered commonly in a general conversational way by many families.[5]

Much of this statistical and obituary information is gathered at the time of the first call by the counselors for the Cosmopolitan Funeral Home. If not, it is recorded by the counselor while making arrangements. Usually, his questions review the information previously gathered, and he quickly goes over pertinent matters to be certain that the forms are correct. It is interesting that a great many families working with the counselors divulge similar extra information as those dealing with the Community Funeral Home directors. Notably, there appears to be a desire to talk about one's problems, and on numerous occasions bereaved families use the counselor as a sounding board for their thoughts about the deceased and his death. They seemed to be seeking some form of personal attention from the counselors. To some extent, they receive it, for the counselors are good listeners and most of them give the impression of being sympathetic and understanding of the problems the bereaved mention. During the course of making arrangements, therefore, the counselors for the Cosmopolitan Funeral Home seem to provide professional services, even though the way in which they foster this impression is through bureaucratically oriented and efficiently conceived procedures.

During this arrangement period, funeral directors at both firms explain as many aspects of the funeral as possible. They offer advice and suggestions when they are solicited. The following questions are typical of the advice sought and questions asked.

"Should we look at the body?"
"Should we have visiting hours?"
"Should we bring the children to the funeral?"
"What should we do when people come into the funeral home?"
"What cemetery should we buy a plot in?"
"Where should we buy flowers?"
"What should we do about the insurance policy?"
"What about social security?"
"What about joint bank accounts?"
"Should we get a lawyer?"

It was observed on many occasions that the bereaved funeral arrangers depended on the funeral director's answers to these questions for much of their subsequent behavior.[6] In most instances, the funeral directors attempted to appear knowledgeable and concerned. For example, there were no outright fabrications to increase either the family's social involvement or their financial obligation.

Of course, by refraining from such fabrications, the funeral director has a chance to demonstrate his professional skill as a nonpartisan funerary specialist. Furthermore, the funeral director, like other professionals, derives a large measure of work satisfaction from actually helping bereaved families.[7]

The above remarks are true for both funeral homes. Throughout the research it was apparent that the image created while making arrangements is deemed by both bureaucrats and servers as being connected to the commonly held professional image of funeral directing as a service occupation. Thus, seldom does the funeral director try to force issues or talk people into decisions of any kind.

In addition to deciding upon the type of service, and selecting the casket, an important outcome of making arrangements is designating the time, place, and date for the funeral service. For the most part this is contingent upon arrangements the family have made or will make with a clergyperson. At this point an interesting difference between the Community Funeral Home and the Cosmopolitan Funeral Home stands out.

Apparently, because of the Community Funeral Home directors' wish to please people and to gain respect, they seem to bend over backwards to make the scheduling of the funeral compatible with everyone's wishes, largely excluding the convenience or inconvenience to themselves. They schedule funerals to suit the family, the clergy, and the cemetery, and, then, they manipulate their staff and facilities to fit. This emphasizes that the Community Funeral Home directors aim their behavior at and modify it primarily for the bereaved and the public rather than themselves or other funeral directors.

Such a practice stands out as one of the unique features of funeral directing as a service occupation, especially since it disrupts their personal lives. For instance, they all mentioned how much they dislike to be called out on weekends; however, they always added the postscript, "Well, that's just the nature of things, people can't help it when they die."

The scheduling of funeral services for the Cosmopolitan Funeral Home is geared to the desires of the bereaved family to some extent. However, the concerns of the firm are more important in determining the exact time of the funeral. In one sense, this is a matter of logistics, because to handle a large number of services in a given amount of time requires precise scheduling to eliminate overlap.

The counselors handle this organizational necessity in an interesting fashion. When talking with the bereaved family they unobtrusively check the master schedule which shows the times and locations of funeral services, and then they suggest the time to the family by asking a question such as this: "Now, let's see, today is Monday. This means you would probably want the funeral Wednesday or Thursday. Possible Wednesday afternoon at 3:00 or Thursday morning at 10:00?" In most cases, the family feels that it has a choice between two times, a morning service or an afternoon service, and they seem pleased when they make their final decision, as if the time had been their idea in the first place.

There is another aspect of such scheduling at the Cosmopolitan Funeral Home. Each counselor is on duty only for an eight-hour shift five days a week, so the schedule has little bearing on his other activities. Thus, unlike the funeral directors in the Community Funeral Home, the funeral schedule does not disrupt his other activities, either at work or at home. This means that he can afford to schedule a funeral service for any time that conforms to the master schedule, and he need not be concerned that it might be inconvenient for anyone. This is possible because the only times available on the master schedule are such that some of the staff always is available to handle them. In these ways, then, the personnel of the Cosmopolitan Funeral Home foster the impression of providing personal services to bereaved families; however, it is always in the context of their bureaucratically organized operation.

Making arrangements for a funeral involves more than merely scheduling the time for the actual services. One of the important results of making arrangements is the selection of the casket to be used for the service. Although the casket is a mercantile item, it has become an integral part of American funeral service, and funeral directors at both firms look upon its selection as an important element of making arrangements.

Selecting the Casket

In almost all instances, the casket is selected by the next of kin of the deceased. There is a wide range of available types, styles, and prices of caskets, and both funeral homes display a fairly large selection of caskets and other funeral merchandise in their selection rooms.

The funeral directors in the Community Funeral Home believe that it is not their job to try to "sell caskets," but they do feel that it is part of their job to explain the differences between caskets for the family's information if requested. Most of the time, however, they merely enter the selection room with the family and mention that each casket is marked with a price card showing its cost. They go on to explain that any questions the family may have will be answered willingly. Generally, at this point, they allow the family to browse through the casket selection room and make their own choice.

Importantly, the caskets are purchased by the funeral director for their attractive qualities, and the differences in price stand out rather obviously even to the inexperienced eye. All of the caskets are shown in the same room and are not separated into sections by price or quality. The Community Funeral Home directors believe that the attractiveness of their selection room and the appearance of the caskets will help in the sale and "allow the family to make this decision without pressure and yet be aware of the different values that exist."

On one occasion a bereaved family commented that they were shocked that they were left to themselves in the selection room and that the funeral director did not try to force the sale of a casket. They were so surprised and put at ease by this lack of pressure to "buy an expensive casket" that "we spent more than we had planned to, and after looking everything over, we are glad that we were able to do so." Thus, it may be that presenting themselves as professionals who are not concerned with sales, the funeral directors in the Community Funeral Home are able to handle their sales more effectively; however, they never consciously spoke of "sales" in these terms.

The counselors at the Cosmopolitan Funeral Home are considerably more professional than one would expect given the size of the operation and its form of organization. Notably, the counselors are not paid commissions for caskets sales, which means that to some extent they are able to effect a detached air about the purchase. It is important that the firm keeps extensive business records which analyze the quality of sale made by each counselor over a six-month period. So, although a specific sale is relatively uninfluenced by efforts to sell expensive caskets, the records of the firm are such that the counselor admitted that in the long run they are concerned with sales, but that it really does not influence individual transactions.[a] Of course, this enables them to behave as concerned professionals, not overly interested in selling expensive merchandise.

The selection room of the Cosmopolitan Funeral Home is separated into several sections. The largest section includes a wide range of differently priced caskets, but there are small annexes in which there are extremely low-priced and extremely high-priced caskets. It was explained that those people wishing to select an especially expensive casket deserved to be treated exclusively and to be taken to a room in which only the best were shown. Conversely, anyone wanting the cheapest casket possible also deserved to be so segregated. The room is small and crowded because it is not profitable to display inexpensive merchandise to the exclusion of moderate to more expensive merchandise. Thus, the Cosmopolitan Funeral Home also uses the physical setting and appearance to help make casket sales and still appear as a professional operation.

Let us turn from the sales techniques used by funeral directors and focus on some observations regarding funeral director orientations toward merchandise, caskets, and funeral sales. First, families assumed to have limited funds generally were discouraged by the funeral directors from purchasing beyond their assumed limit of paying ability, although they were encouraged to spend up to that limit. This observation is counter to the criticisms leveled at funeral directors for overselling their merchandise. All the funeral directors claimed that there is little sense in making big sales for which they never will be paid; therefore, concerted efforts seem to be made to encourage families with "less than adequate means" to select something within (up the limit of) their financial reach including available insurance and bank accounts.

For both firms, the great bulk of funeral purchases fall into the middle price range. There were no obviously negative feelings on the part of the funeral director toward this large portion of his business enterprise, even though they do not spend "above average." Families who are seen as having considerable buying power and who purchase a well-below-average casket are seen as being "strange" and possibly even "disrespectful" of the deceased.

Often, there is surprise when families behave in an unexpected manner. For instance, a family expected to buy a moderately priced casket even though they might have more than adequate means takes the funeral director by surprise when they purchase a considerably more expensive casket. The reaction of pleasure with a "good" purchase is coupled with that of surprise. Witness such remarks as, "I certainly didn't expect these people to choose this kind of a casket!"

Good purchases elicit behavior from the funeral director which is similar to that of attorneys and physicians when confronted with a client or patient whose ability to pay is well above "average."[9] While the actual services rendered may be essentially similar and there is not necessarily a deliberate effort to give these "more fortunate" people more or better service, the cordiality with which service is given is the most noticeably different thing. Wealthy families with high social status generally are treated not just to the best services available by the funeral director, but also they are treated by him in a most felicitous way.[10]

Such treatment stems somewhat from the funeral director's desire to enhance his own status. By providing his services in a superlative fashion, he hopes to gain or increase his acceptance by the bereaved family. This hope is not ill-founded, for his efforts often are rewarded with social relationships that did not exist prior to his professional dealings with such people.

Such practices were true for individuals connected with both firms. It was interesting that on several occasions members of the owning family of the Cosmopolitan Funeral Home served as counselors and carried out director activities for specific funeral services. This is an unusual occurrence and was marked in each instance by the regular counselors and directors commenting about how badly these arrangements were handled by these figureheads. These same people occasionally took over making arrangements when a very well known dignitary died.

The Cosmopolitan Funeral Home impressed high status or important people with its organizational mode of personal service by such practices. It did so by having someone step out of the hierarchy and perform in a nonbureaucratic fashion, thereby effecting a sense of personal service. This may be contrasted with the Community Funeral Home in which the owner participated to about the same extent in every case, except that the level of attention and personal involvement increased as did the social status or importance of the bereaved family. Both firms made efforts to give the appearance of increased personal service for certain families, but they did so in different fashions.

Visitation

Once the arrangements are made and the body prepared, generally the next event is "visitation." Visitation is that period during which family and friends of the deceased and of the bereaved come to "pay their respects" and to offer condolences. This period is alternately called the "wake," "visiting hours," "calling hours," or "viewing." It is the time for the regathering of scattered units, whether these be familial or friendship relationships.

Visitation usually commences with the first viewing by the immediate next of kin. This is an upsetting time for most families. It is their first exposure to the deceased either since sometime before death, or just after death occurred. The fears that "Daddy won't look the same anymore," or that "Dad was such a mess," or that "Mother had lost so much weight and had gotten so wrinkled" all loom before the family prior to the first viewing. In general, the first viewing allays many of the fears of the bereaved. Due to the restorative efforts of both firms, this first exposure generally produces a positive reaction, with surprise at "how well he looks," and relief because "things aren't as bad as I expected."

This time is also a chance for the family to break down openly and to display grief reactions to each other. Such reactions, however, must be modified fairly quickly to accommodate friends and relatives who are also interested in being involved. Throughout this period of time the Community Funeral Home directors generally remain in the background ready to assist if needed and ready to answer questions. The Cosmopolitan Funeral Home personnel merely check on how things are arranged and then leave the bereaved alone when all seems satisfactory.

Normally, there is very little reaction with the exception of tearful comments such as, "You've done a magnificent job," or, "You certainly

have done more than I ever expected." It is common for the funeral director to try to learn if the deceased looks the way the bereaved want him to
look without asking in so many words. Most families get the message, but
some, however, see his probes differently. For instance, they make
statements such as: "No, everything's not the way I want it. He's dead!
Isn't he?" or "I thought the casket was darker," or "I didn't realize that
flowers made such a difference. It will be nice when some more get here."
If this occurs, the funeral director may drop the subject or probe a bit
further and ask, "Is your mother's hair the way you want it?"

The funeral director's concern with the appearance of the dead body
eventually seems to get communicated to the bereaved. The awareness of
such a concern is an important aspect in helping the bereaved know just
what the body of the deceased actually "should" be to them. The concern
with the appearance is made openly by the funeral director and draws
attention to his work, his importance, and his practical value, as well as to
the lifeless body of the deceased. Thus, although the funeral director's
reasons for emphasizing the dead body actually may not be the same as the
social-psychological value of viewing the dead, the result often is the same.
His efforts enable the family to come to an acceptance of death that would
not occur if the funeral director did not attend to or concern himself with
such appearances.[11]

Once the family gets the message that the funeral director's questions
are concerned with the appearance of the body, they usually make it clear
that they are pleased or that something could be modified. Such
modifications are handled in an interesting fashion. In most cases, the
family is asked to leave the room while the funeral director makes an effort to correct things. Change at this time often is not easy, and it is common that the funeral director actually does not do much. He might make
minor readjustments in the vicinity of the requested change, or, as is more
common, he does almost nothing at all. In the vast majority of the cases
observed, the family came back and said, "Oh, that's wonderful. That's
just perfect. That makes so much difference." This strategy was used by
funeral directors in both firms.

Visiting hours produce many observable changes in the bereaved. They
seem to become more relaxed. They often converse in great detail about
the deceased. In the Community Funeral Home, there seems to develop a
relaxed group participation atmosphere, and the funeral director's conduct
has a lot to do with this change.

Even if the funeral director has a warm personality, the surrounding
environmental factors have an influence, and the ability to relax seems to
depend to some extent on the physical setting. For example, in the
Cosmopolitan Funeral Home, the entryway, lobby, and hallways have
marble floors and walls and formal chandeliers. However, the arrangement offices and reposing rooms are carpeted, warmly decorated, and con-

tain such things as comfortable chairs and small tables to foster the impression of the warmth and friendliness of a private home. The Community Funeral Home effects a warm, friendly setting throughout. Thus, in the funeral home in which he operates, the funeral director uses the physical setting to help present himself as a professionally cordial participant in the funerary activities.

In the Community Funeral Home, during visiting hours, the funeral director functions as a doorman, confidant, supervisor, friend, and, in general, host. His primary responsibilities are to the bereaved; however, a large portion of his time is spent talking with friends of the family. The Community Funeral Home directors see this as a period during which they can become acquainted with other friends and family members and have a chance to impress them with their skill as professionals. People actually do utilize this exposure to make judgments about the funeral director, his operations, and his talents. This finding gives credence to the notion that the funeral director is a professional being judged by the lay public. Funeral directors recognize this on a practical level and are concerned with how their public behavior inside the funeral home is viewed by the bereaved and by society at large. For example, while greeting visitors, the Community Funeral Home directors and assistants are careful to mask a before dinner cocktail so as to smell as sober as possible.

At night, when the bereaved leave the Community Funeral Home, it is common for the funeral directors not to turn off the parking lot lights until after the family leaves the yard. They do this even though it is annoying to have to sit around the semi-darkened funeral home waiting for them to leave. The idea is to give the bereaved the impression that they have not been rushed in the exit from the funeral home. Also, the Community Funeral Home directors feel that it might be "upsetting" to the bereaved family to see the room in which the deceased is laid out to be plunged into darkness. Such things might be overlooked or thought to be irrelevant by the bereaved, who may not be nearly so concerned with the dead body as is the funeral director. In any case, by attending to such concerns of his own making, the Community Funeral Home director continues to foster a definition of the funeral that emphasizes the importance of his service position. Moreover, his very attention to such details helps make them a more important part of the funeral situation.

In the Cosmopolitan Funeral Home, visitation is attended to by a number of people. When people enter the lobby, they are greeted by either the switchboard operator from her cubbyhole in the lobby wall or more commonly by the lobby attendant. They are directed to the floor on which visitation is taking place. There, they are greeted by a floor attendant who ushers them to the appropriate room.

When the family initially arrives, one of the counselors attempts to check on their satisfaction with the arrangements and attends to any corrections to the body that are requested by having someone come up from the preparation room to make these changes. The family is then left alone. During the course of the visiting hours, they come and go as they wish with no effort made by the funeral home personnel to monitor or participate in their activities.

There is a practical device which is used to effect a sense of personal service by the Cosmopolitan Funeral Home. On the night before the funeral, a counselor goes to each family explaining that he is "one of the managers" and that he has come to make certain that everything is going as scheduled and that the arrangements continue to be satisfactory. He sits for a few minutes with the family and chats in a friendly fashion with them. In his hand is an arrangement sheet on which are all the details of the funeral. He inconspicuously mentions the cemetery to be used, the time of the service, what vehicles have been hired, and other pertinent arrangements that are noted on the arrangement sheet. He does so in a seemingly casual, personally interested fashion, but he actually is making sure that the records are accurate. Numerous bereaved families were heard to exclaim after the counselor left that "it certainly is amazing that such a large place can be so personal."

It is customary in both firms for visitation to end the day before the funeral ceremony, which is the next matter of concern for the funeral director. It is important to point out that many of the public activities we have been discussing occur simultaneously with nonpublic ones and not necessarily in the order presented. This is crucial because the funeral service itself does occur subsequent to all other activities in the funeral home. Let us now turn to an examination of the funeral as the culmination of all that has gone before.

The Funeral

When funeral directors refer to "the funeral" they mean the actual funeral process, including the social psychological events for acting out feelings that are basic to therapeutic intervention.[12] The funeral may occur in the funeral home, in the home of the deceased, in a church or other public building, at the cemetery, or any place the bereaved decide to carry out the commemorative service. Whatever the setting, funeral behavior is essentially the same.

On the day of the funeral, the funeral director and his assistants are prepared well in advance, and they stand ready to greet people long before they are due to arrive. Wherever the funeral takes place, it is customary for the funeral director to seat the bereaved family in the front of the room. Usually, they usher them to this position in a slow and deliberate fashion. The front location of the family is thought to be an important part of the funeral, and on the few occasions when families seated themselves elsewhere, the funeral directors made certain that they moved to the front.

The funeral director in the Community Funeral Home is easily identifiable not only because he acts as a doorman and head usher for the bereaved family, but also because he is well known to the townspeople. Many years ago, the earlier Community Funeral Home directors made certain that they would be identifiable by wearing morning dress. Today, they emphasize their identities by their actions and reputations.

At the Cosmopolitan Funeral Home, some of the funeral directors still wear striped pants and black jackets to identify themselves. Others identify themselves by their actions. One of the commonly used devices to foster the appearance of being the funeral director is to carry an arrangement card containing notations about the funerals. In almost all instances observed, the director knew all he needed without the card; thus, it had little functional value except to identify him as the director of the service.

Funeral directors in both settings work hard to make the funeral go as smoothly as possible. This includes maintaining an orderly seating arrangement and making certain that the participants in the funeral do not do something unexpected, for surprise easily upsets the event.

One of the important but too often overlooked elements of the funeral is that it allows the bereaved to behave in a death-appropriate mask. In the setting of both funeral homes, it is appropriate for men to be seen with tears in their eyes, for women to be disheveled, and otherwise obviously affected by the death.[13] Prior to and during the funeral, all such behavior is not merely allowed, but it is encouraged by the funeral director through his activities and procedures. Thus, to some extent, it is because of his behavior that the bereaved come to have a definition of the funeral as a useful social process to attend death.

When a bereaved family chooses to remain outsiders to the funeral, the funeral director is unable to define and carry out a "complete and proper funeral." This is an imposition on him and is a source of problems between the funeral director and families whose wishes do not allow him to work through the funeral. This aspect of death-related behavior is touched on by Everett Hughes (1958: 16-17, and 1971: 128), who points out that we Americans have tried hard to do away with death, saying:

> If there be any triumph in death, our generation will not be there to see it. As for mourning, we are so fearful of wearing sorrow upon our sleeves, that we eat our hearts out in a mourning which cannot be brought to a decent end, because it has never had a proper beginning. I have had dear friends who have done it so; and so has anyone who is of that well-meaning generation who believed that all good things could be attained by science and all bad things avoided by emancipation from old formulae and freedom from old distinctions; the people who got it into their heads that anything formal is cold—not sensing that ceremonial may be the cloak that warms the freezing

heart, that a formula may be the firm stick upon which the trembling limbs may lean; that it may be a house in which one may decently hide himself until he has the strength and courage to face the world again.

Such a situation is clearest in the Community Funeral Home because the completion of a funeral depends upon the funeral director's institutionalized treatment of it, and although there are many possible versions of how a funeral gets carried out, there is a more or less clear-cut idea of the proper way.

For instance, when a body is donated to medical science by a family, the Community Funeral Home director usually plays very little part in the definition of the funeral situation. The family may decide to go through some kind of memorial service, but seldom do they ask the funeral home to help them arrange for such a service. This makes problems not just for the funeral director, but for the community as well, for in such an instance, it is impossible for friends and acquaintances to act out many of the parts that they usually do when someone dies.[14]

For example, the obituary which announces the death almost never mentions that the body has been donated to science. Thus, although word about the death may spread, it remains little more than news floating in space with no actual connection to "acceptable" funeral behavior. At times there may be a memorial service handled by the family and a church or other organization. Because such organizations are not usually familiar with publicity about funerals or memorial services in the same way the Community Funeral Home is, very seldom are such services adequately publicized to allow attendance of all those concerned with the deceased.

Naturally, this means that the funeral is never likely to be completed in the "standard" way. Of course, it is possible to offer condolences in other settings; the point is that it is not commonly done. Even in the funeral home setting, it is difficult enough to offer useful consolation to the bereaved, and without such a setting, the problems become considerably greater. While such problems often are treated as unimportant for society, they are always important for the funeral director whose main concern is with defining and carrying out the necessary steps to complete the funeral.

The situation of the Cosmopolitan Funeral Home regarding such an event as the donation of a body to science does not have the same impact for the funeral directors. Since each of them only attends to specific aspects of the funeral, there tends to be little feeling about not completing one. The donation of a body to science merely means that the removal man does all the work. He goes to the hospital and makes the removal and takes the body to the institution to which it was donated. He is not distressed that he does not get a chance to meet the family face to face, for he never deals face to face with families. The counselor handling the family also is not distressed not only because his work is briefer than usual, but also because he is never concerned with the completion of the funeral ceremony. Thus, none of the specialists of the Cosmopolitan Funeral Home feel the impact of a donation to science in the same way that the total practitioner does in the Community Funeral Home.

It makes sense that the funeral director's public behavior inside his funeral home helps foster and encourage many aspects of the lay public's funeral behavior. This is not to say that the funeral director's motivations for doing so are necessarily in the best interests of the bereaved in every situation. Rather, it is through his dramatic presentations that he helps implement their funerary activities. Let us now turn our attention to the ways the funeral director manages the impressions of funeral performances others receive.

Funeral Directors and Impression Management

When the funeral director is able to work on his own home ground inside his funeral home, he is under relatively little pressure and is able to practice to the full his arts of impression management.[15] Important in this regard is the fact that the funeral director no longer goes forth to meet families in their homes as he did years ago, for it is to the funeral home that they come to make funeral arrangements.

Impression management, however, involves more than the spatial location of the funeral director's workshop, just as it involves more than the hospital as the physician's workshop, or the courtroom as the attorney's workshop, or the schoolroom as the teacher's workshop. Notably, there are a number of techniques which are commonly used to carry out impression management by funeral directors. Tact is important to the funeral director. He is careful not to offend or otherwise adversely impress the family which comes to make the funeral arrangements. This means that his attitudes, actions, and behavior are carefully modulated to reflect an aura of tact and cooperativeness that might not otherwise exist.

Such attributes are intended to support the performance and to prevent jeopardizing the appearance that is intended. Goffman (1959: 212) explains:

> In order to prevent the occurrence of incidents and the embarrassement consequent upon them, it will be necessary for all the participants in the interaction, as well as those who do not participate, to possess certain attributes and to express these attributes in practices employed for saving the show.

Tact is not the only attribute required of the funeral director. Loyalty to the overall funeral is another. This refers to funeral directors strictly adhering to and remaining loyal to all of the dramaturgical demands of the funeral. For funeral directors in both firms, an important aspect of maintaining the loyalty of team members is that they are not allowed to become too sympathetically attached to the bereaved. In this way, funeral directors are seldom tempted to be disloyal to the overall funeral.[16]

The funeral team also is likely to develop considerable internal solidarity and an image of the bereaved as an audience which tends somewhat to dehumanize them and allows the funeral directors to deal with them on an impersonal emotional basis.[17] In this sense, it is important that funeral directors form a complete social unit, and that the funeral team as a society has built-in sources of support which allow its members to be protected from the doubts of the bereaved audience. This sort of esprit de corps is very important to all professional groups, and it is not merely a defense mechanism. Moreover, to the extent that funeral directors conceive of their professional role as members of an important caretaking occupation, their team behavior is built around respect and appreciation for their common role.

Funeral directors also are prevented from developing strong affective ties with the bereaved because they deal with each bereaved family separetely either only once, or, on rare occasions, a few times.[18] For example, a widow arranging for her husband's funeral will not arrange for her own funeral as well, although she may act as an arranger for some other family member. The number of contacts between even the Community Funeral Home director and a particular family are limited considerably; thus, the affective contacts with the bereaved have little chance to become well developed. However, even though the length of time of any funeral is quite brief and would appear to leave little room for the development of strong affective ties between the funeral director and bereaved families in either setting, the distinction between chronological time and psychological time considerably modifies the situation. Emotional movement is rapid in times of crisis and stress, and the time the funeral director spends with a bereaved family, although short in hours, may be highly privileged and meaningful in terms of impact and development.

Another important element in maintaining the stability of the overall funeral is that the funeral team has dramaturgical discipline.[19] Funeral directors must be disciplined not to break their role, and they must be consistent in their part and not give the show away by disclosing secrets that are pertinent to it. Thus, a funeral director who observes an assistant making a blunder must be careful not to shout or run wildly to the assistant's aid, thereby drawing attention to the error. He must carry out the funeral by adhering to the strictest discipline possible, and an important part of the training of funeral directors involves imparting to them a sense of calm during the service. Thus, apprentice funeral directors are cautioned: "Never run, even when something drastic happens, such as someone fainting beside the casket, or somebody knocking over a basket of flowers."

It is also important that the funeral director not allow his personal problems to intrude upon his performance. Again, he must be disciplined and keep them hidden especially from the bereaved, because they are believed to have enough burdens to bear. Goffman (1959: 217) explains:

> The focus of dramaturgical discipline is to be found in the management of
> one's face and voice. Here is the crucial test of one's ability as a performer.
> Actual affective response must be concealed and an appropriate affective
> response must be displayed.

In this sense, an important part in the training of a funeral director is
that he learns how to appear to be appropriately solemn and yet not
somber or depressing to the bereaved. His facial expression must be
managed so as to give the impression of care, interest, and understanding,
not dismay, fear, or panic.

It is necessary for the funeral director to make prudent preparations
for the funeral itself. He must prepare in advance for contingencies which
could disrupt the process. For example, someone fainting during visiting
hours disrupts the supposedly smooth operation of the funeral home. In
both organizations, it is common for funeral directors to be prepared for
such swooning people by having small kits of ammonia capsules, and they
are quick to hand these out to those members of the family who are expected to be best able to "take" the stress.

Another way the funeral director is prepared for such contingencies is
by having loyal and experienced assistants. They are quick to notice
breakdowns or disruptions in performances and take immediate steps to
prevent them from happening or immediately to repair the damage when
possible.

A technique that is commonly available to professional practitioners
staging an occupational performance which allows for dramaturgical circumspection is not always available to the funeral director. Since people
come to him, the funeral director is unable to select the kind of bereaved
audience that will cause a minimum of trouble in terms of the kind of
funeral service he wants.[20] Clearly, it makes it difficult that the funeral
director must perform before audiences that are not necessarily optimally
selected. The Cosmopolitan Funeral Home is not nearly so limited in this
regard as is the Community Funeral Home. In large urban areas it is common for people to select funeral directors based on such things as ethnic
ties, religious affiliation, and social status. Thus, although the funeral
director in the Cosmopolitan Funeral Home does not select his bereaved
families specifically, there is usually a process of self-selectivity which
often affords him a certain amount of dramaturgical circumspection
regarding audience selection.

Another technique which allows for dramaturgical circumspection is
that of limiting the size of the audience to as few as possible, for as Goffman (1959: 220) says, " . . . other things being equal, the fewer the
members, the less possibility of mistakes, 'difficulties,' and treacheries." It
is while making funeral arrangements that the problem of audience size

looms largest for funeral directors. Specifically, decisions about funeral arrangements may be seriously complicated by trying to please or pay heed to several arrangers at once. In general, the funeral director has little control over the size of such audiences; however, they tend to be made up of very few people in both settings.

Normally, it is important for an audience to have some knowledge of the performer in advance of any staged or real-life performance. In the Community Funeral Home this is commonly the case, for it is operated by people whose reputations are "good," practices well known, and community relationships highly developed; however, in the Cosmopolitan Funeral Home the situation is considerably different, and only the firm possesses such attributes. In either event, when the bereaved family enters into a relationship with the funeral director, familiarity with his (or his firm's) techniques and practices is often such that it allows them to judge his work as he carries it out. Because of this relationship with the bereaved, and because the funeral director is judged by laypeople rather than other funeral directors, it is important for him to make obvious the important aspects of the funeral performance by his front, his manner, and his appearance.

Funeral directors are also dramaturgically circumspect and prudent in that they adhere to a rather strict agenda; thus, funerals seldom are run in a haphazard fashion.[21] Naturally, this reduces the possibility of disruption of the overall funeral. Paradoxically, the funeral director also must be careful to stick to his plan with greater diligence than if he ran things with considerable leeway.[22] Funerals are scheduled for specific times with many other operations contingent upon that time. For instance, the use of the church, arrival at the cemetery, arrangement for vehicles, etc., are set in advance; therefore, funerals do not get "rained out," postponed, or similarly disrupted because of a change in plans.

Thus, no matter what conditions arise that conceivably could disrupt a funeral, "the show must go on." For instance, cemeteries which are unable to open graves because of frozen ground during the winter notify funeral directors well in advance that the grave opening is impossible, and arrangements are made to store the deceased in a receiving vault until the ground allows the grave to be opened. Never does the cemetery wait until the funeral procession arrives for the burial, for to them then would completely disrupt the performance, and the entire funeral would be blown to pieces. Thus, the funeral team cooperates.

Most of the defensive techniques of impression management are accompanied by a tendency on the part of an audience or an outsider to act in a reciprocally protective way, thereby allowing the performers to save their own show.[23] One of the common techniques that allows for such protection is that individuals voluntarily stay away from those regions to which they have not been invited. For instance, the bereaved would not enter into the preparation room and accidentally stumble onto an embalming, even if the funeral director did not specifically exclude them from there. Thus, tact on the part of the funeral audience as well as exclusions by the funeral performer serve to protect the performer from disruptive behavior.

The audience also may generously forgive slips, errors, or mistakes made by the performer.[24] Thus, when a funeral director inadvertently and accidentally buries the deceased with jewelry on that was supposed to be removed, the audience may forgive him, saying such things as, "Well, she would have wanted it that way anyway, so it's probably for the best;" or, "God meant for her to have those things anyway."

There seem to be a number of reasons why bereaved audiences behave in such a tactful manner. First, the bereaved may identify with the funeral director and be hesitant to expose him because of knowing how badly he would feel. Second, it may be that the bereaved do not want to have an unpleasant scene which would prove little or nothing; therefore, they just accept things as being accidental. Third, it may be that the bereaved intend to exploit the funeral director by ingratiating themselves to him, and it may be that they display good humor and tact in hopes of reducing the funeral bill or otherwise compromising the funeral director.

In order for tact to be effective, it is necessary that the funeral director and the bereaved have a clear understanding of and awareness about the way in which tact may be demonstrated. Thus, if the funeral director gets cues, he must take warning when his show is unacceptable. If he wants to save the situation, he must modify his behavior by considering the meaning of the warning.[25]

In funeral-related social interaction, as well as most other types, it appears that the fundamental dialectic when one individual enters into the presence of other individuals is that he wants to know all the relevant social facts of the situation, but to know all such facts is rare.[26] Thus, the individual tends to utilize indicators in order to make predictions. He uses cues, hints, expressive gestures, signs, and symbols and concentrates his attention on appearances. The indicators of reality used by funeral directors and bereaved people emphasize their general concern with the staged funeral performance. Such use, therefore, demonstrates that it is the impression given to others that counts rather than the actual carrying out of specific exigencies involved in the funeral situation.

We contend that it is the appearance created, expressive behavior emitted, and the impression fostered by funeral directors that are of the utmost importance to the funeral performance. We also contend that it is the manner in which firms are organized which to an important extent determines the way in which funeral directors carry out such performances.

Notes

1. For a complete treatment of the "Social Construction of Illness" see Eliot Freidson, *Profession of Medicine: A Study in the Sociology of Applied Knowledge*. New York: Dodd, Mead, and Co., 1970, pp. 203-331.

2. For a discussion about general hospital death-related behavior see Freidson, *op. cit.*, pp. 109-36; for death-related behavior and communication see Barney G. Glaser and Anselm Strauss, *Awareness of Dying*. Chicago: Aldine Publishing Company, 1965; David Sudnow, *Passing On*. Englewood Cliffs, N.J.: Prentice-Hall, Inc., 1967; and Vanderlyn R. Pine, "Institutionalized Communication About Dying and Death," *Journal of Thanatology*, forthcoming.

3. Such arrangements are historically common to funeral behavior. A possible explanation for this is offered by Parsons and involves the concept of "keeping going" even under great stress through customary ritualized behavior. For a related theoretical discussion of this concept see Talcott Parsons, *The Social System*. New York: The Free Press, 1951, p. 304.

4. The questions include the deceased's name, age, sex, marital status, date and place of birth, parents' names, social security number, veteran's status, place of burial, etc. The cause of death is entered by the attending physician, coroner, or medical examiner.

5. The situation is similar to the case of physicians learning confidential information about their patient's private life. See Parsons, *op. cit.*, p. 452.

6. This contributes, of course, to the funeral director's ability to help the family construct funerary reality and is similar to the physician's ability to do so with a patient's illness. For a discussion of this aspect of medicine, see Freidson, *op. cit.*, pp. 286-88.

7. This is a source of satisfaction for some bureaucratic officials as is pointed out by Peter M. Blau, *The Dynamics of Bureaucracy*. Chicago: University of Chicago Press, 1955, pp. 83-86.

8. For an interesting comparison about the effect of such organizational pressures in bureaucracies see Blau, *op. cit.*, pp. 36-56; and in medicine see Freidson, *op. cit.*, pp. 98-105.

9. For comparison see Freidson, *op. cit.*, pp. 30-36, 90-93, and 362; also see Erwin O. Smigel, *The Wall Street Lawyer*. Bloomington: The Indiana University Press, 1969, pp. 176-78 and 200.

10. A similar observation is made about other professionals; see Peter M. Blau and W. Richard Scott, *Formal Organizations*. San Francisco: Chandler Publishing Company, 1962, pp. 74-81.

11. Once again, the funeral director is engaged actively in the construction of funeral behavior much as the physician is with illness. For comparison see Freidson, *op. cit.*, pp. 203-331.

12. For a fuller discussion see Parsons, *op. cit.*, pp. 443-45; and L. E. Abt and S. L. Weisman (eds.), *Acting Out: Theoretical and Clinical Aspects*. New York: Grune and Stratton, 1965.

13. For comparison with the "funeral show" see Parsons' discussion of "expressive symbolism," *op. cit.*, pp. 510-13.

14. For an additional perspective on this very problem see Parsons, *op. cit.*, pp. 443-45.

15. See Erving Goffman, *The Presentation of Self in Everyday Life*. Garden City, New York: Doubleday Co., Anchor Books, 1959, pp. 208-37.

16. For a fuller discussion see Goffman, *op. cit.*, p. 214.

17. This is similar to the way in which jazz musicians deal with their audiences. See Howard S. Becker, *Outsiders*. New York: The Free Press, 1963, pp. 79-120.

18. This is very different from what happens to physicians. See Freidson, *op. cit.*, pp. 109-36.

19. For a full discussion see Goffman, *op. cit.*, pp. 216-18.

20. For a full discussion of this sort of problem see *ibid.*, p. 219.

21. For a more detailed discussion of this aspect of occupational difficulties *ibid.*, pp. 218-28.

22. In this sense, as well as for other reasons, funerals can be thought of in terms of "routine and emergency," for even though time is not usually a crucial factor, once the funeral schedule is established it becomes more important. For comparison see Hughes, *Men and Their Work*, Glencoe, Ill.: The Free Press, 1958, pp. 54-55, and *The Sociological Eye:* Book 2. Chicago: Aldine-Atherton, 1971.

23. For an expanded treatment of how the audience protects the performer see Goffman, *op. cit.*, pp. 88-101.

24. For a discussion about occupational mistakes see Hughes, *op. cit.*, pp. 88-101.

25. As pointed out earlier, such behavior contributes to the construction of social reality much as similar patterns do for physicians. For comparison see Freidson, *op. cit.*, pp. 203-331.

26. See Goffman, *op. cit.*, pp. 248-51.

Chapter 6
Nonpublic Behavior
in the Funeral Home

This chapter describes, discusses, and analyzes the various ways in which the funeral director presents himself when carrying out certain aspects of his job that are not easily visible to the public. To do this, we examine some common shortcuts, tricks, and everyday practices of funeral directors, paying special attention to these as nonpublic occupational activities.

Removals

Every death requires that the funeral director remove the dead body from the place where death occurs to some other place, usually the funeral home.[1] This is commonly called a "removal."

It seems a simple task, but the removal can involve considerable dirty work. For instance, on one occasion, a family had gone to several funeral homes during the three days following the death of their father. When they finally chose the Community Funeral Home, which made the removal, the deceased had been dead in bed in his well-heated room for three and one half days, and his putrefied condition was enough to make most people gag upon entering his death room. After completing the removal, the owner commented to the man helping him, "Those bastards, if I had had the slightest idea of the condition of that body, I would have refused the call or

108

would have charged them a fortune just for the removal."

Most of the time, however, removals are not unique or spectacular. They may be categorized as being (1) from an institution such as a hospital or nursing home, (2) from a private home, or (3) from the scene of an accident or emergency. Over 90% of the removals made by the Cosmopolitan Funeral Home are from institutions. Institutional removals constitute slightly more than 50% of the total made by the Community Funeral Home.

When removals are made from an institution, the patterns are essentially similar for both the Community Funeral Home and the Cosmopolitan Funeral Home. Thus, the following discussion about institutional removals conforms in general to what was observed for both firms. Appropriate releases must be secured, and the funeral director must go to the institution at its convenience. Delays may be considerable, for such things as autopsies take a long time. The removal may be further complicated if the physician has gone for the day and a signed death certificate is not available. When death occurs at a distant hospital, it is common to ask a funeral home near the institution to make the removal.

Many institutions have personnel designated to attend to the dead, generally referred to as "morgue attendants."[2] Upon arrival at the hospital, the funeral director secures permission to remove the body through the nursing office, the switchboard, or the admitting office, or sometimes a combination of the three. Then, he must wait while the morgue attendant is inconspicuously paged, often as follows: "Mr. Post, Mr. Post, please report to your office." *Post* is the abbreviated form of post-mortem examination or autopsy, and this page from the P.A. system sends the nonexistent "Mr. Post," the morgue attendant, inconspicuously to his "office," the morgue.

In some instances, the wait for the morgue attendant is longer than one would expect. There seems little reason for this, except that morgue attendants may be excercising a small bit of power over the funeral director. However, things are speeded up considerably, if the funeral director gives a tip or gratuity, which will ensure better and more solicitous service and much quicker action for institutional removals.

Obtaining the signature from the physician for the death certificate is quite another matter. There is very little the institution can do other than try to "nab the doctor" when he passes the switchboard desk. This often means that the funeral director must make a special trip to the hospital or to the physician's office to obtain his signature.

In the case of a close personal friendship between the funeral director and the physician, common in the Community Funeral Home, obtaining the signature for a death certificate is a different matter and takes place quickly. For example, the Community Funeral Home owner utilizes such opportunities to foster his friendship with the physician. Very seldom does the conversation between them have anything to do with the deceased, the bereaved, or the death; rather it is a social interlude for both. The physician and the funeral director use this time as a chance to step out of their professional roles.

There is an additional reason which may help account for the avoidance of the subject of death. It is likely that the physician is not happy with having lost a patient, and unless the circumstances merit special concern, he says very little about the death or the patient's dying condition, seemingly because of a desire not to discuss an occupational mistake.[3] Similarly, the funeral director also seems inhibited primarily because he tends to view his work as considerably different professionally from the physician's, and to discuss the death in any great detail would mean revealing occupational secrets which might be embarrassing to either or both. Such mutual inhibition often seems to place the two on equal grounds.

At no time during the course of the research was a similar situation observed with any of the personnel from the Cosmopolitan Funeral Home. In every instance, the physician's signature was obtained through institutional procedures. The funeral directors from the Cosmopolitan Funeral Home never confronted such high-level institutional personnel as physicians. Moreover, it consistently appeared that the persons making institutional removals for the firm could not help but think of their job in terms of a bureaucratically organized operation. This is notable because it means that they never had to present themselves in any but a bureaucratic role. Also important is that there seemed to be little or no confusion as to exactly what to expect or what their role should be.

A different situation exists in removals from the deceased's own home or other place which is not institutionally structured to handle dead bodies. When the funeral director arrives at the place of death, most of the bystanders are laypeople, unacquainted with the usual practices and procedures. This means that advice is sought and questions asked. The funeral director is quick to seize the situation and to issue reassurance. Furthermore, he tries to display his knowledge, experience, and ability.[4]

The funeral director tries to present himself as knowing what he is doing, but this is not nearly so difficult a task as it may seem, because no one except himself actually knows what knowledge, experience, and ability he is supposed to have. Thus, as long as it appears that he is doing things "correctly," most laypeople see his work as "expert." He protects himself by taking the precaution of asking the bereaved or others present if they care to step to another room. He implies that to see the body moved may be too upsetting for them. However, it also means that he can perform removals as a nonpublic activity.

The funeral directors of the Community Funeral Home believe that the removal of the deceased from a place other than an institution is an important "professional responsibility." They claim that one of the major tasks in this setting is "easing the tension and increasing the peace of mind of the family." Such a concern was held by very few of the personnel of the Cosmopolitan Funeral Home, and the general attitude was that the job ought to be done "efficiently and quickly."

In the presence of lay bystanders, the Community Funeral Home personnel believe that they must be extremely careful how they handle the deceased. The body is manipulated gently and appears to be treated reverently. The hands are placed carefully at the sides and the deceased is covered with a percale sheet. The straps to hold the body onto the stretcher are not belted into place with the same abruptness that is common with hospital removals. The stretcher cover zipper is closed quietly. These precautions are an important part of the way the funeral director constructs his treatment of the dead even though such concern and professional treatment may go completely unnoticed by the family. To swing the body violently onto the stretcher, to yank the straps across the chest and legs, and then to bounce it downstairs probably would draw considerable attention. It seems that what goes unnoticed is importantly different from what is actually done.

A few of the funeral directors of the Cosmopolitan Funeral Home told of their belief in the importance of carrying out a home removal in a seemingly personal fashion. One thing they do in order to effect such an appearance is to refer to the deceased by name. By mentioning the name several times, they believe the family thinks they have a personal interest. They also attempt to appear to be unhurried in their work even though they are trying to move as quickly as possible; thus, they avoid sudden movements of any kind. In these ways, the appearance to a bereaved family of the performance of this nonpublic activity by the personnel of the Cosmopolitan Funeral Home is hoped to be interpreted as discreet and professional.

As the deceased is being taken from the place of death, the Community Funeral Home director often turns and comments, "I'll be back with you in just a moment." After the body is placed in the vehicle, the director returns to the bystanders to reassure them that everything is under control, and that he will be in touch with them if anything arises, but more importantly, "You should feel free to contact me at any time if a question arises, no matter how trivial it might seem." This helps to emphasize his professional capabilities and exemplifies his belief in the value of his work.

The Cosmopolitan Funeral Home personnel attend to this detail in a different manner. Although they return and give attention to the bereaved and emphasize the fact that things are under control, they make certain that the bereaved plan to contact the firm about making arrangements rather than contacting them as an individual funeral director with that firm. In this way, they give the bereaved an initial sense that they are dealing with an attentive yet bureaucratically organized firm.

The third kind of removal is one from an emergency death. This is a rare event for the Community Funeral Home, and it never happens for the Cosmopolitan Funeral Home. This is because county coroners are not as likely to have the body moved by ambulance to the county morgue as are the medical examiners of the large city, who do so in every unexpected death. In an emergency situation, the Community Funeral Home director is to some extent under the control of such agencies as state or local police, and he behaves very differently than in the first two types of removal. He attempts to carry out the removal in a professional fashion, but he is con-cerned differently with the image he portrays. This is largely because he does not see the people present as posing the same threats to him as lay onlookers do. Moreover, he often attempts to portray an image more nearly like that of a public servant, than as a professional service prac-titioner. This role modification helps emphasize that the Community Funeral Home director presents himself according to the situation, and it is his definition of it which determines the appropriate service presenta-tion.

In general, in this kind of removal, he isn't told what to do as far as the dead body is concerned, but rather he is informed that, "You can move the body now." The interested bystanders such as the police generally are ex-perienced with death, and small talk occurs between the funeral director and these people. Relevant anecdotes often are recited. This kind of emergency removal is carried out more mechanically, with greater than usual precision, and something less than the usual reverence observed in those from private homes. In one sense, it is an institutional operation, although not occurring in a usual institutional setting.

Embalming

At the Community Funeral Home, the first task is embalming the body. This is accomplished in the preparation room, which is equipped with special machines. There is a portable embalming machine, which is an hydraulic pump and a liquid container used to inject embalming fluid into the arteries of a dead body. There is an hydraulic body lift used to pick up and move a dead body or a casket.

All of the funeral director's activities surrounding and notions of em-balming relegate it to the state of nonpublic work. For example, although the next of kin legally may request that a family member or their represen-tative witness the embalming, it is almost never done, and funeral directors vehemently discourage participation in the embalming process by anyone except funeral home personnel.[5]

Among the reasons the funeral director keeps such skills secret and nonpublic is that embalming necessitates surgical incisions in the body to gain access to the appropriate arteries and veins to carry out arterial embalming. The embalming machine pumps formalin in solution into the arteries, and the blood is drained from the veins of the dead body.⁶ The fluid mixes with and forces out the blood contained in the arteries during life. Since embalming is complicated by such things as clots, aneurysms, and other vascular obstructions, it is common practice to allow the blood to drain openly on the embalming table. This means that the task of embalming is rather messy, and this helps locate it as nonpublic work. The funeral director procedurally demonstrates his concern with the sight of blood and works hard to hide what he is working with.⁷

This is different from the practice of obstetricians who deliver babies with very little mess, and then deliberately smear blood on their delivery gown before going to greet the father of the newborn.⁸ Supposedly, to the new father this sight of apparently dangerous bleeding helps demonstrate the crucial nature of the obstetrician's job, and helps make those who see him come out of the delivery room aware of his importance in the process of birth.

The funeral director behaves in just the opposite fashion. He is afraid that the sight of blood on his gown might indicate less than the "proper" amount of care and diligence in the process of embalming, and thereby might indicate that he has been derelict in his duties. This may be because embalming is not a life-saving measure. When the Community Funeral Home director appears as the embalmer, he tries to do so in an immaculate surgical gown, as if to indicate that the embalming procedure is not messy, troublesome, or in any way offensive to the dead or to the bereaved.

Embalming is handled similarly in the Cosmopolitan Funeral Home but for different reasons. In the first place, the preparation room is very large and contains two embalming tables and a dressing table, all of which at times may be occupied simultaneously. Such an abundance or potential abundance of dead bodies is seen by the personnel as "too much" for the bereaved to see. In the second place, it would considerably reduce the efficiency of their embalming operations if they had to stop and start because people were coming into the room.

Finally, the people carrying out the embalming are considerably less careful about the cleanliness of their gowns and messiness of their work than are those in the Community Funeral Home.⁹ However, they never appear before a bereaved person in an embalming gown, whereas it was common for those in the Community Funeral Home to do so. Part of this is a result of the funeral directors in the Community Funeral Home having to appear as embalmer, counselor, and director simultaneously, while in the Cosmopolitan Funeral Home this is never the case, and at no time do they attempt to play more than one role at a time. Thus, embalming must remain secretive at the Cosmopolitan Funeral Home as much or more for organizational reasons as for professional ones.

There is the further connotation that embalming is nonpublic work because to observe such activity is thought to be repulsive to the unhardened eye. Most funeral directors see it as an activity which should be denied to the eyes of the bereaved and the general public. Naturally, this means that all activities in the funeral home which revolve around embalming are carefully kept out of sight of lay people.

Embalming can be carried out by one person, and at the Cosmopolitan Funeral Home it usually is done by a single embalmer working alone. However, in many instances at the Community Funeral Home two men work together so as "to facilitate" the embalming procedure. Such doubling up on work actually serves as a chance for sociability. It gives the workers an opportunity to withdraw from their work while doing it and helps protect them from becoming too deeply involved with the deceased as an individual.

There is an interesting contrast between the way two people work together and the way single operators work. Most single operators were observed to work with great speed, and their efforts were to complete their activities as quickly as possible. Theoretically, working in a team ought to speed up the process. Almost never, however, was this the case. Doubling-up seems to be less a practical work consideration than a social activity which to a great extent serves to make the work less dirty. Thus, the Community Funeral Home directors are able to locate embalming as nonpublic to lay people, but as public to colleagues. In this way, they are able to emphasize to each other the value of their services as professional embalmers.[10]

Seldom did people work together on an embalming at the Cosmopolitan Funeral Home. However, because of the number of bodies that needed attention, it was common that they worked in the presence of other embalmers and in this setting had open conversations with each other. Little effort seemed to be made by these embalmers to judge each other's work. Their main concern was in getting done as quickly as possible, sometimes finishing in as little as three quarters of an hour and never in more than two and one half hours. This is considerably less than the length of time taken for the embalmings observed at the Community Funeral Home. There such work ranged in time from an hour and one half to as much as three or four hours, and once even a full six hours. These differences are not so much because of the skill of the embalmers in the Community Funeral Home, but rather because of their great concern with the appearance of the dead body. Such appearance was less important for the embalmers at the Cosmopolitan Funeral Home. Concern with the appearance of the dead brings us to another important aspect of the funeral director's nonpublic activities.

Presenting the Dead

Painstaking efforts are made to "restore" the face of the deceased to a "natural likeness," and although the funeral director's embalming creed is for "Sanitation, Preservation, and Restoration," foremost in his mind is the ultimate restorative result that will be seen by the family, friends, and the general public coming to view the face and hands of the fully dressed dead body.

There are a number of reasons why restoration is so important in presenting the dead. First, when death occurs, the surface capillaries which largely contribute to the normal skin coloring of live humans lose their blood content because the blood drains to the lowest parts of the body. This leaves the flesh putty colored and strangely ghostlike. Second, without closing by the embalmer, the mouth gapes and the eyes stare with open lids.

If there has been an autopsy, there are additional problems. A large incision is made across the top of the head through the hair, and the entire top of the skull is detached to gain access to the brain, which is then removed. The pathologist's handiwork is not hidden in any way by the personnel of the hospital. At worst, without restorative efforts, the embalmer would display a dead body with a gray-white face, gaping mouth, staring eyes, and a strangely dislocated and blood stained scalp. Even without trying to enhance the importance of their own job by taking on tasks such as restoration, funeral directors expressed a concern about "how bad" the unrestored dead body looked. They went on to explain that part of their pride of workmanship resides in making the deceased appear as much like himself as possible.

As mentioned above, the embalmers in the Cosmopolitan Funeral Home are concerned with the appearance of the dead bodies to a lesser extent. Many of these embalmers seem to feel that is is important to make the deceased presentable, but that "the family wouldn't realize the difference between a masterpiece and a lousy job." Another reason for their lack of concern in this regard is that it takes a long time to carry out cosmetic work, and to take such time upsets the firm's routine. Moreover, not all of the personnel are qualified to do more than "a barely decent job." It takes time to apply the cosmetics on each individual case, and often time is a problem for these people, for on numerous occasions the removal men arrived with a dead body very close to the time it was supposed to be ready for viewing. This meant that those carrying out the embalming and restoration had to move very quickly in order to make the schedule for presenting the body in the reposing room.

It is interesting that the professional culture of funeral directing has not developed expert embalming and restorative specialists to any great extent, even in large metropolitan areas. The Community Funeral Home personnel fancy themselves as being competent in this capacity, and this seems to be true for most funeral service practitioners. Thus, unlike most aspects of medicine, which are highly specialized, embalming is carried out by each individual practitioner without expert help from outside his own firm. Even with a terribly mutilated case, it is the embalmer's own discretion rather than the opinion of a restorative expert which determines whether or not he will carry out a full-fledged restorative effort in an attempt to open the casket. Clearly, the funeral director has little professional visibility in the same sense that physicians do.[11] This problem was mentioned numerous times, for this lack of professional recognition was annoying to many of the funeral directors.

This also has another interesting ramification. It means that the expert orientation of the funeral director exists on an individual basis, and that he directs his expert work at an audience which is not professionally trained to judge such efforts.[12] The bereaved family and the general public which comes to view the deceased make judgments about the practitioner's work not based on standards of competence established in the profession but rather from outside it. In this regard, it was common to have people well acquainted with the work of the Community Funeral Home explain that they had recently visited another firm and that the work did not compare at all favorably with that of "my own funeral director." On several occasions, there was an opportunity to compare such opinions because of access to the other named funeral director. In each instance, what resulted was a favorable judgment on the part of those judging the person of the their acquaintance compared to "the other funeral director" whose work was deemed to be unsatisfactory in the eyes of an unacquainted lay public.

In light of these circumstances, it is not surprising that the Community Funeral Home directors take care and pride in their presentation of the dead body. Not only is it an important element in their conception of the funeral, but also in helping them to have a satisfying professional self-image. This is especially relevant because of the lack of professional judgment of their work.

The Community Funeral Home directors' primary concern when embalming is to restore the deceased's face and hands to as natural a likeness as possible, and to present the dead in this fashion. Observations of the bereaved indicate that this truly is the primary concern of the family too, and that the funeral directors' efforts are not misplaced in this regard. Their concern with these potentially visible areas is a cosmetic rather than a sanitary one. This is true to a lesser extent for the embalmers at the Cosmopolitan Funeral Home, who are more concerned with speed and efficiency.

It is not strange that after the embalming process is completed and the deceased is fully dressed, further efforts are made to help the face and hands appear as natural as possible by the use of externally applied coloring agents and cosmetics. Most funeral directors want to have the body look good when finally placed in the casket. The cosmetic appearance involves the overall body, the flesh, the clothing, the casket in which the body is lying, the lighting in the room in which the casket in placed, and the general decor of that room and its surrounding environment. The Community Funeral Home directors believe that all of these contribute to the way in which the bereaved surviving relatives visualize the deceased as a dead entity, and they pay considerable attention to these details.

The embalmers at the Cosmopolitan Funeral Home are concerned about the appearance of the body; however, this concern is based on the belief that it is "a real pain to go up and change something that doesn't please somebody." Therefore, most of their efforts at restoration and cosmetizing the dead are in the interest of expediency more than in the actual appearance. Not all of them took this attitude, however, and a few of them became very annoyed when called upon by the personnel supervisors to go and do another task just when they were about to complete their work. They gave as reasons that, "I do not like to leave a job undone," or "There's no one else who really cares as much as I do about these sorts of things, and I hate to leave before I'm finished."

After the body is embalmed and cosmetized, the deceased must be casketed and everything "set up" for viewing and visitation. The set up is considered very important by most funeral directors; however, the actual casketing of the body as an activity is relatively unimportant to the funeral director. Rather, it is the overall impression once completed in which he is most interested. His main conern is how the complete set up will appear to the bereaved and the visiting public, but his activities surrounding the setting up are crucial in locating his definition of the "appropriate" funeral setting. His placement of the casket in the reposing room, the arrangement of the chairs and pieces of furniture in the room, and other physical concerns receive the funeral director's attention. By attending to these concerns and demonstrating his interest in fostering the satisfactory funeral setting, by his definition, they become an important element in the funeral even if the bereaved and the lay public do not specifically notice his efforts and operational procedures.

The set up is importantly a process which the funeral director does nonpublicly in the privacy of his funeral home; however, it does not need to be a secretive operation. The casket is usually placed on some movable platform and the fully dressed, cosmetized body put in it. The casket on the platform is then moved into the reposing room, where the body will be available for viewing until the time of the funeral service. Once the casket is placed, the funeral director attends to the general setting and to tiny details such as clean eyeglasses, lint-free blue serge suits, polished fingernails, earrings, chairs placed in appropriate places, and flowers put up around the casket, or, if necessary, throughout the reposing room. These details are seen as the artistic "memory picture" aspect of the funeral. Such factors as the position of the body, the level of lighting in the room, the music, and others are considered with the ultimate aim being a satisfactory memory picture of the deceased for the bereaved.

The set up at the Cosmopolitan Funeral Home also is seen as an important element of the work. However, it is done in a fashion which is very different from that in the Community Funeral Home. The people in the preparation room who have done the embalming often do not carry out the dressing and cosmetizing. Often, these are done by one of a few embalmers who consider themselves specialists at cosmetics. Once they finish their handiwork, they may be assisted in casketing the body by an apprentice. The apprentice then transfers the casket to the care of the elevator operator who, with the assistance of the attendant on the floor, takes it to the room in which it is to be on display.

Once in the room, it is up the floor attendant to position the casket in the proper spot and to make certain that the room is arranged appropriately. Usually, this is done very quickly and without great care. When flowers arrive, it is up to the floor attendant to put the flowers up as quickly as possible. Almost all of these efforts are done in the hopes of pleasing the bereaved, but each person is concerned primarily that he need not have to do his job over rather than that it may be of benefit to the bereaved family.

Thus far, we have tried to explain how and why certain activities of funeral directors in their funeral homes are carried out nonpublicly. These activities are not commonly visible to the bereaved or to the lay public, but they are an important aspect of the funeral director's presenting behavior. Let us examine such behavior from the perspective of behavior carried out in secret.

Secretive Behavior

Although secretive behavior usually is thought of as that which is carried out nonpublicly or not in the presence of an audience, it is important to distinguish between two types of secretive behavior. First, there is private secretive behavior. Such behavior is carried out nonpublicly or out of the audience's view and is deemed by both funeral directors and bereaved people as appropriately being performed there. The implication seems to be "out of sight, out of mind," even though there is an awareness that such behavior exists. The clearest example of private secretive behavior for funeral directors is the embalming of the dead. It is recognized as such by both performers and audiences, and the funeral director never performs an embalming before anyone.

Second, there is public secretive behavior. It is that behavior in the presence of the bereaved which has the potential of disrupting the overall funeral by discrediting the funeral director's performance. The removal of the dead body from the home in the presence of the bereaved family is an example of public secretive behavior. A more subtle example, but one which emphasizes the importance of this concept, occurs while the funeral director is "helping" the family to select the casket. When the funeral director deals with bereaved families during this selection, he is on display and behaving in a public fashion. However, many of his sales techniques and handling of the bereaved audience could discredit his performance as a "professional personal servant." Therefore, the funeral director treats these interests as secrets, but he does so in full view of the bereaved audience.

Private and public secretive behavior are subtle modifications of presenting behavior. We contend that the way in which the individual service practitioners perform is influenced by the intricacies of their tasks and by elements which may or may not be related to the funeral performance itself.

There is a second circumstance which deserves our attention. On numerous occasions, people were observed performing in a manner which was unfamiliar in a situation which was familiar. In every instance when this was the case, it was observed that the practitioner was attempting to behave as a funeral director but not in his usual fashion. At times servants were observed behaving as if they were bureaucrats, and vice versa. The reasons for such transformations were not always clear. One thing consistently appeared when this was the case, however, and that was that the funeral director carried out deliberately contrived behavior. It seems that when situations arise which are exceptionally difficult to cope with, service practitioners may handle them by hiding their usual selves in full view of the audience by presenting themselves as model opposites.

An example may help clarify this. The owner of the Community Funeral Home was about to go on vacation, and he knew that getting involved with a funeral would take more of his time than was available. Therefore, he carried off his behavior as a bureaucrat. A similar example from the Cosmopolitan Funeral Home occurred when a normal bureaucrat became deeply involved with a bereaved family for whom he "felt very sorry," and he attended to them as a service professional.

The distinction between these discrepancies and usual performances is that such discrepancies happen on rare occasions. It seems appropriate to conceive of them as being a funeral director's attempt to hide his usual self through contrived behavior. Thus, on occasion, practitioners were observed to be hiding in full view of the audience when confronted with situations of uncommon difficulty.

In sum, we may say that in the Community Funeral Home when funeral directors are working nonpublicly, they tend to present themselves as serious service practitioners working primarily in the best interests of the bereaved. In the Cosmopolitan Funeral Home, funeral directors working nonpublicly behave as well trained technicians trying to implement their work as efficiently and expeditiously as possible primarily for the sake of the funeral home's operation.

Notes

1. The only exception is if someone dies in the funeral home. Over a 15 year period in the Community Funeral Home, this happened twice; the first was one of the funeral home owners, and the second was a woman attending her sister's funeral. According to those interviewed for this research that is more than is common because only two people remembered it ever happening at the Cosmopolitan Funeral Home.

2. For a detailed discussion of morgue attendants see David Sudnow's discussion of "John" in *Passing On*. Englewood Cliffs, N.J.: Prentice-Hall, 1967, pp. 51-60.

3. For a discussion about such mistakes see Everett C. Hughes, *Men and Their Work*. Glencoe: The Free Press, 1958, pp. 88-101.

4. This and the following discussion may also be viewed from the perspective of the construction of social reality. For example, this is the way in which illness can be examined; see Eliot Freidson, *Profession of Medicine: A Study in the Sociology of Applied Knowledge*. New York: Dodd, Mead and Co., 1970, pp. 203-331. Such treatment under the rubric of the sociology of knowledge is useful to bear in mind throughout the following section. In this regard see Peter L. Berger and Thomas Luckman, *The Social Construction of Reality*. Garden City: Doubleday and Co., Anchor Books, 1967; and Burkart Holzner, *Reality Construction in Society*. Cambridge: Schenkman Publishing Co., 1968.

5. Goffman points out that a similar point is made by Robert Habenstein, explaining:

> If the bereaved are to be given the illusion that the dead one is really in a deep and tranquil sleep, than the undertaker must be able to keep the bereaved from the workroom where the corpses are drained, stuffed, and painted in preparation for their final performance.

Erving Goffman, *The Presentation of Self in Everyday Life*. Garden City: Doubleday Co., Anchor Books, 1959, p. 114.

6. This situation bears close resemblance to that of physicians regarding "Access to the Body," which is described in more detail by Talcott Parsons, *The Social System*. New York: The Free Press, 1951, pp. 451-54.

7. For a discussion of this sort of circumstance in broader terms see Hughes, *op. cit.*, pp. 71-75.

8. This was personally described to me by an obstetrician who was surprised that funeral directors usually appeared before him in *immaculate* embalming gowns.

9. Such a situation is similar to the one which Gouldner found among mine

workers involving their apparent detachment from, yet actual connection to, the rest of the gypsum plant. See Alvin Gouldner, *Patterns of Industrial Bureaucracy*. Glencoe: The Free Press, 1954, pp. 105-54.

10. This finding supports the contention that professionals are more influenced by colleague control in certain work settings than in others; see Freidson, *op. cit.*, pp. 137-57.

11. For a helpful discussion of professional visibility and organizational setting see Peter M. Blau and W. Richard Scott, *Formal Organizations*. San Francisco: Chandler Publishing Company, 1962, pp. 60-64.

12. For comparison see Freidson, *op. cit.*, pp. 87-108; also see Eliot Freidson, "Client Control and Medical Practice," in the *American Journal of Sociology*, LXV. 1960, pp. 374-82.

Chapter 7

The Funeral Director
and the Presentation of Self

One of the distinctive characteristics of the Community Funeral Home is that all behavior is geared to the totality. Efforts are made to make every aspect of the operation of the funeral home compatible. Responsibility is borne by all members of the staff, and they consciously strive to present themselves as masters of every facet of the firm. This includes public and nonpublic behavior in the funeral home and general behavior out of it. Moreover, the Community Funeral Home directors believe that they should attend to every aspect of their lives in a "proper" professional fashion.[1]

This emphasizes the distinctiveness of not having specialists for various tasks. Each member of the staff is capable of carrying out numerous tasks and duties, and they all do so without fanfare or exclusivity. Thus, when people come for services, they are rendered by whoever is on hand at the time, for each person is capable of handling all clients. It is implicit in such behavior that the Community Funeral Home directors have a service orientation. For, in addition to being concerned with the overall impression fostered by the funeral home, they are also concerned with behaving as all-knowledgeable, all-capable service practitioners.

It is also distinctive of the Community Funeral Home that each person does not merely exemplify the organization, but in a very real sense actually is the organization. Thus, even though there may be several people providing services, each one of them does so as if he were the total

122

organization. This means that questions and problems are dealt with individually as they arise and are not referred to another part of some hierarchy. It also means that the behavior of each individual at any given time represents the characteristic behavior of the organization as a unit.

This trait of the Community Funeral Home directors also influences the way in which they act in all aspects of their lives. Since the individual is the organization and since the organization is service oriented, the individual funeral director also is service oriented. Moreover, the organization of the funeral home fosters the impression of professional personal services. In this way, it is important that the funeral directors are members of the funeral home's staff rather than that they are funeral directors in general. Thus, the work setting in which one practices helps determine one's orientation toward one's profession.[2]

Another important characteristic of the Community Funeral Home directors is that they appear to have little awareness of the formal aspects of their organization. The members of the staff are not so much concerned with the distinctions between employer-employee, and the hierarchy of the organization is relatively unimportant to the members of the staff. To be sure, an hierarchy does exist, and to say that it is not attended to is false; however, the hierarchy plays a very small part in a formal way. Each practitioner is to a great extent free to conduct himself as a full-fledged professional member of the organization without having to cope with notions of superiority or inferiority.[3]

Similarly, there is very little awareness of the informal aspects of organization. The members of the staff of the Community Funeral Home do not think of themselves as "part of an organization," but rather that they are individual, although not independent, service practitioners. Thus, organizational activities are not seen as being formal or informal, but all are part of their jobs as professional personal servants.[4]

The personnel of the Cosmopolitan Funeral Home primarily gear their behavior to the specific area with which they are concerned. Counselors present themselves as counselors, funeral directors as funeral directors, and so forth. Thus, the way in which they present themselves is determined largely by their particular job.

This does not mean that they do not have a conception of the totality of their funeral organization, but rather that they attend primarily to a specific part of this totality. They are concerned with the totality, but this concern is not paramount to the way in which they conduct themselves; rather, it serves in a general orienting way. Their primary concern is that their job is an integral part of the overall operation. As individuals, they are not nearly so important as is their actual work. The area in which they are employed is the important thing rather than them as individual practitioners of a particular occupational specialty.[5]

The Cosmopolitan Funeral Home is characterized by many such

limited specialists. There is enough work to do in each specialty so that each practitioner, although aware of the general operation, attends to his specialty as an expert. In the Community Funeral Home, in addition to being geared to the totality, funeral directors are not specialists as such. This difference between the two organizations is important in that it helps foster a sense of one's job in such a fashion that the members of the Cosmopolitan Funeral Home, largely because of the way in which it is organized, come to believe in themselves as experts in a bureaucracy.

The organization of the Cosmopolitan Funeral Home has no "personality" in the same sense that the other funeral home does. The large organization is the organization, and individuals are part of it in an almost anonymous way. Thus, rather than exemplifying the organization, they are little more than workers in it. Naturally, these individuals do not tend to see the organization in as personal a way as do those with the Community Funeral Home.

In the Cosmopolitan Funeral Home there is a keen awareness of the formal aspects of the organization. The hierarchy, table of organization, titles, positions, specific areas of competence, rules and regulations, all are important to the way in which the individuals conduct themselves. Interestingly, the formality of the organization emphasizes its informal aspects. For example, individual personalities and the compatibility of colleagues are considerably more important than in the other funeral home. Moreover, informal control and sanctions considerably modify the effectiveness with which many of the employees of the Cosmopolitan Funeral Home operate.[6]

The providing of services by those practitioners is accomplished efficiently, and people are handled quickly and with precision. Little time is devoted to nonessential amenities, and bereaved families are dealt with as speedily as possible without seeming haste by experts. Little effort is made by each specialist to provide services in more than his own aspect of the operation. Thus, although the services are intended to appear to be professional and personal, they are provided only when and where appropriate. This is very different from the Community Funeral Home where every activity is conceived of as contributing to or being part of professional personal services.[7]

Perceptions of Funerary Behavior

The Community Funeral Home directors to a great extent believe in themselves as professional personal servers whose work is important to the bereaved and valuable to society. They like to believe that their work is a humanitarian service, and they try to foster the appropriate appearance. Moreover, they claim that one of the most important interpersonal relationships is with those for whom they work and the public at large. This relationship may be thought of as a continuum ranging from the intimate funerary dealings with the bereaved next of kin to the somewhat more public ones with the general public who come to visiting hours or who are met at social events out of the funeral home. It is this lay relationship rather than one with colleagues which the Community Funeral Home directors cherish, nurture, and develop to the highest degree possible. The relationships the funeral directors develop with the public are different from ones generally developed by other professional personal servants.[8]

The personnel of the Cosmopolitan Funeral Home see themselves as employees of an organization whose job it is to provide services to individuals who request them. The emphasis, however, is on the firm's providing of services rather than on the individual practitioner's providing of personal services. These funeral directors are concerned about fostering the appearance of being servants when they are in public in the funeral home. When they are not in public or are out of the funeral home, their behavior is considerably different, and most of the time they behave as bureaucrats.

Even though this is the case, they, as do the Community Funeral Home directors, tend to consider the relationship with the people for whom they work to be important and a source of satisfaction.[9] Importantly, the Cosmopolitan Funeral Home directors are not unconcerned with the general public, but their concern is essentially public relations oriented and is attended to by advertising and promotion rather than by the personal contacts of individual practitioners.

Practitioners in the Cosmopolitan Funeral Home also are concerned about relationships with colleagues, especially in their own organization. They work together on a friendly basis, and as funeral directors generally treat each other as equals, interacting extensively while on the job, each hoping that the others will see his work as being of high quality.[10] Generally, however, such ties do not carry beyond the organization, and between competing firm employees in the city, there is very little colleague judgment because of the competitive nature of the different firms.

It is interesting that apprentice funeral directors in the Cosmopolitan Funeral Home are treated not just like fledgling funeral directors, but rather like inferior beings. They are asked to carry out jobs involving considerable dirty work and which are quite boring.[11] Such tasks as cleaning the morgue table after an embalming or suturing the cranial, thoracic, and abdominal incisions of an autopsy are set aside largely for apprentices. The general attitude is that apprentices need to do this work because, "This is the kind of thing I had to do, and you don't really know what sort of job funeral directing is unless you do it."

In the Cosmopolitan Funeral Home, the relationships between funeral directors and unlicensed funeral personnel generally tend to be confined to rather lax supervision and unspecified leadership. When there is work to be done the funeral director almost informally tells the other employees what, when, and how to do it. However, he sees himself in a position of authority even though the system is very lenient and relatively indulgent.[12]

Funeral directors in both firms consider it more important that those who buy and pay for their services be satisfied than that their colleagues know or care whether they have "done a good job." One of the determinants as to whether a funeral director is doing a good job in the eyes of his colleagues is related to the dollar amount of his average funeral sales. Ironically, this depends upon client rather than colleague satisfaction.

The funeral directors of the Cosmopolitan Funeral Home have little need for advice from consultants or other experts. They merely do their job as set forth by the organization. It may be that management turns to experts, but when it does so, policies are established and procedures implemented on the basis of management decisions. Funeral directors in this setting do not see themselves as pacesetters in any way.

The Community Funeral Home directors consider themselves to be experts in their own right and pay little heed to outside advice except that which they gain through seminars such as those sponsored by NFDA.[13] Even at these seminars, the advice offered tends to come from experts from other fields. Presently there are very few acknowledged "funeral service experts" whose training and background is broad enough to enable them to give generally valuable advice to funeral directors on a wide range of related matters.

It is interesting that most personal service occupations have developed sets of specialists who do nothing but render advice. Not only are there very few specialists of a funeral service advisory nature, but also there seems to be considerable hesitancy about utilizing those who do exist. This does not mean that funeral directors do not take advice, for certainly they do. However, decisions generally are predicated on advice rendered by such experts as business management consultants rather than funeral service advisory specialists. This is true for both of the funeral homes. It will be interesting to note in coming years whether such specialists arise, and, if so, what their backgrounds will be.

There is a difficult problem for funeral directors of the Community Funeral Home and for those deciding management procedures for the Cosmopolitan Funeral Home working with anyone on a consulting or advisory basis. Namely, both organizations believe that their operation and the families served are unique and that an advisor would be worthless unless he were totally familiar with the nature of their particular population and its peculiarities, plus being fully acquainted with all aspects of funerals service. This feeling seems to exist because most of the present consultants seldom if ever have dealt with dead bodies or bereaved people, and in the eyes of many funeral directors, this automatically disqualifies them as experts in funeral service. This attitude exemplifies the earlier finding that funeral directors deal with lay people rather than colleagues on an expert basis.

Although the funeral director sees himself as the expert regarding funeral matters, the ancillary occupations such as florist, cemeterian, and so forth, present a strange situation.[14] The Community Funeral Home director tends to treat such people in a friendly, businesslike way, and he usually requests rather than commands that something be done. In this way he tends to have less control over the ancillary occupations than one might expect. Although he is the highest level of the funeral field, he is dealing with people who can make his lot rather uncomfortable. For instance, uncooperative florists can deliver flowers in the middle of visiting hours, thereby increasing the problems of placing them around the casket.

In the Cosmopolitan Funeral Home, dealings with these ancillary personnel are almost nonexistent, for most such people are also employed by bureaucracies and there is little or no contact between individuals. However, it is quite possible for members of these occupations to "make life miserable" for the funeral directors of his firm. For instance, cemetery gravediggers' and flower car drivers' strikes have had a deleterious effect on funeral service in many cities.

The way in which the bereaved perceive the funeral director depends to a great extent upon the kind of organization in which one is practicing as well as upon the region in which one is carrying out his activities. Recall that there are commonly practiced sets of behavior that funeral directors use while dealing with the bereaved. For example, when bereaved families call on the telephone, either to announce a death, or to ask questions about an already announced death, the Community Funeral Home directors or the funeral counselors at the Cosmopolitan Funeral Home are solicitous, kind, and generally attentive. Their voice and conduct suggest an effort to be personal and intimate.

At times, some funeral directors even take on familial characteristics and act like a member of the family. For example, funeral directors were heard to call the deceased "Father" while talking about him with the family. When confronted with such behavior, bereaved families were observed either to ignore the funeral director's attempt to assume a family position, or to be offended by it, although they seldom said so to the funeral director. Several were heard to comment that "he isn't part of the family, why is he talking that way?" The reason is clear if we realize that funeral directors in both settings attempt to be personal with bereaved families in an effort to gain acceptance.[15] However, the way in which the bereaved perceive a funeral director's presentation is not necessarily the same as his own perception of it.[16]

The policies at both funeral homes are to have a licensed funeral director conduct and direct the funeral. However, it is important that the licensed director at the Cosmopolitan Funeral Home fulfills his duties primarily as a bureaucrat. He is not the same person with whom the family made the arrangements or selected the casket. Furthermore, seldom during visiting hours are funeral directors present. Thus, even the location of certain activities is organizationally based.

One of the crucial determinants of the way in which others preceive the funeral directors' presentations involves prior exposure to funeral directors in both professional and nonprofessional activities. This means that if a person has experienced at an earlier time the death of a close relative or friend and has dealt with a funeral director, that person will have certain preconceptions about how the funeral director will behave. These prejudgments seriously modify how other people perceive the presentations of the funeral director. Individuals who have a preconceived notion of the funeral director as a server are likely to be confused if the funeral director is perceived as a bureaucrat, while those expecting a bureaucrat are likely to be just as confused by an individual perceived to be a service professional.

Locations and Behavior

The ways in which funeral directors present themselves are modified by the region of the funeral home in which they are active. Their behavior also is modified by the type of organization in which they practice.[17] Our intention now is to construct some typical presenting characteristics which will enable us to understand more clearly the joint effects that regions and organizations have on the presentation of self.

Table 1 shows six types of presenting characteristics in the two kinds of firm organizations, based on the three regions of the funeral home in which the actors perform.[18]

Cell 1 shows that when members of the simple service organization present themselves publicly in the funeral home, they tend to foster the appearance of being personal servers. This may be contrasted to those members of the complex service organization, who while in the funeral home publicly present themselves as impersonal servers, as shown in Cell 2. It is important to note that the impression in both instances is intended to be as a server, and to a great extent the differences lie in whether the practitioner behaves in a personal or impersonal fashion. The services may be just as "satisfactory" in either instance. However, a personal server fits the model of a professional personal service occupation while an impersonal server fits the model of a bureaucratic occupation.

Importantly, it is possible that bureaucratic organizations may be able to provide a wider range of services to bereaved people than can personal service organizations. Such provision may be accounted for by the fact that in a bureaucratic organization there are more available servers. Thus, as needs become greater, either because of difficult tasks or because of many people to be served, the bureaucratic organization often is better able to cope with such problems. However, even though this may be the case, the very existence of an impersonal server is a contradiction of both models.

Table 1
Ideal Presenting Characteristics of Funeral Directors,
Firm Organization, and the Regions of the Funeral Home

Regions of the Funeral Home	Firm Organization	
	Simple	Complex
Publicly in the Funeral Home	Cell 1 Personal Server	Cell 2 Impersonal Server
Nonpublicly in the Funeral Home	Cell 3 Technical Server	Cell 4 Expert Technician
Out of the Funeral Home	Cell 5 Occupationally Concerned Server	Cell 6 Occupationally Unconcerned Individual

When working nonpublicly in the funeral home, the members of a simple service organization tend to foster the appearance of being technical servers, as shown in Cell 3. Their efforts, practices, and emitted expressive behavior indicate that their task orientation is geared to providing services, and they practice in this capacity even though carrying out technical tasks. Cell 4 shows that their counterparts in a complex organization tend to appear as expert technicians. Thus, they, too, are carrying out technical tasks calling for a high degree of skill and expertise. However, the way in which they conduct and present themselves is less oriented to the notion that their tasks are services and more geared to the notion that their tasks are essentially technical ones. In most instances, the expert technician does not attempt to appear as a server in any sense of the word.

Cell 5 indicates that out of the funeral home members of the simple organization tend to foster the appearance of being occupationally concerned servers. They maintain the aura of service, even though they are not performing in their funeral home. They care about the expressive behavior they emit because of its occupational connections. Members of the complex organization are quite different, as can be seen in Cell 6, and they appear as occupationally unconcerned individuals. This is not meant to imply that they live deviant existences or that they ignore community customs or mores, but rather that their activities are completely disoriented from having an influence on their occupation. As individuals, they behave as they wish and present themselves in whatever manner they see fit. This may include attending to some occupational or professional concern, or it may mean that they pay absolutely no attention to creating the impression that their job is an important service one.

Funeral directors present themselves differently according to the region of the funeral home in which they are practicing. There are, however, greater differences in the way in which they present themselves based on the type of organization in which they are practicing. This means that it is the difference between being in a simple contrasted to a complex service organization which produces the most distinct differences in the presenting behavior of funeral practitioners. We believe that the kind of organization is which one participates is the most important determinant of one's behavior. Moreover, it appears that one's occupational orientation and funerary behavior to a large extent are dependent ·upon the organizationally relevant aspects of one's work and not just upon the work itself or its demands in society.

A Continuum of Behavior

Thus far, our discussion has treated the perception of funeral director presenting behavior as if there were two clear-cut categories of the presentation of self, namely, bureaucrat and server. Life is not so simple, however, and it requires little imagination to think of funeral directors appearing as various combinations of bureaucrats or servers. In other words, the above two types are merely two categories of the funeral director's presentation of self.

In order to analyze more completely the implications of funeral directors as presenters, it is essential that we expand our treatment and include some combined types of self presenters. This can be accomplished by examining the continuum of relationships between firm organization and the presentation of self as shown in Table 2.[19]

It is important to emphasize that all four types were observed empirically; however, our main point is not so much to count them as it is to categorize them. Moreover, there are too few people in the simple organization to allow valid enumeration. Instead, this continuum helps illustrate some of the complexities of presenting behavior.[20]

Cells 1 and 4 contain two pure types of self presenters. In Cell 1 are those who present themselves as servers in simple organizations, the pure servant. They are common to most firms such as the Community Funeral Home. In Cell 4 there are those practitioners who work in a complexly organized firm, the pure bureaucrats. They are common in firms such as the Cosmopolitan Funeral Home. Such pure types may be contrasted to two mixed types of self presenters, the service bureaucrat in Cell 2, and the bureaucratic server in Cell 3.

Those practitioners who fall into Cell 1, the pure servers, are the least problematic of the four types. Such people behave appropriately for the model of their occupation and work in a firm which is appropriately organized to allow them to do so. A structural assessment of the people who fall into Cell 4, the pure bureaucrats, indicates that they, too, are appropriately located. However, when scrutinized according to the notion of occupational models, such practitioners may be seen as problematic, for they do not fit the service occupation model. Thus, even though they are likely to be highly valued by the organization, they may fall short of what is expected of them by the families they serve.

Table 2
A Continuum of Behavior by Firm
Organization and Presentation of Self

Firm Organization	Servant	Bureaucrat
Simple	Cell 1. Pure Server	Cell 2. Service Bureaucrat
Complex	Cell 3. Bureaucratic Server	Cell 4. Pure Bureaucrat

Cell 2 contains the service bureaucrats. These are practitioners in a simple service organization who present themselves as bureaucrats. When the bereaved audience confronts funeral directors such as this, although they may appreciate the efficiency and speed of their services, they may be disturbed by such things as impersonality and an apparent lack of individual concern.

Cell 3 contains the bureaucratic servers. There are a few practitioners who appear to provide more personal services in the firm with a complex organization. Of course, there is the possibility that people who select bureaucratic firms do not want this type of treatment and might find bureaucratic servers unexpected and disturbing. However, there are a number of reasons why it appears that bereaved familes are most desirous of services rather than efficiency. We contend that the bereaved audience enters into the funeral home because they need death-related services, not because they want to deal with a bureaucracy, even if they select a bureaucratically organized funeral firm.[21]

Similar problems arise when the bereaved audience enters into a simple service organization and confronts bureaucrats. Servers in a bureaucratic organization may engender greater client satisfaction than when there are bureaucrats in a service organization. Again, this is largely because people come to funeral homes for services, not for bureaucratic treatment. To reiterate, our greatest concern is the audience's perception. Thus, when the bereaved expect bureaucratic treatment but perceive personal service treatment, it is likely to be more positively affected than when the bereaved expect service but perceive bureaucratic treatment.

It would be possible, of course, to expand the continuum using various dimensions pertinent to presenting behavior and firm organization. Suffice it to say, that to fail to recognize that the presentation of self may occur along a sizable continuum of performances is an error of oversimplification. The essence of the four types of presenting behavior just described is that funeral directors may confront the bereaved with orientations different from expected, and the bereaved may find not just the unexpected, but also the insincere.

The Funeral Director and the Bereaved

In team efforts, it is common that someone has the right and responsibility to direct and control the progress of the dramatic action. The individual who dominates the funeral is not only its director, but also plays an actual part in the overall activities. The funeral director may be thought of both as a team member and as the director. In the latter capacity he wants the overall funeral to go as smoothly as possible.[22] He is the director of a team effort, but he is also an active member of the team.[23] It is quite understandable that the funeral director must attempt to keep other team members behaving adequately as well as allocating the parts for each funeral. Thus, the attitudes of the bereaved as participants toward the funeral director as director are different from what they are toward other active teammates.

The funeral director considers the bereaved to be participants with whom and before whom he is behaving. Furthermore, the bereaved realize that the funeral has a director, and it is likely that they hold him more responsible for the success of the funeral than if he were a mere participant. The funeral director responds to this by making dramaturgical demands on the bereaved that he might not make on himself. It is quite possible that this might add to the estrangement the bereaved feel for him.[24]

It is important that a funeral team is understood to be a set of individuals who must cooperate intimately if a given projected definition of the situation is to be carried off. A funeral team is a grouping, not in relation to the funeral home social organization, but in relation to an interaction or a series of them in which that definition of the funeral situation is maintained. Thus, the funeral team constitutes a society which is separate and distinct from the larger society of which the participants and team members are a part. This is true, of course, for all the possible team combinations which exist in the funeral setting, and it may be that several teams work together to act out the entire funeral.

The situation is something like this. The funeral director and the bereaved form a team whose task at hand is to carry out the entire funeral process. Both the funeral director and the bereaved tend to see themselves as mutual participants in the funeral process. The funeral director believes that the funeral audience is composed of the bereaved and the other people who observe or take part in the funeral. The bereaved, on the other hand, believe that they are performing before the other people in attendance at the funeral. Additionally, the bereaved gear part of their behavior to what they expect to be the demands of the funeral director as part of their audience. However, he is not just a member of the audience, and in many ways he is the director of the funeral process, for both he and the bereaved usually believe that he is the only one who knows all aspects of the funeral well enough to coordinate them in a "proper" fashion. Naturally, this means that the funeral director is in the difficult spot of having to behave in what he sees as the right ways for the funeral process.

An example of how there may be a gulf between the funeral director's behavior and the bereaved's expectations of it involves the way in which the funeral director conducts himself with the dead.[25] The funeral director is socialized to think of every dead body as the "remains of a human being." He feels a responsibility to it, and he seeks signs and symbols from the dead body so as to make judgments about how he should carry out the funeral. His public efforts to be genteel in the presence of the dead body, his efforts to restore it to a somewhat lifelike appearance, his supposedly reverent treatment of it, and his vested interest in it, all make his relationship with the dead body somewhat unusual.

Not surprisingly, this relationship seems difficult to understand for those neither connected to nor familiar with funeral directing. To anyone who believes that death terminates life and that the remaining body is an empty, useless shell, the behavior of the funeral director regarding the dead body seems pretentious and the basis for it confusing. Thus, the very naturalness of the way in which funeral directors conduct themselves during their work with the dead may appear to the bereaved and the unconcerned lay person to be unnatural.

Let us examine how the funeral director implements his work with the dead. Quite obviously, there can be no verbal communication between the funeral director and the dead body. However, there is a strange kind of one-way communication which is similar to that which often exists between living people, and it operates to make the dead body a team member. For example, upon the completion of the restoration and casketing of the body funeral directors have been heard to say, "Well, Mr. Smith, I think you look fine. I hope that your wife does, too." At night when closing the funeral home, funeral directors occasionally have been heard to say, "Goodnight" to no one in particular. Such remarks are spoken with no expectation of eliciting a response, or for that matter, of being heard by the bereaved or others. From the perspective of everyday living, this may sound a bit strange, but it is not when one realizes just what an important part the dead body plays in the funeral process.

There is an important way in which the dead body is used by the Community Funeral Home directors to help them behave in the most "appropriate" fashion possible. Specifically, their intimate dealing with the corpse allows them to make observations of secret signs and symbols. These often are used to guess how the funeral arrangers will behave when making funeral arrangements. For instance, dead bodies wearing old, tattered clothing or having uncared for fingernails or toenails indicate a certain lack of concern about personal well-being. The kinds of belongings of those who die in the hospital are signs which may help to guess the manner of living conceived of as "appropriate" by the deceased and the bereaved family.

Such signs and symbols are more than merely observed artifacts by the Community Funeral Home directors. They must physically carry the belongings of the dead and actually undress their bodies. It is largely through these intimate, interpersonal contacts with the dead that these funeral directors foster their active relationship with them. The Community Funeral Home directors often are able to behave before a bereaved family which they have been able to somewhat prejudge. They are thus able to modify their behavior to provide at least their version of appropriately dealing with a particular family.

The bureaucratic funeral directors of the Cosmopolitan Funeral Home seldom have this advantage. Their behavior tends to be more stereotypical, and they are geared to reacting to immediate and apparent audience demands and requirements. Thus, the contrast between the two kinds of funeral directors is that the Community Funeral Home director responds to the bereaved based on not just audience-emitted symbols, but symbols gleaned from a relationship with the dead team member. This suggests that the Community Funeral Home director has the advantage over his Cosmopolitan Funeral Home counterpart, in that he is able to utilize more physically observable characteristics in determining the most appropriate funeral behavior.

Another example of the gulf that exists between funeral directors and bereaved people involves the presenting of the dead. On numerous occasions people were heard to remark, "I want to remember her as she was." This feeling is common among some bereaved families as well as many other people. However, most of the time, the dead body is restored and presented in a casket which quite obviously leaves the body unlike "she was." Recall that presenting the dead in a restored state is an important aspect of funeral directing, and most funeral directors believe that it is important to make some efforts at restoring the dead to as "lifelike" an appearance as possible.[26]

The funeral director presents the dead publicly. Although the preparations needed to make them ready for their silent appearance are done nonpublicly, their presence in public is an important aspect of the overall funeral process. The question here is not whether the bereaved see the restoration and presentation as nonpublic activities, but rather that they may question the need for them as activities at all. There is little public awareness that the unrestored dead body would have a putty colored face with gaping mouth and eyes. Most funeral directors feel that for a bereaved family to confront their dead member in this condition would be neither pleasant nor beneficial. The funeral director is aware of the way the dead body appears before and after it has been embalmed, restored, and presented. The restored body looks dead but at least somewhat more like itself alive than would the unprepared dead body.

Many bereaved families do not understand the need for the presentation of the dead as a part of the funeral process; however, the funeral director does because of the secret knowledge he holds. When he presents himself as a restorer of the dead, there is possible confusion as to the value of his presentation, even if he presents himself "smoothly and appropriately." This emphasizes some of the difficulties that may arise because of conflicting expectations of the way in which one should present himself as compared to the actual perception of the presentation.[27]

In the Community Funeral Home, where people are at least somewhat familiar with the funeral director's customs and procedures, it is likely that there is less chance for misinterpretation. This results, of course, from the coinciding of expectation and perception. In the Cosmopolitan Funeral Home there is a much greater chance that expectations and perceptions will not coincide. This does not mean that the funeral directors in the latter setting do not present themselves "as well as" the funeral directors in the former, but rather it is the perception of their presentation compared to the expectation of it that may cause a gulf in understanding.

The logic of presenting the dead has been discussed from several perspectives.[28] Observations in both settings indicate that there is a sound argument for such presentation. All of us have memories about people and places which are not easily forgotten. Such memories about dead people are in this category. For example, most of us remember our fathers when we were children, when we were adolescents, and as adults. Each of these memories is distinct and separate, yet they all involve the same individual. To have a memory of the deceased while he is a dying patient is still another memory. However, "to remember him as he was" after he is dead is in a sense unrealistic, simply because he is not as he was. After death, he is a dead thing, and life is no longer present. His body is a reminder of his presence which incorporates most of our conscious awareness of him as an individual, for our memories include not only his personality and character traits, but also images of his person as a physical being. To try to remember him as he was means to try to remember him alive; however, since he is no longer alive, it is an unrealistic memory.[29]

We believe that this helps to account for the nearly universal practice of viewing the dead body. In order to have a complete memory of someone, we must remember him through the stages of life and, then, as a still, lifeless, dead thing. Without his final memory, we weaken not just our ties to reality but also our ties with other people. Thus, it is an important aspect of the funeral to present a dead person in a manner that will elicit a memory of that person as a dead body. When the bereaved do not abide by this logic, and yet they perceive the funeral director performing in a manner which indicates his belief in this restoration of the dead, it is quite possible to develop confusing and ambivalent feelings about the funeral director as a participant in the funeral process.

We have indicated some ways in which participants may be thought of by the presenter and how he perceives himself in this role compared to the way in which he is perceived by the audience before whom he is performing. Recall, it is the appearance intended by the funeral director, the appearance expected by the bereaved audience, and the appearance perceived of each in which we are interested. It is important that both the funeral director and the bereaved audience are inherently interested in completing the funeral process in a fashion satisfactory to both. Each has a vested interest in the funeral as a ceremony as well as a process. When the funeral director's presentation is consistent with the bereaved audience's expectation, it often is completed without a hitch and both sides come away well satisfied with the entire process.

However, when the funeral director's presentation is perceived by the bereaved audience as conflicting with their expectation of it, the success of the funeral process is seriously threatened. We contend that most bereaved audiences expect the funeral director to provide personal professional services. If and when they perceive him as a bureaucrat providing such services, there may develop a gulf between them and him which is difficult to bridge no matter how well the bureaucracy handles the service.

When people seek the services of a service occupation, it is important for the organization providing these services to give the appearance of being other than a bureaucracy. Naturally, when a firm has a complex service organization, to give such an appearance is a difficult, if not impossible, task. Therefore, even though the Cosmopolitan Funeral Home provides efficient, well-organized, and expediently conducted services, it may fall short of appearing to be an ideal service organization. Let us now examine what often happens when expectations and perceptions do not coincide.

Notes

1. For a treatment of this topic and the "whole man concept" see Howard C. Raether, *Successful Funeral Service Practice*. Englewood Cliffs, N.J.: Prentice-Hall, Inc., 1971, pp. 19-24.

2. For a similar view concerning medicine, see Eliot Freidson, *Profession of Medicine: A Study in the Sociology of Applied Knowledge*. New York: Dodd, Mead & Co., 1970, especially pp. 85-201.

3. Similar circumstances are reported about lawyers by Erwin O. Smigel, *The Wall Street Lawyer*. Bloomington: Indiana University Press, 1969, especially pp. 171-204.

4. For comparison see Peter M. Blau, *The Dynamics of Bureaucracy*. Chicago: The University of Chicago Press, 1955, especially pp. 250-65.

5. For a pertinent comparison see Blau's discussion of "Conflict With Clients," *The Dynamics of Bureaucracy*, pp. 100-117.

6. *Ibid*., pp. 250-65.

7. For comparative purposes, it is useful to consider Hughes' treatment of such services. See Everett C. Hughes, *Men and Their Work*. Glencoe: The Free Press, 1958, especially pp. 68-77.

8. For example, with the exception of general practitioners who do care what their clients thinks, physicians tend to be more concerned about judgment by and interaction with other physicians. For example, after an operation most laypeople are not capable or thought to be competent to judge how "good" the surgeon was, except that they lived through it and do not seem to have serious complications. See Eliot Friedson, "Client Control and Medical Practice," *American Journal of Sociology*, LXV (January, 1960), pp. 374-82.

9. Such a concern with families and satisfaction from such work is similar to bureaucrats deriving work satisfaction from helping clients. For a discussion see Peter M. Blau, *op. cit*., pp. 83-87.

10. Such a finding supports Blau's formulations about interpersonal relations in bureaucracy, *ibid*., pp. 144-64.

11. Such an initiation is also common in professions such as medicine and law. See Eliot Freidson, *op. cit.,* especially pp. 47-84; and Erwin O. Smigel, *The Wall Street Lawyer.* Bloomington: Indiana University Press, 1969, especially pp. 72-112.

12. The situation resembles that of other patterns of indulgency such as the one

described by Alvin W. Gouldner, *Patterns of Industrial Bureaucracy*. Glencoe: The Free Press, 1954, pp. 45-56.

13. An example of such guidance is the book edited by NFDA Executive Director Howard C. Raether.

14. For a contrasting discussion about the way in which a profession's division of labor is allocated consider the very different situations of medicine and law. See Freidson, *op. cit.*, pp. 47-70; and Smigel, *op. cit.*, pp. 205-48.

15. Such personal intimacy resembles the physician's intimate access to the human body and other aspects of confidentiality. For a full discussion see Talcott Parsons, *The Social System*. New York: The Free Press, 1951, pp. 451-54.

16. The perception of one's occupational role performance also has been noted by other social researchers. For example, see Gouldner, *op. cit.*, pp. 232-34, and Freidson, *op. cit.*, pp. 121-51.

17. It is analytically useful to note that these differences in presenting behavior can be characterized in terms of whether the presenter appears to be personal or impersonal. To be sure, there are some very clear distinctions in this regard as well as some rather shaded ones.

18. These characteristics are analytic rather than descriptive ones. It would be possible, of course, to categorize funeral directors descriptively; instead, we have chosen to analyze what it is about the presentation of self in each cell which distinguishes it from the other cells. Thus, rather than examining an "inside-public-service-presenter," the table indicates that the ideal presenting characteristic of funeral directors in Cell 1 is that they appear as "personal servers." All of the cells are analytically listed according to the firm organization and the regions of the funeral home. For a similar treatment see Freidson, *op. cit.*, pp. 231-52.

19. This and the following discussion bears a close resemblance to the analysis of professional and bureaucratic orientations based on Scott's investigation of "County Agency," presented in Chapter Three of Peter M. Blau and W. Richard Scott, *Formal Organizations*. San Francisco: Chandler Publishing Company, 1962, especially pp. 60-74.

20. The value of such analytic descriptive tables is that they allow us to examine more clearly the possible sorts of behavioral characteristics of people. Similar use of such tables is made by Freidson, *op. cit.*, pp. 231-52; and Howard S. Becker, *Outsiders*. New York: The Free Press, 1963, p. 20.

21. For a fuller treatment of this matter see Hughes, *op. cit.*, pp. 78-87; and Erving W. Goffman, *Asylums*. Garden City: Doubleday and Co., Anchor Books, 1961, pp. 323-86, especially p. 354.

22. Goffman explains it as follows:

> Whether it is a funeral, a wedding, a bridge party, a one-day sale, a hanging or a picnic, the director may tend to see the performance in terms of whether or not it went "smoothly," "effectively," and "without a hitch," and whether or not all possible disruptive contingencies were prepared for in advance.

Erving Goffman, *The Presentation of Self in Everyday Life*. Garden City, New York: Doubleday and Co., Anchor Books, 1959, pp. 97 and 98.

23. Contrast this with the work of attorneys and physicians. See Smigel, *op. cit.*, pp. 141-70, and Freidson, *op. cit.*, pp. 109-36.

24. Goffman, *op. cit.*, p. 99, explains:

A director, hence, starting as a member of the team, may find himself slowly edged into a marginal role between audience and performers, half in and half out of both camps, a kind of go-between without the protection that go-betweens usually have.

25. A useful perspective along these lines involves "license and mandate" and is set forth by Hughes, *op. cit.*, especially pp. 78-87.

26. In this regard, the funeral director demonstrates his belief in his work much as is done in medicine. For comparison, see Freidson, *op. cit.*, pp. 158-84.

27. Pertinent here is Hughes' discussion, *op. cit.*, p. 70, about work done "for or to" people. He puts it this way:

The danger of major distortion of relationship and function within the framework of a formal office lurks wherever people go or are sent for help or correction: the schoolroom, the clinic, the operating room, the confessional booth, the undertaking parlor all share this characteristic.

28. For example, see Bronislaw Malinowski, *Magic, Science and Religion*. New York: Doubleday & Company, Inc., 1948; Raymond Firth, *Elements of Social Organization*. Boston: Beacon Press, 1964; Robert Habenstein and William Lamers, *Funeral Customs the World Over*. Milwaukee: Bulfin Printers, Inc., 1960; and Jack Goody, *Death, Property and the Ancestors*. Stanford, California: Stanford University Press, 1962.

29. For pertinent discussions about this very problem, see Hughes, *op. cit.*, pp. 16-17, and Parsons, *op. cit.*, pp. 443-45. Also pertinent in this regard are two works with a very different perspective. First, Weisman's *On Dying and Denying: A Psychiatric Study of Terminality*. New York: Behavioral Publications, Inc., 1972. Second, Becker's *The Denial of Death*. New York: The Free Press, 1973.

Chapter 8

The Role
of the Funeral Director

In Chapter 2, we indicated that the role of the funeral director is claimed to be one of the problematic aspects of the occupation. Previous research emphasizes that the funeral director is used as a scapegoat for American society's attitudes toward death, and that he is seen by many as being unclean and possibly tainted. Furthermore, feelings toward him seem to be ambivalent, with considerable confusion surrounding his role. The sources cited treat the funeral director as if he were produced by one mold, and none of them makes an adequate effort to specify the conditions under which funeral directors have difficulty in carrying out their role.

The present study differs considerably in this regard. By examining the behavior of the funeral director in everyday settings, we found that the role characteristics are specified to a great extent by such things as the organization of and the location in the firm in which he works. We now turn to an examination of some of the problems of funeral directing which exist on a practical everyday level. To do so, let us first examine the duties and activities of the funeral director.

The Duties and Activities of the Funeral Director

The funeral director performing as a server in a simple organization plays his role as a professional with little or no ambiguity or confusion. By conducting himself as a professional, the Community Funeral Home director enjoys high social status, considerable community prestige, political power, and personal respect. This may be contrasted with the Cosmopolitan Funeral Home director, whose activities tend to be as a bureaucrat and whose work generally is anonymous and impersonal and often is subject to criticism by the public. Even though bereaved families expressed satisfaction with the services at the latter firm, such an organization is likely to contribute to much of the ambivalence discovered by previous research.

Public behavior in the Community Funeral Home is very personal. The funeral director develops close ties with bereaved families and is involved with them as a friend as well as a service professional. To some extent, this results because he acts in terms of the totality of the funeral operation. This may be contrasted to the Cosmopolitan Funeral Home director, whose public behavior is efficient but impersonal. In this bureaucratic setting, the funeral director does not develop close ties with bereaved families. He tends to deal with the loss of the deceased in a somewhat routinized fashion, and he is oriented to his specific task. By playing his role in this fashion, the Cosmopolitan Funeral Home director heightens the criticism and ambivalence mentioned earlier.

Although we observed considerable differences between the nonpublic activities of the funeral directors in the two settings, by definition these activities are not perceived by the bereaved or the general public. However, the impact of such activities on people fosters impressions which support the previously reported findings that the funeral director's nonpublic role is not well understood and that his backstage activities often are perceived as not necessary professional tasks by the public. This is the case, even though the Community Funeral Home director is concerned with the professional aspects of his work and their place in American funeral service and acts appropriately. It is important to point out that the funeral director in the Cosmopolitan Funeral Home is more concerned with the problems of the organization and the exigencies of task completion and scheduling and performs his nonpublic activities accordingly.

Over the years, the funeral director has incorporated more and more duties into his role. Robert Fulton and Gilbert Geis (1965: 72) explain: "With the exception of the funeral eulogy, which is the responsibility of the clergy, the modern-day funeral director is prepared to assume all activities associated with death, even to the point of providing 'chapel' facilities for the holding of the service." Additionally, in the recent past many funeral directors have taken on a new duty, that of grief therapy. This has been seen by funeral critics as an attempt to raise the status of funeral directing through identifying with those professions which do engage in therapy.[1]

Grief therapy is one of the more controversial of the duties which has been assumed by the funeral director. Some professional therapists are concerned because funeral directors are not necessarily trained to practice therapy. In reality, however, the funeral director does not actually carry out therapy in a traditional psychotherapeutic sense. The funeral service version of therapy consists of advice concerning funeral practices, the creation of a suitable atmosphere for bereavement, and the providing of counseling services aimed at helping the bereaved to understand loss through death. Thus, it bears only a resemblance to traditional therapy.[2]

The Community Funeral Home director more often than his Cosmopolitan Funeral Home counterpart plays the role of grief therapist seriously and consistently. His self-conception as a service professional seems to be responsible for this aspect of his behavior. His concern with the overall problems of the bereaved family rather than specific aspects of funeral-related tasks also contributes to his diligent efforts to be a satisfactory grief therapist. For example, it is common for the Community Funeral Home director to be consulted for advice about grieving and bereavement by bereaved families and their friends. At no time did we observe or hear about similar requests from the bureaucratically organized counselors or funeral directors at the Cosmopolitan Funeral Home.

Disagreement exists not only over such duties as grief therapy, however, but also over a task which the funeral director considers basic to his role, that of embalming and restoration of the body. Funeral directors and most of the public believe that this is a task which the funeral director ought to perform. Critics who question the value of embalming and restoration claim that embalming is not necessary as a public health measure even if the deceased has been ill. They argue that there is no reason for embalming if the corpse is buried soon after death. However, it is not accurate that embalming does not perform a health function. A number of microbiological studies have indicated that bacterial infection may be spread by dead bodies.[3] To solve this health problem by burial soon after death is not necessarily in accord with many customs and traditions which may be important to the bereaved next of kin.

Critics also claim that a corpse which "looks like he did when he was alive" does not serve as a memory picture which is of benefit to the bereaved. Such criticisms which question the value of the funeral director's attempt to restore the dead also have a counterpoint which emphasizes their positive value.[4] Whatever the case, our present point is that since the value of such a basic task as embalming and restoration is questioned, it is not surprising that duties such as grief therapy are criticized.

As with grief therapy, the Community Funeral Home director is convinced that embalming and restoration is a very important aspect of his work both as a nonpublic activity and from the public perspective of presenting the dead. Furthermore, he behaves in a manner that helps convince the bereaved audience of his worth and contributes to their construction of the funeral situation as appropriately including such an activity. In the Cosmopolitan Funeral Home, the task of embalming and restoration is performed nonpublicly by a funeral director who does not appear later in public. The bereaved audience is not as likely to be convinced of the value or necessity of the task.

This difference has been emphasized a number of times in conversations with bereaved families, relatives, and friends in the Community Funeral Home who have voluntarily exclaimed about the excellent appearance of the dead body. The very fact that they observed the product and could then verbalize their opinion of this job contributes to locating it as an important professional activity. This may be contrasted to the situation in the Cosmopolitan Funeral Home in which no one on the staff interacts extensively with the bereaved family, and the funeral director is detached from all but his specialized activities. Moreover, in this setting the presentation of the dead is not the crucial matter that it is for the Community Funeral Home director, who takes great personal pride in his skill at restoration.

Confusion about the funeral director's duties arise not only because those duties are not clearly defined, but also because they, or at least the underlying rationale for them, often are contradictory. For example, the funeral director is expected to mask the reality of death for the survivors, but he must also call attention to the special services which he is rendering. Thus, he must both blunt and sharpen the realities of death at the same time. In order to do so, the Community Funeral Home director performs as a professional personal server both in and out of his funeral home. His community prestige and his close ties with bereaved families enable him to blunt and sharpen simultaneously with less chance of offending or engendering ambivalence and hostility. Such simultaneously ambiguous performances are not as easy for the bureaucrat whose anonymity and detachment more readily foster hostility from the bereaved, as is the case with the Cosmopolitan Funeral Home director.

The very activities that the funeral director's role encompasses makes his job a complex one, and the way in which the public sees him may easily be confused or misconstrued. It is our contention that most of us have certain preconceived ideas about how people in given positions will behave. Thus, we expect typical patterns of behavior from those occupying certain statuses. We tend to deal with them on whatever level may exist at that time and in that setting, and they tend to deal with us in a reciprocal role-related fashion.

Herein resides a problem for the funeral director. Because he does a combination of many things, his role is not a unified kind of action, but rather it is a set of actions which revolve around numerous activities. This poses a major question—just what is a funeral director? Among other things, he has been positively and negatively described as a professional, businessman, manager, merchant, tradesman, and industrial worker. Clearly, there is considerable confusion. Regardless of such confusion, all sources indicate that the funeral director is a wearer of many hats, and to place him in a niche is difficult.

The Multiple Dimensions of Funeral Directing[5]

To say that the funeral director directs funerals does not suffice. To say that the funeral director handles all the details that go into the final disposition of the dead is a bit better, but still does not give a complete and accurate description. It is helpful in describing the funeral director to refer to what it is he does according to his own notion of the occupation. The National Funeral Directors Association provides a rather complete definition of the "Practice of Funeral Service" in their *Proposed Single License Law* which so describes the American funeral director.

> [The funeral director is] a person engaged in the care and/or disposition of the human dead and/or in the practice of disinfecting and preparing by embalming or otherwise the human dead for the funeral service, transportation, burial or cremation, and/or in the practice of funeral directing or embalming as presently known, whether under these titles or designations or otherwise. It shall also mean a person who makes arrangements for funeral services and/or who sells funeral supplies to the public or who makes financial arrangements for the rendering of such services and/or the sale of such supplies whether for present or future need.

In this context, the American funeral director sees himself carrying out a mixture of roles, including those of professional, administrator, coordinator, and businessman. Naturally, he believes that he provides an important function in American society, the overall responsibility for combining and integrating the elements of the funeral. Furthermore, he feels that his role is of the utmost importance to the mental health and well-being of the bereaved families with whom he works, especially considering the long-range social-psychological problems which may arise from mishandling the death situation.

The above definition and portrait of what the funeral director sees as his duties and responsibilities can be used to compare the two funeral firms. The Community Funeral Home director sees his role as all-inclusive, and he willingly and knowledgeably carries out each aspect described above. The Cosmopolitan Funeral Home director, realizing full well that all of the described activities and responsibilities pertain to the overall completion of the funeral, sees himself as rightfully performing only those aspects which comprise his specific job. Thus, even though the definition and description of the American funeral director is acceptable to practitioners in both settings, the treatment of the job as either all-inclusive or bureaucratically subdivided seems to be a powerful factor contributing to the acceptance of the role of the funeral director.

Although many occupations are made up of subdivisions, we do not tend to think of them piecemeal; so also with the funeral director. Ideally, he plays the single role of funeral director in which he combines and integrates a multiplicity of tasks.[6] This role includes (1) the professional tasks of providing advice and counsel to bereaved families and caring for their dead member, (2) the administrative tasks of managing the intertwined elements of the funeral and providing a setting in which funeral arrangements may be carried out, (3) the coordinating tasks of handling the movements and activities of those involved in the funeral, and (4) the business tasks of handling the merchandise sales and the economic interconnections which arise because of the overall combinations of arrangements.

Of course, such a combination of tasks is problematic for the bereaved funeral arrangers as well as for the funeral director in any organizational setting. This largely is because bereaved people tend to behave erratically and often unpredictably, and the funeral director must react quickly to any change. Thus, he must be able to modify his task orientation and role behavior as the situation necessitates.

The duties of the funeral director include a wide range of services which require specialized training, expertise, and a knowledge of death-related matters. The Community Funeral Home director takes pains to be prepared to advise, counsel, and console bereaved families about funeral practices and related matters. He also has to take care of the dead person. The performance of these sorts of tasks implies a professional role, and the Community Funeral Home director sees himself as a "caretaker," or one who provides aid and care to those who need them at the time of someone's death.[7] The Cosmopolitan Funeral Home divides such tasks among counselors, funeral directors, and embalmers. The duties and services are the same, but the organizational setting in which they are carried out is very different, and each task is handled by a separate specialist.

In addition to such professional duties, there are administrative tasks which include managing and administering the specialized facilities and personnel which are needed to carry out funeral arrangements. The Community Funeral Home director acts as a host, who provides facilities and equipment in the setting of his funeral home. At the Cosmopolitan Funeral Home, there is a specialist in charge of these tasks, and he is not too concerned with other aspects of the operation. Once again, there is a difference between funeral directors in the two settings, and it involves the separation of business management from the overall operation. The Community Funeral Home director is concerned with this administration as part of his professional duties, while the Cosmopolitan Funeral Home director considers it a nonprofessional managerial task.

It also is necessary to coordinate the movements and activities of those involved in the funeral. This means the deceased, the bereaved family, the clergyman, and the social group which gather to surround and support the family at this time. To coordinate the activities of this diversified group of variously bereaved people is a difficult task, and the Community Funeral Home director pays heed to the differences between them when he is called upon to provide coordinating activities contrasted to professional or administrative activities. In the Cosmopolitan Funeral Home, the coordination of people and activities is carried out by the dispatchers, who are not part of the professional staff except in their own eyes.

Lastly, there are several business tasks which to a great extent are a product of the combination of services, facilities, and merchandise provided. The Community Funeral Home director provides funeral merchandise and tends to the economic and related elements of his work. In the Cosmopolitan Funeral Home, these tasks are carried out by the business and accounting personnel. Even though the counselors are involved in the selection of funeral merchandise and deal with bereaved families on matters concerning funeral arrangements and financing, the actual implementation of these tasks is left to the firm's secretaries, bookkeepers, and accountants. When a bereaved family wishes to obtain information about the economic aspect of a funeral, the request is routed not to the professional counselors but to the business office. This is considerably different from the Community Funeral Home, in which bereaved families are well acquainted with the funeral director and deal with him about economic and business matters in a personal and friendly fashion. In this firm, payment and financing are handled not by a routinized, computerized accounting system, but rather depend upon personal arrangements and mutually understood business agreements.

Given the multiple dimensions of funeral directing, there may be differing conceptions of just what aspect of the role is the proper one for the funeral director to carry out. Thus, the orientation to the field of funeral service may serve as a source of confusion. Let us now consider the conflict between professional and bureaucratic orientations.

Professional-Bureaucratic Conflict

Although there is a variety of professional situations which conforms more or less to both models, the practitioner who conducts his practice as a service professional and behaves as such is less likely to experience problems than a practitioner who provides his services through a bureaucratic organization and who tends to behave as a bureaucrat.[8] This is an issue with which we have been concerned throughout the book.

In addition to some of the problems common to the traditional professions, there are a number of unique features of funeral directing. The efforts to make funeral directing a profession have been seen as a form of collective status-seeking and mobility and an attempt to elevate the funeral director in the eyes of the public.⁹ Such goals, however, are not accomplished easily, for funeral directing does have the business elements mentioned above, and the values and practices of the business person often are at odds with those of the professional. For instance, businesses traditionally have a profit structure with mercantile overtones, while professions are expected to provide services which are primarily for their client's welfare and, then, to "make their living" from fees.¹⁰

Funeral directors in both settings must contend with this problem. As indicated earlier, the situation of the Community Funeral Home director is such that the families he serves are considerably more aware of his service provision than his merchandise sales because of his personal involvement with each funeral. Therefore, to pay for his services, facilities, and merchandise may engender feelings of hostility only because of the nature of the purchase, but it is not as likely to influence adversely community feeling. Moreover, the Community Funeral Home director, much like the solo medical practitioner, is seen as receiving financial reward for his providing of valuable services. The funeral director in the Cosmopolitan Funeral Home is not so fortunate because his personal involvement is so limited that the bereaved may never recognize his work as worth its cost. Thus, the anonymity and impersonality of the bureaucratic organization contributes to the potential problems in terms of the profit structure of funeral directing.

Another general problem for the American funeral director as a professional is that the educational requirements are rather scant, compared, for example, to medicine and law. Some states have no educational requirements for funeral directors but only for embalmers. Generally, funeral service education consists of one or two years of college plus one year of mortuary science courses and one or two years as an apprentice or trainee. Education is not likely to have as great an influence on the assessment of the Community Funeral Home director as it has on his Cosmopolitan Funeral Home counterpart. Primarily, this is because the former enjoys high social status and is thought to be well educated and professionally trained for his field. However, no matter what his educational background may be, the Cosmopolitan Funeral Home director does not necessarily have high social status, and he is not known intimately by the families he serves. Thus, their judgment of him is based more on how he carries out his work responsibilities. In the case of the Community Funeral Home director, judgment is based upon the knowledge by the bereaved family that he is a well-educated, prestigious member of the upper social status in his community. Once again, the problems confronting the funeral directors in the two settings are dissimilar because of the organization in which such practitioners work.

An additional problem for the Cosmopolitan Funeral Home director is that even though embalming is a funerary task which requires technical knowledge or special skill, the firm does not treat embalmers completely as professionals. Their work is merely "part of the job." This problem is not one which must be faced by the Community Funeral Home, for each member of the firm is able to carry out embalming, and it is considered by all of them to be an important professional service. Embalming in the Cosmopolitan Funeral Home is handled as a bureaucratically allocated aspect of the job and not all of the practitioners carry it out with enthusiasm or take special pride in their craftsmanship as embalmers.

Unlike the traditional free professions, the funeral director does not claim competence in one well-defined area, but in many, including some, such as grief therapy, for which he has somewhat limited professional training.[11] In addition, the context of the funeral and its brief duration do not easily foster the development of the usual professional relationships for the Cosmopolitan Funeral Home director. For the Community Funeral Home director, however, it is not too important that the funeral itself is brief, for he is able to develop professional relationships with the public and the bereaved at times other than a specific funeral. This suggests that because of his involvement in the totality of the funeral operation, and his extensive community participation, the Community Funeral Home director enjoys professional relationships of a traditional sort. On the other hand, the Cosmopolitan Funeral Home director is likely to have a different sense of obligation to his clients than have other professionals, primarily because he attends only to those matters which directly concern his position in the bureaucracy.

Whether or not the funeral director in either setting qualifies as a professional is influenced by the fact that he, like the physician, has access to the human body.[12] This occupational right considerably modifies whatever else it is that the funeral director possesses or does not possess in the way of professionalism.[13] Although there is no fear that the funeral director may injure the body as a physician might, when the dead human body is entrusted to him, the bereaved family implicitly (if not explicitly) believes the funeral director's professional competence to be such that he will not "injure" the body and that he will do no more than is necessary to carry out his occupational duties. This lay vulnerability and professional right elevate the funeral director's occupational position to a height not easily attainable by other similar jobs.[14]

Even though it has business elements, funeral directing is not a typical mercantile business. For example, the funeral director has certain advantages and disadvantages in the buyer-seller relationship which do not exist in other businesses. Specifically, the buyer may be vulnerable because of the grief and guilt feelings which he may have.[15] Even though this is the case, the funeral directors in both firms did not appear to try to force, coerce, or cajole families into spending excessive amounts.

The Community Funeral Home director does not do so because such behavior is inappropriate for a professional. The Cosmopolitan Funeral Home director does not do so because, even though sales records are maintained, the organization of the firm does not force him to make "good sales" on a commission basis. Even though the bereaved are at a disadvantage, it is likely that they themselves bring about high expenditures which then appear to be the direct fault of the funeral director. In both firms it is largely through the setting of the selection room that the funeral director is able to differentiate between his expensive and inexpensive merchandise. The grief of the bereaved coupled with the setting of the selection room may lead the bereaved to spend up to the limit of their paying ability.

The Community Funeral Home director has other advantages, which resemble those of professions such as medicine or law. For example, he often has a chance to look at the arranger's home when he comes to make the removal or to make funeral arrangements. He may be able to assess approximately the family's taste and potential spending ability, as do doctors and lawyers, who have the same advantage in assessing the ability to pay for their services. Most other businesses do not have such advantages in the sale situation.

On the other hand, all funeral directors have certain disadvantages which are not present in other businesses. The bereaved arranger may uncomfortably speculate and fear what will happen to the body of the deceased. The market for funerals cannot be stimulated artificially. The "product" is a handicap in that the funeral director cannot repossess if the family later fails to pay. Finally, unlike most other businesses, the funeral director is caught between two pricing philosophies. The typical business operates on a *quid pro quo* basis with everyone paying the same. The funeral director, however, also must make special arrangements for the poor or indigent, which is part of the noblesse oblige rationale.[16]

In addition to such problems common to all funeral directors, there are other less tangible but just as crucial ones which may place a strain on them. We pointed out earlier that in the past funerals were carried out by relatives and neighbors of the deceased. With the increase of industrialization and urbanization, most interpersonal relationships have become more impersonal and anonymous, and secondary relationships have increased in number while primary relationships have decreased. Faunce and Fulton (1958: 206) explain that funeral directors not only reflect this

> pervasive development of secondary group relationships but also symbolize (as well as bear the brunt of) the conflict, frustration, and anxiety which accompany bereavement in our society. To a certain extent this tension, as well as the ill-defined nature of the funeral director's role in the urban communi-

ty, appears to be a consequence of this transition in the nature and essence of interpersonal contact.

The situation described by Faunce and Fulton is used commonly in describing the plight of the American funeral director. The present findings indicate, however, that it is the case largely for funeral directors who work in a bureaucratic setting. Community oriented funeral directors, on the other hand, cherish and nurture primary group relationships with a wide range of people. Furthermore, the funeral director's role in the community is such that it affords him status similar to that of the traditional free professions.

Jessica Mitford (1963) asserted that American funeral directors manipulate our "way of death" in an undesirable fashion, and that they generally force people into unpopular customs and decisions. However, the present findings as well as some other recent studies indicate considerable individual satisfaction regarding funerals and funeral directors and that Americans tend to regard favorably present funeral practices.[17] Cultures develop unique funeral practices which may change from time to time, but their drastic revision or exploitation cannot be blamed easily or logically solely on a small group of individuals such as funeral directors. Our findings also suggest that previous research reflects a metropolitan, bureaucratic bias. Specifically, we found that funeral directors who work in simple, service-oriented organizations do not fit this negative description. This may be contrasted with the plight of the complex funeral organization bureaucrats who often do fit the description and who tend not to enjoy the advantages of "professional" status. Furthermore, our findings suggest that people change their attitudes depending on the occupational model they perceive. That is, there often is a redefinition of the funeral situation.

Confusion and Redefinition

People have occupational models in advance of the events and processes in which they participate. They expect certain forms of presenting behavior when entering a specific setting.[18] People entering the funeral home have expectations about various aspects of the funeral director's presentations.

Expectation may be thought of in terms of the kind of organization to which an audience turns for services. When people select funeral organizations they are likely to do so knowingly. If people select a bureaucratic firm, they probably expect bureaucratic treatment and anticipate dealing with bureaucratic funeral directors. Those people who select service-oriented firms probably do so knowingly, and expect service, anticipating that it will be provided by personal servers. In large urban areas there are some funeral homes with a simple and some with a complex organization, but in most small towns only a simple service organization exists.

When the expectation of the audience and the perception of the funeral director do not mesh, the audience may be confused. In the case of bureaucratic servers, it is likely that the bereaved will be satisfied and will develop the feeling of having gotten more service than was bargained for. On the other hand, when service bureaucrats appear, the reaction of the bereaved is likely to be dismay at having been treated impersonally by such a practitioner.[19]

When confusion does exist, there appears to be a redefinition of the situation. However, the redefinition is such that what actually occurs is a realignment of occupational models by the bereaved. When they are confused, they do not actually revamp their notion of the funeral situation, but rather they modify and realign their model of funeral service practitioners as servers or bureaucrats.[20]

The bereaved may come up with a combined definition of servers and bureaucrats, or they may change their notion altogether. This helps account for the fact that even in the Cosmopolitan Funeral Home, there are families which come away feeling that they have been treated in a service fashion. Conversely, in the Community Funeral Home, there are occasions in which services are doled out scantily by an overly busy staff. Thus, there are instances in which a family comes away feeling that the organization provided bureaucratic services.

The realignment of occupational models need not be conceived of positively or negatively. However, it is likely that those dealing with a bureaucratic organization, who realign their model of the occupation to a service one, are better satisfied than those individuals who utilize a service organization and realign their model to a bureaucratic one. This is largely because people seek the services of funeral directors rather than the efficient operation of their firm's organization.[21]

When model realignment takes place, expectations are reconstructed after the fact and funeral directors are adjudged as having been either one type or the other. After such realignment, when bereaved people recall their prior model, they refer to a specific individual in their former notion.[22] Thus, it is common to hear remarks such as the following:

> It's been my experience with funeral directors in general that they're impersonal and cold and tend to handle everybody the same. *However*, our funeral director isn't that way at all. He's on call night and day and treats everybody as if they're important, but I guess he's just an exception.

Such a characterization indicates the sort of model realignment that perceived behavior often brings about. Even when there is not a complete realignment, a mixture of occupational behavior emphasizes the allowances that exist for bereaved audiences when perceiving a funeral director in action. This potential for variation is an important element when it comes to bereaved-funeral director relationships, especially if there needs to be any adjustment on the part of either.

The Significance of Performances

The ways in which funeral directors perform exist in the "real world." Moreover, such presentations are observable in everyday actions and behaviors. We emphasized this as well as having pointed out that the empirical realities of everyday life are modified to a great extent by conceptual models which people hold about such things as occupations. These models are the result of a great many factors, most of which reside in the various processes which serve to socialize and condition us.

Admittedly, there are alternative models about almost all phenomena, and individuals select one, the other, or a combination thereof in their construction. However for analytical purposes, we have chosen to divide service occupations into two types. First, service occupations may conform to the model of professional personal services, in which case the practitioners were described as servers. Second, service occupations may conform to the model of bureaucratic organizations, in which case the practitioners were referred to and described as bureaucrats.[23]

Whatever the occupational models may be, there must be trained people who practice the occupation and who are perceived by lay people who seek their services. Such lay people have their own models about the occupation as well as perceiving the performance of it. Furthermore, trained practitioners enter the relationship with their own models. Thus, the entire occupational process is tempered by various sets of models about the behavior as well as the lay person's perception of what is performed.[24]

The situation is something like this. Models exist in the minds of both professionals and lay people, and when the two meet, the professional has a chance to present himself. In so doing, he attempts to abide by his notion of the occupational model. At the same time, lay people perceive and experience his presentation, holding their model in their mind's eyes. Thus, what we have is an intricate meshing of models with emitted and perceived behavior. This is importantly different from the notion of the presentation of self as a somehow unconnected mode of behavior or as a purely theatrically staged performance.[25] The intention of the present elaboration has been to capture a more complete and more realistic glimpse of the behavioral characteristics of those people who perform in a service setting.

It is the relationship between occupational models and the perception of them which is of considerable practical utility to people. Although most of us do not divide life into variables and categories in a formal fashion, we tend to do so informally. Thus, by translating presenting behavior and occupational models into variable-like phenomena, we have demonstrated that the relationships between firm organization and the presentation of self combine on an empirical level to influence occupational models on a theoretical level.

In the eyes of the funeral director, errors of commission or omission are not possible if he is to accomplish his work appropriately.[26] It is possible that the funeral director and the bereaved audience are not similarly oriented, and the bereaved might not be aware of his errors. That the bereaved are likely to be disturbed because of errors of commission or omission, however, is emphasized by their very unfamiliarity with funeral customs and procedures. The bereaved depend upon the funeral director to help carry out the tasks and activities that he considers customary and necessary when death occurs.[27] Thus, that the bereaved become upset over such errors may reflect their taking the cue from the funeral director's expressive behavior, and his very distress over his errors are likely to help the bereaved agree with his judgment and see them as such.

Given such a possibility, it is easy to understand why bereaved people who are not familiar with many aspects of a given funeral may judge it to be inadequate and inappropriate, not so much because of some deviation from usual behavior, but rather because the funeral directors give themselves away and fail to accomplish the funeral successfully. This suggests, therefore, that errors by service practitioners are not absolutely measurable in terms of customs or traditions, but that they may be the result of a poorly completed performance on the part of the practitioner.

This leads to our notion of the realignment of occupational models. Model realignment is the modification of held conceptions one has about an occupation.[28] One of the most important reasons for the realignment of occupational models is because an audience perceives behavior and modifies its models both of the worker and his occupation.

Audience perceptions are not static, but rather are dynamic, and it is through the dynamics of behavior that one's configuration of models is affected. Thus, one of the important features of behavior as a social phenomenon is that it has the power to help mold people's minds. This has been recognized, of course, from many perspectives by numerous social observers; however, the overall focus is sharpened by explicating the relationships between such things as firm organization, occupational orientation, and the presentation of self in greater detail.

Notes

1. It is common tactic of people in low-status occupations to seize upon some aspect of their work which is highly valued, whether throughout the society or in the work subculture, and build a self-image around it. For a discussion of this tac-

tic see R.L. Simpson and J. Simpson, "The Psychiatric Attendant: Development of an Occupational Self-Image in a Low Status Occupation," *American Sociological Review*, **24** (1959), pp. 389-92.

2. The detractors of modern funeral service are quick to criticize such tasks as grief therapy as being superfluous and an effort to justify higher funeral costs. However, most funeral directors believe that their work is useful to bereaved families, and they generally work hard to master skills which can be of such benefit. The funeral director's concept of therapy may be compared and contrasted to the death-related views expressed in Weisman's *On Death and Denying: A Psychiatric Study of Terminality*. New York: Behavioral Publications, Inc., 1972, and Kubler-Ross' *On Death and Dying*. London: The Macmillan Company, 1969.

3. For more complete discussions see Vanderlyn R. Pine, "The Effectiveness of Embalming On Microbes Isolated From The Mouth," *The Director*, **XXXVIII** (January, 1968), pp. 12-14; Pine, "Comparative Studies of the Anti-Microbial Effects of Selected Antibiotics Against Micro-Organisms of Embalmed and Unembalmed Human Bodies," *The Director*, **XXXVIII** (September, 1968), pp. 15-17; Gordon W. Rose and Alice K. Bicknell, "The In Vitro Effect of Certain Antibiotics on Cultures Isolated From the Unembalmed Body," *Antibiotics and Chemotherapy*, **3** (September, 1953), pp. 896-98.

4. See Howard C. Raether, *Successful Funeral Service Practice*. Englewood Cliffs, N.J.: Prentice-Hall, Inc., 1971.

5. The following discussion is based to some extent on my paper, "The Multi-Professional Dimensions of a Funeral Service Practice," given at the annual meeting of the National Funeral Directors Association, Portland, Oregon (October 9, 1969).

6. For a fuller discussion see Raether, *op. cit.*, pp. 19-24.

7. Funeral directors are quick to emphasize this and often refer to the following comment by Earl Grollman, a noted authority on grief, who says, "The funeral director is someone who cares about, who takes care, and who takes care of. He is called upon to cure, to encourage as well as to console, to overcome soul-wounds. His is part of a meaningful, caretaking profession." Raether, *op. cit.*, p. 21.

8. The problems of professionals working in bureaucratic organizations often have been analyzed empirically from the perspective of formally organized work units. For recent studies treating this general problem see George A. Miller, "Professionals in Bureaucracy: Alienation Among Industrial Scientists and Engineers," *American Sociological Review*, **32** (October, 1967), pp. 755-67; Richard H. Hall, "Professionalization and Bureaucratization in Large Professional Organizations," *American Journal of Sociology*, **74** (September, 1968), pp. 138-45.

9. Bowman points out that in recent years,

> A persistent drive to gain recognition as a profession is met everywhere among the leaders in the associations of funeral directors, in the trade periodicals, in the announcements of the mortuary schools, and among some of the successful proprietors of establishments.

LeRoy Bowman, *The American Funeral*. Washington, D.C.: Public Affairs Press, 1959, p. 77-78.

10. To be sure, certain professions such as medicine and law have been severely

criticized in recent years for allowing the profit-motive to assume too great an importance in their practices, but they still are seen as "providing necessary services for a fee."

11. Efforts to clarify the status of funeral directing through the courts have met with conflicting results. The following, for example, as Bowman (*op. cit.*, p. 79) points out, is part of the New Jersey "New Mortuary Science Act:"

> In the interest of, and to better secure, the public health, safety and welfare, and for the more efficient administration and supervision of sanitary codes and health regulations, the practice of mortuary science and the practice of embalming and funeral directing are hereby declared to be a profession.

Mitford, *The American Way of Death*. New York: Simon and Schuster, 1963, p. 190, points out, however, that the Florida District Court of Appeals said in February, 1962:

> Undertaking or mortuary practice is a business rather than a profession, and the fact that it is referred to in certain instances in the regulatory statute as a profession does not make it so.

12. For a detailed discussion of this "right" in medicine see Talcott Parsons, *The Social System*. New York: The Free Press, 1951, pp. 451-65.

13. Parsons points out that the amount and occasion of bodily exposure and contact are regulated carefully in all societies, especially so in ours; furthermore, such contacts "are expressive symbols of highly strategic significance." *Ibid.*, p. 451.

14. For instance, it is considerably different from that of hospital attendants who merely move already wrapped dead bodies to the morgue but do not do things to or for those bodies. For a fuller discussion see David Sudnow, *Passing On*. Englewood Cliffs, N.J.: Prentice-Hall, 1967. Also see Everett C. Hughes, *Men and Their Work*. Glencoe: The Free Press, 1958, p. 70.

15. Bowman argues that the funeral director takes undue advantage of this vulnerability. He says:

> Grief on the part of the family is recognized by undertakers as a disabling factor, but the number of cases in which it leads them to moderation in recommendations for elaborate funerals seems to be very small. For the majority of them the vulnerability of the family due to grief is an advantage in the bargaining situation not to be neglected.

Op. cit., p. 32.

16. For a more complete discussion of this problem see the treatment in Chapter 2; and also see Robert Fulton, "The Sacred and the Secular: Attitudes of the American Public Toward Death, Funerals, and Funeral Directors," *Death and Identity*, especially pp. 104-105.

17. For complete discussions see Robert Fulton, "The Clergyman and the Funeral Director: A Study in Role Conflict," *Social Forces*, 39 (May, 1961), pp. 317-23; and Jerome Salamone, "The Status of Funerals and Funeral Directors," *The American Funeral Director*, 90 (October, 1967), pp. 69-74.

18. See Hughes, *op. cit.*, pp. 78-87; and Erving Goffman, *Asylums*. Garden City, New York: Doubleday & Co., Inc., Anchor Books, 1961.

19. For a discussion of another example of client conflict see Peter Blau, *The Dynamics of Bureaucracy*. Chicago: The University of Chicago Press, 1955, pp. 100-17.

20. This notion of redefinition may also be seen from the perspective of reality construction. For comparison see Eliot Freidson, *Profession of Medicine: A Study in the Sociology of Applied Knowledge*. New York: Dodd, Mead & Co., 1970.

21. For a pertinent discussion see Hughes, *op. cit.*, pp. 78-87.

22. For another discussion of a similar observation about this occurrence see Salamone, *op. cit.*, pp. 69-74.

23. For the sake of analytic simplicity, we chose not to elaborate mutant forms or the many combinations of the two.

24. All of us hold mental images (models) of occupations with which we are familiar. These images are based to some extent upon the tasks called for by the occupation; however, they are also based on the masks worn by those who perform those tasks. This means that our occupational models are based on both tasks and masks, and in order to analyze service practitioners, we must attend to both.

25. The presentation of self in particular and presenting behavior, in general, are conceptually crucial to almost all analyses of human interaction, for, by definition, interaction involves face-to-face reciprocal encounters between people in everyday life. The perception of such behavior depends not just upon audience and actor connections, but also upon the conceptual models about presenting behavior held by both.

26. For instance, if the funeral director were to laugh loudly enough so that he knows the bereaved hear him, he would believe this to be the commission of a serious error. Likewise, if he fails to order a hearse for the funeral or fails to order the grave to be opened, he would believe these to be blatant ommissions upsetting the overall funeral.

27. This is similar to Freidson's argument about the social construction of illness. See Eliot Freidson, *op. cit.*

28. For instance, if one initially believes funeral directors to be bureaucrats, but after dealing with them changes one's mind and considers them to be servants, one has experienced model realignment.

Chapter 9

Caretakers
and Personal Service

This book has been a case study of the relationship between occupational models and the behavior of people carrying out their work in the organizational setting of the funeral home. Our examination and analysis of the ways in which service practitioners present themselves in two considerably different organizations has provided a glimpse of how these various factors operate in everyday life.

Our objective has been to examine analytically the relationship between the typical conceptions of servers and bureaucrats on the basis of an investigation of the everyday behavior of funeral directors. A number of questions have arisen during the study; some have been answered in the preceding analysis; other remain unanswered. The purpose of this final chapter is to discuss some of the ramifications of these questions.[1] Let us turn, therefore, to some remarks which will conclude this book but which we hope will open some new avenues both in terms of analyses of human behavior and in terms of those groups which provide personal service.

Our central argument throughout this book has been as follows: The way in which service practitioners present themselves depends upon how their firm is organized, their orientation to the occupation, and the exigencies of task performance on an everyday basis. Such a thesis has at least two important ramifications. First, service occupation behavior is as much a function of the setting in which practitioners find themselves as it is of a certain orientation to the service occupation itself. Second, segments of the general public may have problems dealing with those service practitioners whose firm organization and occupational orientation are such that they present themselves differently than expected.

Our observations indicate that presenting behavior exists in a matrix of other forms of social behavior. We have documented that the firm organization of a service practice influences the ways in which the practitioners present themselves. We have tried to take into account the variations that exist among individuals by constructing a continuum of presenting behavior for service practitioners. By so doing, we have attempted to utilize the conceptual notion of the presentation of self with an empirically rooted base and have provided at least one version of how such behavior may be examined from an empirical-analytical viewpoint.

Our concern also has been with the service and bureaucratic models. Our analysis provides additional information about the intricacies of service occupations, emphasizing that professional personal services are not provided in one uniform fashion. It is important that the occupational models are but the classical form of behavior for such occupations. Moreover, the actual occupational behavior of people is not only influenced by the models thereof, but also the models are influenced by the behavior.

The way in which the funeral director presents himself depends to a great extent upon his definition of the funeral situation. This situation, however, is not a singular, all-encompassing one which is identical in every case. Thus, the funeral director has grounds on which to base decisions that help him locate the relevant conditions of the situation for each funeral. Service practitioners look for cues and other characteristics of their audiences in order to help them define the situation appropriately.

The integration of the three concerns, personal service, bureaucracy, and the presentation of self, allows us to treat theoretical and practical concerns simultaneously and yet to maintain some connections to social reality, thus increasing the relevance of our study. Furthermore, this combination helps emphasize that social structure has an important and analyzable influence on social-psychological phenomena. Such a result is, of course, the rationale behind most social research. However, it is not always possible to see such connections so clearly. This is not so much the product of an especially clever research design, but rather that the characteristics and phenomena observed were amenable to analysis and that they blended well together.

An example of how our combined analysis provides possible answers to some common sociological questions emphasizes the value of integrative efforts. We noted that funeral directors who present themselves successfully as servers occupy a considerably higher position in the social stratification system of their community than their bureaucratic counterparts. We explained that the funeral director's location is dependent not just upon the common index characteristics of social status, but also on the way in which he behaves before various audiences, and this is influenced by his firm's organization. It is a combination of factors, therefore, which emerges as important from an analytical viewpoint.

Professional personal service occupations tend to have a standard socialization training period and an organized regulative licensing procedure. Furthermore, practitioners in all kinds of settings attend to similar tasks and provide similar services. We contend that since the variety of behavior is considerable, it is influenced by such things as the firm's organization. It is also dependent upon there being a limited market of available personnel for a given occupation and upon firms having to recruit and select from qualified individuals. Given such a situation, we believe that the selection fit for service practitioners is tighter in a service organized firm than in a bureaucratically organized firm in which it is more important to fit the person to the job.

Our analysis allows for a theoretical expansion of both the service and the bureaucratic models. We are able to portray them as being complex rather than simple matters. Our construction of the continuum of behavior enables us to view such theoretical models more realistically. It is common to reduce such complexities to a summarized state and merely to speak about servers and bureaucrats. We emphasized that practitioners behave along a continuum. We believe that it is possible to use models to speculate and theorize about them as they relate to empirical reality. Furthermore, we believe that the connections between the two are a constant and important concern of sociologists and feel that it is urgent to attend to both.

There are some practical implications of this study which are pertinent to service practitioners in particular and all people in general. When people present themselves, it is important for them to be cognizant of the orientation they hold toward their behavior, whether it is an occupational matter or not. This means that the careless presentation of self, with little attention paid to performer orientation and audience expectation and perception, has the potential of disrupting the overall relationship. Servers and bureaucrats would do well to assess themselves according to their location on a continuum. Even though unable to interpret their own behavior meaningfully, by so doing they at least will be able to better understand how they wish to attempt to present themselves. This would give them a greater measure of control over their work and various aspects of it; thus, it ought to reduce some of the tensions which may exist.

There are also certain implications for organizations as servers. For example, personal service firms, whether small or large, simply or complexly organized, private or public, ought to take cognizance of the fact that their primary function is to provide services. At first glance, this may appear redundant, for by definition such organizations provide services.

However, the important point that has emerged from the present study is that some organizations which provide services have the problem that above all else they tend to be organizations rather than servers. If such an organization is bureaucratic, certain service needs may be bypassed for the sake of efficient and expeditious operation. That this happens is not necessarily so problematic, except when it influences the ways in which the services are perceived. Thus, if audiences perceive "inefficiency" as indicative of personal service, in the long run, it may be that inefficiency is more beneficial than efficiency.

In the final analysis, organizations are represented by individuals, and it is the individual presenters who foster the impression of that organization. This means that training programs for positions in a bureaucratic organization must take into account not just bureaucratically relevant information but also must be geared to the occupational necessities called for if it is a service occupation. Put differently, it is not sufficient to have an extensive division of labor which is bureaucratically organized around an efficient hierarchy of offices to provide what people count to be professional personal services. What is required has its roots in the personal service occupational model.

It may be that bureaucrats can foster a service impression through their behavior. Such actions may raise questions. It is conceivable for large bureaucratic service organizations to modify slightly their procedural activities, however, and to take into account some of the important typical values of a service organized firm. By so doing, it may be that large bureaucracies can address themselves more personally to the needs of those served. In the long run, the benefits of greater personal contact may be worth the cost to efficient operation.

A final question emerges from the considerations treated in this book, but it has not been answered herein. When the need arises for personal services, people are generally in a vulnerable position. This lay vulnerability at the hands of expert service professionals is not necessarily the result of the contorted minds or orientations of such practitioners, but has to do with the severity of the need in question and the lay public's inability to cope with it alone. This vulnerability can be attenuated only by increasing the lay public's awareness of the everyday concerns of those people who are the caretakers of the problems which call for personal services. Conversely, however, lay familiarity may reduce the effectiveness of the presenter's services.

This brings us to that final question which we mentioned above, and which, for now, must remain unanswered. How can service practitioners behave most satisfactorily to serve the needs of their clients without sacrificing the effectiveness of their services?

Note

1. The discussion and citations throughout the study have set the stage for this chapter, and most of the present remarks stem directly from the foregoing chapters.

Funeral Director Questionnaire

DEPARTMENT OF SOCIOLOGY

DARTMOUTH COLLEGE

HANOVER, N.H.   03755

June 1, 1967

Dear Funeral Director:

This questionnaire is part of a study being carried out in the funeral service profession. Its intention is to learn about the attitudes of people in funeral service.

Please answer all of the questions exactly as you wish. The answers will not be connected with your name, and will be used for an impersonal analysis only. PLEASE DO NOT OMIT ANY ITEMS.

This is an attitude questionnaire, not a test. There are no right or wrong answers. You may make comments at the end of the questionnaire. ALL INFORMATION WILL BE HELD IN THE STRICTEST CONFIDENCE.

Most questions may be answered either by putting a check in a box, like this: ☒, or by numbers on short lines, like this: _3_, or by answers written out by you on a line, like this: _Saleseclerk_. Please do not pay any attention to the numbers on the left of each box, they are merely for tabulating purposes.

Thank you very much for your help.

Van R. Pine

Van R. Pine
Survey Director

1-2. Where were you born? (Write state or foreign country.)

_____

3. What kind of community was your home town?
    (Check one.)

    1[ ] Rural area
    2[ ] Small town
    3[ ] Small city
    4[ ] Metropolis
    5[ ] Suburb of a Metropolis

4. What is your age? (Check one.)

    1[ ] Under 25
    2[ ] 25-31
    3[ ] 31-35
    4[ ] 36-40
    5[ ] 41-45
    6[ ] 46-55
    7[ ] 56-65
    8[ ] 65 or over

5. How many years have you personally spent in funeral
    service? (Check one.)

    1[ ]   0 - 5 years
    2[ ]   6 - 10 years
    3[ ] 11 - 15 years
    4[ ] 16 - 20 years
    5[ ] 21 - 25 years
    6[ ] 26 years or more

6. Have you ever pursued a career in another field of
    endeavor? (Check one.)

    1[ ] yes
    2[ ] no

7-8. If yes, which one? Please be as specific as possible.
      (e.g., salesclerk in a clothing store, mechanical
      engineer, etc.)

_____

      What sort of business is that (bank, factory,
      government, etc.)?

_____

9. What is your religious preference? (Check one.)

    1[] Protestant (what denomination?)
    _____

    2[] Roman Catholic
    3[] Jewish
    4[] Other (what? _____)

10. How frequently do you attend religious services at
    your own church? (Check one.)

    1[] Never
    2[] Seldom
    3[] Occasionally
    4[] Fairly regularly
    5[] Regularly, almost without exception

11-17. How active have you been in the organizations to which
        you belong? (Check one box for each activity listed
        below.)

	Do not belong	Nominal member	Active member	Extremely active, i.e. officer, etc.
a. Fraternal organizations (Elks, etc.)	[]	[]	[]	[]
b. Civic or service clubs (Lions C of C.etc)	[]	[]	[]	[]
c. Religious social groups (. of C. etc.)	[]	[]	[]	[]
d. Political clubs (Republican Club, etc.)	[]	[]	[]	[]
e. Veterans' organizations (VFW, etc.)	[]	[]	[]	[]
f. Youth organizations (Scouts, etc.)	[]	[]	[]	[]
g. Miscellaneous	[]	[]	[]	[]

18. How much formal education have you had (not including
    funeral service school)? (Check one.)

    1[] Some grade school
    2[] Finished grade school
    3[] Some high school
    4[] Finished high school
    5[] Some college
    6[] Finished college
    7[] Attended graduate school

19. What kind of training-education did you receive for
    funeral service? (Check one.)

    1[ ] Traineeship only (apprenticeship, etc.)
    2[ ] 6 month course plus traineeship
    3[ ] 9 month course   "   "
    4[ ] 12 month course   "   "
    5[ ] College affiliated course plus traineeship
          (How long was that? _____)
    6[ ] Other, specify
    _____

20. How would you rate the funeral service education
    program that you received? (Check one.)

    1[ ] Superior
    2[ ] Good
    3[ ] Average
    4[ ] Poor
    5[ ] Inferior
    6[ ] Had none

21. What educational level do you feel should be required
    of students entering funeral service schools?
    (Check one.)

    1[ ] Entrance examination only
    2[ ] High school graduate
    3[ ] Some college
    4[ ] College graduate
    5[ ] Some graduate school
    6[ ] A grduate degree

22. Approximately what is the average number of clock
    hours per week that you devote to the funeral
    profession? Include all the time spent on activities
    which are required or definitely expected of your
    as part of your job whether you do the work at the
    funeral home, or elsewhere. (Check one.)

    1[ ] Less that 30 hours
    2[ ] 30 -39 hours
    3[ ] 40- 44 hours
    4[ ] 45 - 49 hours
    5[ ] 50 - 54 hours
    6[ ] 55 - 64 hours
    7[ ] 65 or more hours

23. How do you lean in national politics? (Check one.)

1[] Toward the more liberal Democrats
2[] Toward the more conservative Democrats
3[] Toward the more liberal Republicans
4[] Toward the more conservative Republicans
5[] Toward a third party (which? _____)

6[] I have no party leanings.

24. If you had it to do over again, would you enter funeral service? (Check one.)

1[] Definitely yes
2[] Probably yes
3[] Uncertain
4[] Probably no
5[] Definitely no

Please explain briefly:

_____

_____

25. How much financial security do you feel you have as a funeral director? (Check one.)

1[] Very little security
2[] Some security
3[] Moderate amount of security
4[] Considerable security
5[] Very much security

26. How much prestige does your position as a funeral director give you in your community? (Check one.)

1[] Very little prestige
2[] Some prestige
3[] Moderate amount of prestige
4[] Considerable prestige
5[] Very much prestige

27-28. How much formal education did your parents receive?
        (Check one.)

        FATHER   MOTHER
        1 [ ]   1 [ ]   Some grade school
        2 [ ]   2 [ ]   Finished grade school
        3 [ ]   3 [ ]   Some high school
        4 [ ]   4 [ ]   Finished high school
        5 [ ]   5 [ ]   Some college
        6 [ ]   6 [ ]   Finished college
        7 [ ]   7 [ ]   M.A., Ph.D, M.D., etc.

29-30. What is your father's occupation (if unemployed,
        retired, or deceased, what was his usual occupation?)
        Please be as specific as possible: (e.g., clerk in a
        clothing store, mechanical engineer, etc.)

        _____

        What sort of business is that (bank, factory,
        government, etc.)?

        _____

31.   How does your style of life compare with your
        father's? (Check one.)

        1 [ ]   Much better than father's
        2 [ ]   Some better than father's
        3 [ ]   The same as father's
        4 [ ]   Some worse than father's
        5 [ ]   Much worse than father's

32.   How do you feel that your community prestige compares
        with your father's? (Check one.)

        1 [ ]   Much lower
        2 [ ]   Some lower
        3 [ ]   About the same
        4 [ ]   Some higher
        5 [ ]   Much higher

33.   Which of the following possibilities would you say
        most influenced your decision to enter the funeral
        profession? (Check one.)

        1 [ ]   Family
        2 [ ]   Friend (s)
        3 [ ]   Always interested
        4 [ ]   Business opportunity
        5 [ ]   Other, specify

        _____

34-38.   Rank the following rewards of funeral directing
         in terms of their importance to you. (Rank from 1
         through 5.)

         _____ High income
         _____ High community prestige
         _____ Security of a needed occupation
         _____ Professional affiliation
         _____ The work is important and gives a feeling of
               accomplishment and a sense of value.

39-43.   Rank the following five occupations in terms of
         their desirability to you. (Rank from 1 through 5.)

         _____ Stock Broker
         _____ Architect
         _____Business Executive
         _____ Doctor
         _____ Retail Store Owner

44.   If "funeral director" were ranked along with these
         five, according to its desirability, which rank would
         you assign to it? (Circle the appropriate number.)

               1   2   3   4   5   6

45.   If a child of yours were seriously considering his
         occupational future, would you ....? Check one)

         1[ ] Encourage him to enter funeral service
         2[ ] Tell him to make his own decision
         3[ ] Discourage him from entering funeral service

         Please explain briefly: _____

         _____

46.   How much opportunity to be helpful to other people
         does your position as a funeral director provide for
         you? (Check one.)

         1[ ] Very little opportunity
         2[ ] Some opportunity
         3[ ] Moderate amount of opportunity
         4[ ] Considerable opportunity
         5[ ] Very much opportunity

47. When you receive a funeral call at 3 o'clock in the
morning, and the removal must wait until the hospital
releases the body at 9 o'clock, what is your feeling?
(Check one.)

1[ ] Anger at being disturbed
2[ ] Annoyed that they called at that hour
3[ ] Just consider it part of the profession
4[ ] Pleased to have had them call

48. Which of the following do you feel is the most
important in determining present funeral customs?
(Check one.)

1[ ] Geographical location
2[ ] Mass media, i.e., press, radio, TV, etc.
3[ ] Nationality and Religion
4[ ] Social status
5[ ] Influence of funeral directors

49-53. Why do you feel families choose your funeral home?
(Rank from 1 to 5: 1 for the most important, 2 for
the next, etc., and on to 5 for the least important.)

_____ Economic consideration

_____ Geographical location

_____ Nationality or religion

_____ Physical facilities

_____ Reputation

If you think there are other very important reasons
for choosing your funeral home, please list them
below: _____

_____

54-B?   As you see it in the last 5 years are there any
         indications of change in people's attitudes and
         practices regarding funerals? (For each religion,
         check one square in the ritual section and one
         square in the Expenditure section.)

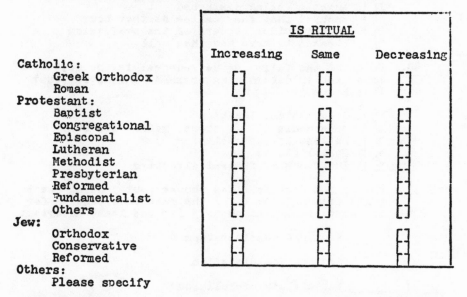

Catholic:
     Greek Orthodox
     Roman
Protestant:
     Baptist
     Congregational
     Episcopal
     Lutheran
     Methodist
     Presbyterian
     Reformed
     Fundamentalist
     Others
Jew:
     Orthodox
     Conservative
     Reformed
Others:
     Please specify

IS RITUAL

Increasing   Same   Decreasing

What are the major changes that you have noticed? (Explain
briefly.)

_____ _____

_____

Are there specific denominations which seem most prone to
changes in funeral customs?

[] yes
[] no

If yes, list which ones.

_____

_____

	IS EXPENDITURE		
	Increasing	Same	Decreasing
Catholic:			
Greek Orthodox	[]	[]	[]
Roman			
Protestant:			
Baptist	[]	[]	[]
Congregational	[]	[]	[]
Episcopal	[]	[]	[]
Lutheran	[]	[]	[]
Methodist	[]	[]	[]
Presbyterian	[]	[]	[]
Reformed	[]	[]	[]
Fundamentalist	[]	[]	[]
Others	[]	[]	[]
Jew:			
Orthodox	[]	[]	[]
Conservative	[]	[]	[]
Reformed	[]	[]	[]
Others:			
Please specify			

Are there specific denominations which seem most prone to changes in funeral customs?

[] Yes
[] No

If yes, list which ones.

_____

_____

84. In light of the recent criticisms of funeral service and considering some of the proposed changes, are there some trends that worry you?

1 [] Yes
2 [] No

Please briefly explain these trends, and which you fear the most:_____

_____

_____

85-86. Suppose that funeral customs change, and your work is
        reduced to removal, disposal, and limited funerary
        counselling. What would you do if, A, your income drops;
        if, B, your income remains unchanged? (Check one for
        each.)

Income   Income
 Drops   Same
1 [ ]   1 [ ]   Leave the profession
2 [ ]   2 [ ]   Change practices
3 [ ]   3 [ ]   Do whatever is asked
4 [ ]   4 [ ]   Try to stop changes
5 [ ]   5 [ ]   Tell people they are wrong

87. How should professional standards be established for
     funeral service? (Check one.)

1 [ ]   By the federal government
2 [ ]   By each state
3 [ ]   By the NFDA
4 [ ]   By the state FDA
5 [ ]   By individuals in funeral service
6 [ ]   By a combination of some of the above

If 6, which ones _____

Please explain: _____

_____

_____

88. How would you rate the National Funeral Directors
     Association? (Check one.)

1 [ ]   Very constructive
2 [ ]   Useful
3 [ ]   Average
4 [ ]   A useless formality
5 [ ]   An obstacle

89. When was the firm with which you're now associated
     founded? (Check one.)

1 [ ]   Before 1900
2 [ ]   1901 - 1929
3 [ ]   1930 - 1940
4 [ ]   1941 - 1945
5 [ ]   1946 - 1955
6 [ ]   1956 - 1960
7 [ ]   1961 - 1966

90. How large is the community that your firm serves?
     (Check one.)

     1 [] Under 2500
     2 [] 2500 - 25,000
     3 [] 25,000 - 100,000
     4 [] 100,000 - 1,000,000
     5 [] 1,000,000 or more

91. How many funerals has your firm conducted during the
     past twelve months? (Check one.)

     1 [] 1 - 50
     2 [] 51 - 75
     3 [] 76 - 100
     4 [] 101 - 125
     5 [] 126 - 200
     6 [] 201 - 500
     7 [] 501 - 1,000
     8 [] 1,000 or more

92-96. Approximately what percent of your business does each
        of the following religious groups represent to your
        firm each year? (Check one box in each column.)

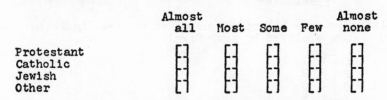

	Almost all	Most	Some	Few	Almost none
Protestant	[]	[]	[]	[]	[]
Catholic	[]	[]	[]	[]	[]
Jewish	[]	[]	[]	[]	[]
Other	[]	[]	[]	[]	[]

97-116. During the past five years, what have been the
         approximate proportions for each of the following
         funeral customs, as you have observed them commonly
         practiced at your funeral home? (Check one box for
         each custom.)

	Almost all	Most	Some	Few	Almost none
Place of death:					
Home	[]	[]	[]	[]	[]
Hospital	[]	[]	[]	[]	[]
Nursing home	[]	[]	[]	[]	[]
Final Disposition:					
Earth burial	[]	[]	[]	[]	[]
Cremation	[]	[]	[]	[]	[]
Entombment	[]	[]	[]	[]	[]

	Almost all	Most	Some	Few	Almost none
Preparation of the dead:					
Arterial embalming	[]	[]	[]	[]	[]
No embalming					
Visiting Hours:					
Public	[]	[]	[]	[]	[]
Private					
None					
Viewing of the Dead:					
Open casket	[]	[]	[]	[]	[]
Closed casket					
Funeral Services:					
With body	[]	[]	[]	[]	[]
Without body					
Graveside only					
None					
Place of Funeral:					
Funeral home	[]	[]	[]	[]	[]
Church					
Private home					

117. How many licensed funeral directors, including yourself, are employed by your firm? (Check one.)

1 [] 1
2 [] 2
3 [] 3
4 [] 4 - 7
5 [] 8 - 11
6 [] 12 - 20
7 [] 21 or more

118. Does your funeral home operate an ambulance service? (Check one.)

1 [] Yes
2 [] No

119. Does your funeral home operate a monument business? (Check one.)

1 [] Yes
2 [] No

120. On the whole, how did you find the questionnaire?
(Check one)

1 [ ] Interesting throughout
2 [ ] Mostly interesting
3 [ ] Half interesting, half dull
4 [ ] Dull throughout

We would appreciate any further comments that you might
have regarding funeral service or this questionnaire which
is relevant to our interests. You may use the remaining
space for such remarks, or, if necessary, an added sheet.

In order to test the statistical adequacy of our sample,
we need to know the name of each funeral director who
participates. The questionnaire will not be identified
with your name; all responses are completely confidential.

Your name: _____

Your address:_____

_____

Comments:

THANK YOU VERY MUCH FOR YOUR COOPERATION,
AND OUR BEST WISHES TO YOU!

Appendix 2:
Funeral Arranger Interview Schedule

DEPARTMENT OF SOCIOLOGY

NEW YORK UNIVERSITY

NEW YORK, NEW YORK 10003

INTERVIEW SCHEDULE

1

NAME OF DECEASED_____

Interview Number	1. Name of Arranger	Sex	Age	Marital Status	Relationship to Deceased
	Residence, State	County	City, Town or Village		Street and Number
	Years of School	Name(s) of School(s)			
	Others Present for Arrangements Name(s) - First, Middle, Last	Sex	Age	Marital Status	Relationship to Deceased

176

2. Did you expect (deceased's name) to die at this time?

( ) Definitely yes   ( ) Did not think so   ) Skip to
( ) Suspected yes   ( ) Definitely no   ) question 4
( ) Had no idea

Notes _____

_____

3. When did you first think (deceased's name) would die at this time?

_____

Was that because of this illness? _____

Notes_____

_____

2

4. What was the matter with (deceased's name)? _____

How long has (deceased's name) been ill? _____

How did you find out what was the matter?_____

Who told you? _____ When was that? _____

Just what did he (she) tell you? _____

Who is your doctor? _____

How long has he been your doctor? _____

How well do you know him? _____

Notes _____

_____

5. Did (deceased's name) know that he (she) was going to die?

( ) Yes: How did he (she) find out? _____

Who told him (her)? _____ When was that? _____

Just what did he (she) tell him (her)? _____

( ) No
( ) Don't know

Notes _____

_____

6. Have you notified a clergyman about (deceased's name) death yet?

( ) Yes: When was that? _____ What did you work out with
him, e.g., what did you tell him, did you ask him to notify anyone
else, etc.? _____

_____

( ) No, but we are about to.
( ) No: Do you want us to do so?
   ( ) Yes: What do you want us to tell him? _____

_____
   ( ) No

Religion of Deceased_____

Religion of Arranger_____

Notes_____

3

7. Have you ever had to make funeral arrangements for someone before?

   ( ) Yes: For whom? _____
      Was that person hospitalized before death?
      ( ) Yes: For how long? _____ (If long hospitalization,
        skip to question 4.)
      ( ) No
      ( ) Don't know
   ( ) No
   ( ) Don't know

   Notes (Try to discuss the arranger's attitude toward funerals) _____

_____

_____

8. Have you ever been through this sort of thing with someone dying before?

   ( ) Yes: With whom? _____
      Was that person hospitalized before death?
      ( ) Yes: For how long? _____ (If long hospitaliza-
        tion, skip to question 4.)
      ( ) No
      ( ) Don't know
   ( ) No
   ( ) Don't know

   Notes (Check out previous funeral director experiences in detail)_____

_____

_____

9. Have you ever had a person close to you hospitalized for a serious illness before?

   ( ) Yes: Whom was that? _____
         For how long? _____
   ( ) No
   ( ) Don't know
   ( ) Not applicable because of unexpected death.

   Notes _____

_____

4

10. Vital Statistics: Deceased

Name: First	Middle	Last	Sex	Race	Age

Birthdate: (Mo., Day, Yr)	Place of Birth: State	Citizen, what country

Marital Status	Name of spouse (If wife, maiden name)	Date married

Residence: State	County	City, Town, or Village	Street and number

Inside Limits? Yes/No	If less than ten years: did (deceased's name) live most of his (her) life in a
Length of stay	( ) very large city ( ) small town ( ) fairly large city ( ) farm ( ) small city ( ) don't know

Usual occupation	Kind of Business or Industry	Social Security #

Years of School	Name(s) of School(s)

Date of death: (Mo., Day, Yr.)	Place of Death: State	County	City, Town, or Village

Hospital, Institution - Street and Number	Length of Stay

Cause of Death

5

11. How did you actually find out that (deceased's name) had died?

_____

Who told you? _____ When was that? _____

Just what did he (she) tell you? _____

Notes _____

_____

12. Family of Deceased:

Father - Name: First, Middle, Last	Birthplace	Occupation
Mother- Name: First, Middle, Last	Birthplace	Occupation

13. Did (deceased's name) belong to any groups or organizations?

( ) Yes: Please list them.

_____

_____

_____

( ) No

Notes_____

_____

14. Would you like us to notify anyone (else)?

( ) Yes: Whom? _____
( ) No
( ) Don't know

Notes _____

_____

15. Have you told anyone (else) about (deceased's name) death yet?

( ) Yes: Whom? _____

    Have you asked them to notify anyone (else)?
    ( ) Yes: Whom? _____
    ( ) No
    ( ) Don't know
( ) No
( ) Don't know

Notes (Discuss the manner in which word spreads about general family
  news_____

_____

16. Surviving Relatives

Name	Address

17. Initiate conversations about the nature of the funeral directors' work
in the context of this and other funerals. Notes_____

_____

_____

_____

_____

Appendix 3:
"Findings": Professional Census

NATIONAL FUNERAL DIRECTORS ASSOCIATION
OF THE UNITED STATES, INC.

OFFICE OF VANDERLYN R. PINE, Ph.D.

P. O. BOX 450, NEW PALTZ, NEW YORK 12561

June 30, 1971

Dear NFDA Member:

This professional census is a part of a study being carried out by the National Funeral Directors Association. Its intention is to learn about the membership of NFDA and to provide a base for scientific sampling for future studies of the association.

Please answer all of the questions as exactly as you can. The answers will not be connected with your name, and will be used for an impersonal analysis only. PLEASE DO NOT OMIT ANY ITEMS.
You are encouraged to make comments at the end of the questionaire.
ALL INFORMATION WILL BE HELD IN THE STRICTEST CONFIDENCE.

Most questions may be answered by either putting a check in a box, like this: [ ], or by answers written out by you on a line like this:
Italian . Please do not pay any attention to the numbers on the leftt of each box, they are merely for tabulating purposes.

Thank you very much for your help.

Yours sincerely,

Vanderlyn R. Pine
NFDA Management Analyst

VRP:kd
Encl.

182

1-2 Where do you practice funeral directing?

State	Total 1970-71 Members	N	Questionnaires Returned % of Total
Alabama	107	63	58.9
Alaska	⁻	3	
Arizona	67	48	71.6
Arkansas	108	71	65.7
California	426	291	68.3
Colorado	89	65	73.0
Connecticut	229	128	55.9
Delaware	65	35	53.8
District of Columbia	15	10	66.7
Florida	232	132	56.9
Georgia	221	130	58.8
Hawaii	-	1	
Idaho	64	44	68.8
Illinois	641	405	63.2
Indiana	560	336	60.0
Iowa	364	235	64.6
Kansas	267	180	67.4
Kentucky	236	194	82.2
Louisiana	121	75	62.0
Maine	157	81	51.6
Maryland	179	96	53.6
Massachusetts	529	310	58.6
Michigan	616	388	63.0
Minnesota	348	242	69.5
Mississippi	115	75	65.2
Missouri	509	284	55.8
Montana	51	35	68.6
Nebraska	169	111	65.7
Nevada	19	10	52.6
New Hampshire	105	59	56.2
New Jersey	584	325	55.7
New Mexico	32	26	81.3
New York	992	613	61.8
North Carolina	255	139	61.8
North Dakota	70	44	62.9
Ohio	967	566	57.5
Oklahoma	216	142	65.7
Oregon	127	90	70.9
Pennsylvania	1529	802	52.5
Rhode Island	105	52	49.5
South Carolina	120	66	55.0
South Dakota	111	72	64.9
Tennessee	204	114	55.9
Texas	490	263	53.7
Utah	54	38	70.4
Vermont	73	35	47.9
Virginia	232	136	58.6
Washington	175	119	68.0
West Virginia	171	98	57.3
Wisconsin	484	334	69.0
Wyoming	25	16	64.0
	13,625	8,227	60.4 %

REGION AND STATE

Total Responses for Each Region

New England   665

    Connecticut   New Hampshire
    Maine   Rhode Island
    Massachusetts   Vermont

Middle Atlantic   1740

    New Jersey   Pennsylvania
    New York

South Atlantic   842

    Delaware   North Carolina
    District of Columbia   South Carolina
    Florida   Virginia
    Georgia   West Virginia
    Maryland

East North Central   2029

    Illinois   Ohio
    Indiana   Wisconsin
    Michigan

West North Central   1168

    Iowa   Nebraska
    Kansas   North Dakota
    Missouri   South Dakota
    Minnesota

East South Central   446

    Alabama   Mississippi
    Kentucky   Tennessee

West South Central   551

    Arkansas   Oklahoma
    Louisiana   Texas

Mountain   282

    Arizona   Neveda
    Colorado   New Mexico
    Idaho   Utah
    Montana   Wyoming

Pacific   504

    Alaska   Oregon
    California   Washington
    Hawaii

3. What is your age?   (Check one.)

    1 [ ] Under 25   5 [ ] 41-45
    2 [ ] 25-30   6 [ ] 46-55
    3 [I 31-35   7 [ ] 56-65
    4 [ ] 36-40   8 [ ] 66 or over

4. How many years have you personally been active in
    funeral service? (Check one.)

    1 [ ] 0-5 years   7 [ ] 31-35 years
    2 [ ] 6-10 years   8 [ ] 36-40 years
    3 [ ] 11-15 Years   9 [ ] 41-45 years
    4 [ ] 16-20 years   10 [ ] 46-50 years
    5 [ ] 21-25 years   11 [ ] 51-55 years
    6 [ ] 26-30 years   12 [ ] 56 or more years

	Mean Age	Mean Years Active
United States	43.5	27
New England	44.7	27
Middle Atlantic	43.5	26
South Atlantic	42.5	27
East North Atlantic	42.5	22.5
West North Central	43.0	26
East South Central	43.0	27
West South Central	42.5	27
Mountain	43.0	27
Pacific	43.5	26.5

5-6. Do you hold a professional funeral service license?
      (Check the appropriate box in each column.)

      A. Which license?   B. In how many states?

      0 [ ] I am not licensed   0 [ ] None
      1 [ ] Funeral director only   1 [ ] One
      2 [ ] Embalmer only   2 [ ] Two
      3 [ ] Single license for both   3 [ ] Three
      4 [ ] Hold both licenses   4 [ ] Four or more

	No License or Funeral Director or Embalmer Only	Single License	Hold Both Licenses
United States	8%	21%	71%
New England	7	19	74
Middle Atlantic	4	49	47
South Atlantic	16	9	75
East North Central	4	13	83
West North Central	8	16	76
East South Central	18	14	68
West South Central	17	4	79
Mountain	3	24	73
Pacific	13	7	80

	0-1	2	3 or more
United States	88%	10%	2%
New England	88	11	1
Middle Atlantic	96	3	1
South Atlantic	89	9	2
East North Central	92	7	1
West North Central	77	19	4
East South Central	86	12	2
West South Central	89	8	3
Mountain	72	23	5
Pacific	88	10	2

7. How much formal education have you had? (not including
   funeral service or mortuary science or embalming school)
   (Check the highest one only.)

   1 [ ] Some grade school
   2 [ ] Completed grade school
   3 [ ] Some high school
   4 [ ] Completed high school
   5 [ ] Some college
   6 [ ] Completed college
   7 [ ] Attended graduate school
   8 [ ] Completed graduate school
   9 [ ] Professional degree (specify, e.g., M.D., B.D.,
         etc._____)

	High School or Less	Some College	College	Graduate School or More
United States	34%	45%	17%	4%
New England	42	35	17	5
Middle Atlantic	45	38	14	3
South Atlantic	41	41	15	3
East North Central	32	49	16	3
West North Central	23	53	21	3
East South Central	42	41	14	3
West South Central	29	47	20	4
Mountain	22	57	17	4
Pacific	22	55	19	4

8. What kind of training-education did you receive for
    funeral service? (Check one.)

    0 [ ] None
    1 [ ] On the job traineeship (apprenticeship, etc.
    2 [ ] 6 month mortuary science or embalming course plus trainneeship
    3 [ ] 9 month mortuary science or embalming course plus
          traineeship
    4 [ ] 12 month mortuary science or embalming course plus
          traineeship
    5 [ ] College plus mortuary science schooling plus traineeship
          (How much college?_____)
    6 [ ] Other, please specify_____

	None, on the job training, etc.	6 or 9 month	12 mo.	College plus mortuary science
United States	12%	40%	22%	26%
New England	9	44	24	13
Middle Atlantic	11	39	35	10
South Atlantic	21	37	27	15
East North Central	7	36	23	34
West·North Central	10	38	7	45
East South Central	20	39	26	15
West South Central	22	48	14	16
Mountain	10	48	8	34
Pacific	14	43	10	33

9. When was the firm with which you're now associated
   founded?   (Check one.)

   1 [ ] Before 1900   5 [ ] 1930-1939
   2 [ ] 1900-1909   6 [ ] 1940-1949
   3 [ ] 1910-1919   7 [ ] 1950-1959
   4 [ ] 1920-1929   8 [ ] 1960-1969
                             9 [ ] 1970- (current date)

	Before 1900	1900-1919	1920-1939	1940-1970 (Current Date)	Mean Year When Founded
United States	22%	22%	31%	25%	1919
New England	31	21	27	21	1915
Middle Atlantic	26	18	27	29	1918
South Atlantic	21	19	27	33	1923
East North Central	25	21	32	22	1916
West North Central	22	26	32	20	1920
East South Central	18	20	34	28	1922
West South Central	13	19	41	27	1923
Mountain	10	31	33	26	1925
Pacific	16	27	31	26	1919

10.   How large is the community (market area) that your firm
      serves? (Check one.)

      1 [ ] under 2500
      2 [ ] 2500 but less than 25,000
      3 [ ] 25,000 but less than 100,000
      4 [ ] 100,000 but less than 1,000,000
      5 [ ] 1,000,000 or more

	Under 2,500	2,501- 25,000	25,000- 100,000	100,000 1 million or more	Mean Community Population
United States	10%	50%	24%	16%	11,250
New England	2	39	41	18	8,400
Middle Atlantic	7	48	28	17	16,000
South Atlantic	7	51	25	17	9,200
East North Central	14	50	20	16	11,500
West North Central	19	59	13	9	11,250
East South Central	5	60	25	10	11,500
West South Central	9	52	23	16	16,750
Mountain	5	57	23	15	13,750
Pacific	2	38	32	28	22,750

11. What is your position with your firm?   (Check one.)

    1 [ ] Owner
    2 [ ] Owner-manager
    3 [ ] Partner
    4 [ ] Manager
    5 [ ] Stockholder only
    6 [ ] Employee
    7 [ ] Other, please specify_____

	Owner	Owner Manager	Partner	All Other Categories
United States	34%	33%	15%	18%
New England	37	29	13	21
Middle Atlantic	39	35	12	14
South Atlantic	26	33	11	30
East North Central	41	28	17	14
West North Central	34	34	17	15
East South Central	26	30	22	22
West South Central	21	37	14	28
Mountain	24	45	13	18
Pacific	21	41	11	27

12. How many <u>other</u> funeral homes serve your community?
     (Check one.)

     0 [] None   4 [] 4
     1 [] 1   5 [] 5 -10
     2 [] 2   6 [] 11-20
     3 [] 3   7 [] 21-50
                                  8 [] 51 or more

	<u>0</u>	<u>1</u>	<u>2-3</u>	<u>4 or more</u>
United States	25%	22%	21%	32%
New England	14	12	20	54
Middle Atlantic	15	18	20	47
South Atlantic	21	24	28	27
East North Central	28	23	19	30
West North Central	40	28	17	15
East South Central	23	28	28	21
West South Central	35	22	23	20
Mountain	36	25	21	18
Pacific	23	22	26	19

13-15.   How many licensed personnel including yourself (if
         applicable) are employed full time by your firm?
         (Check appropriate number in each column.)

Funeral
Directors only   Embalmers only   Single license for both or
                                                    hold both licenses

0 [] None   0 [] None
1 [] 1   1 [] 1   0 [] None
2 [] 2   2 [] 2   1 [] 1
3 [] 3   3 [] 3   2 [] 2
4 [] 4 - 7   4 [] 4 - 7   3 [] 3
5 [] 8 - 11   5 [] 8 - 11   4 [] 4 - 7
6 [] 12- 20   6 [] 12 - 20   5 [] 8 - 11
7 [] 21 or more   7 [] 21 or more   6 [] 12 - 20
                                                    7 [] 21 or more

Table 8

	0	1	2-3	4 or more
United States	5%	55%	31%	9%
New England	5	60	29	6
Middle Atlantic	3	62	28	7
South Atlantic	7	47	32	14
East North Central	2	57	32	9
West North Central	6	59	31	4
East South Central	10	46	34	10
West South Central	6	40	36	18
Mountain	5	46	39	10
Pacific	9	57	26	10

16. How many non-licensed personnel including yourself (if
     applicable) are employed full time by your firm?
     (Check one.)

     0 [] 0   4 [] 4
     1 [] 1   5 [] 5 - 10
     2 [] 2   6 [] 11 -20
     3 [] 3   7 [] 21 or more

	0	1	2-3	4 or more
United States	36%	27%	25%	12%
New England	51	28	18	3
Middle Atlantic	50	25	18	7
South Atlantic	17	20	38	25
East North Central	40	30	22	8
West North Central	41	30	23	6
East South Central	14	21	40	24
West South Central	13	25	36	26
Mountain	29	29	28	14
Pacific	26	25	33	16

17-18. Approximately, how many complete adult funerals did your
        firm conduct during the past year? (Check one.)

	More than	but	Less than		More than	but	Less than
01 [ ]	1	-	25	13 [ ]	326	-	350
02 [ ]	26	-	50	14 [ ]	351	-	375
03 [ ]	51	-	75	15 [ ]	376	-	400
04 [ ]	76	-	100	16 [ ]	401	-	425
05 [ ]	101	-	125	17 [ ]	426	-	450
06 [ ]	126	-	150	18 [ ]	451	-	475
07 [ ]	151	-	175	19 [ ]	476	-	500
08 [ ]	176	-	200	20 [ ]	501	-	525
09 [ ]	201	-	225	21 [ ]	526	-	550
10 [ ]	226	-	250	22 [ ]	551	-	575
11 [ ]	251	-	300	23 [ ]	576	-	600
12 [I	301	-	325	24 [ ]	601	or	more

If over 601, please specify
how many_____.

	1-50	51-75	76-100	101-150	151-200	201-300	301-600	601+
United States	23%	21%	18%	17%	9%	7%	5%	2%
New England	18	27	18	19	10	7	1	0
Middle Atlantic	28	23	18	15	8	4	3	1
South Atlantic	14	15	21	20	10	8	8	4
East North Central	30	22	17	14	7	6	3	1
West North Central	30	24	19	14	5	4	3	1
East South Central	11	18	19	23	12	9	6	2
West South Central	14	17	14	20	13	11	7	4
Mountain	10	16	20	23	11	10	6	4
Pacific	5	8	15	21	18	16	10	7

	Mean Range Number of Funerals*	Median Number of Funerals**
United States	104 - 123	85
New England	82 - 89	83
Middle Atlantic	88 - 102	75
South Atlantic	136 - 158	100
East North Central	88 - 103	48
West North Central	81 - 93	46
East South Central	123 - 141	104
West South Central	140 - 165	115
Mountain	137 - 168	105
Pacific	190 - 221	152

*One way to measure the "typical size" funeral home is to utilize the arithmetic mean (the average) number of funerals conducted annually. The mean number of funerals conducted is the total number of funerals reported divided by the total number of firms reporting. The "Mean Range" shows the lower and upper limits between which the exact arithmetic mean falls. A range is reported because Question # 17-18 calls for respondents to indicate the approximate number of funerals their firm conducted during the past year by checking the appropriate interval (range) in which this number falls, i.e., "More Than   ?   but Less Than   ?   ."

**Because extremely large firms tend to "pull up" the mean, it is useful also to examine the median number of funerals conducted annually to measure the "typical size" funeral home. The median number of funerals conducted is the middle number of funerals reported when the firms reporting are ranked from low to high. In other words, the number of firms conducting less funerals than the median is equal to the number of firms conducting more funerals than the median. Thus, there are the same number of funeral homes which report conducting less funerals than the median as there are which report conducting more funerals than the median.

19-22. Does your firm operate or is it in any way associated
with any or all of the following? (Check one in each
column.)

Ambulance Service	Monument Business	Cemetery	Furniture Store	
1 [ ]	1 [ ]	1 [ ]	1 [ ]	Yes
2 [ ]	2 [ ]	2 [ ]	2 [ ]	No

	Ambulance Service		Monument Business		Cemetery		Furniture Store	
	Yes	No	Yes	No	Yes	No	Yes	No
United States	29%	71%	16%	84%	4%	96%	7%	93%
New England	9	91	5	95	2	98	2	98
Middle Atlantic	9	91	5	95	1	99	9	91
South Atlantic	32	68	17	83	6	64	3	97
East North Central	46	54	14	86	1	99	9	91
West North Central	29	71	26	74	2	98	18	82
East South Central	50	50	21	79	9	91	2	98
West South Central	48	52	34	66	9	91	5	95
Mountain	24	76	37	63	10	90	3	97
Pacific	10	90	22	78	12	88	1	99

23-36. Approximatley what proportion of your funerals does each
        of the following represent to your firm each year? (Check
        one box in each row.)

	Almost None	Few	Some	Most	Almost All

Religions Served:

	Almost None	Few	Some	Most	Almost All
Protestant	[ ]	[ ]	[ ]	[ ]	[ ]
Roman Catholic	[ ]	[ ]	[ ]	[ ]	[ ]
Jewish	[ ]	[ ]	[ ]	[ ]	[ ]
Other	[I	[ ]	[ ]	[ ]	[ ]

(Please specify_____)

Services Provided:

	Almost None	Few	Some	Most	Almost All
Public viewing with a public service and public committal service	[ ]	[ ]	[ ]	[ ]	[ ]
Public viewing, public service, private committal	[ ]	[ ]	[ ]	[ ]	[ ]
Private viewing, public fuenral	[ ]	[ ]	[ ]	[ ]	[ ]
No viewing, but a public service	[ ]	[ ]	[ ]	[ ]	[ ]
No viewing and a private funeral	[ ]	[ ]	[ ]	[ ]	[ ]
Graveside service only	[ ]	[ ]	[ ]	[ ]	[ ]
Immediate disposition with a memorial service.	[ ]	[ ]	[ ]	[ ]	[ ]
Immediate dispositon without any kind of service	[ ]	[ ]	[ ]	[ ]	[ ]
Other	[ ]	[ ]	[ ]	[ ]	[ ]

(Please describe_____)

PROTESTANT

	Almost None	Few	Some	Most	Almost All
United States	4%	4%	17%	37%	38%
New England	12	14	27	31	16
Middle Atlantic	7	7	26	35	25
South Atlantic	1	1	7	30	61
East North Central	3	3	18	39	37
West North Central	1	2	13	42	42
East South Central	1	0	4	22	73
West South Central	1	2	9	32	56
Mountain	8	4	17	52	19
Pacific	1	1	16	61	21

ROMAN CATHOLIC

	Almost None	Few	Some	Most	Almost All
United States	19%	24%	38%	13%	6%
New England	9	13	32	27	19
Middle Atlantic	12	19	37	21	11
South Atlantic	38	26	31	4	1
East North Central	17	26	42	11	4
West North Central	19	31	39	8	3
East South Central	47	28	22	2	1
West South Central	27	33	29	8	3
Mountain	13	24	54	6	3
Pacific	5	21	63	9	2

JEWISH

	Almost None	Few	Some	Most	Almost All
United States	89%	7%	2%	1%	1%
New England	89	8	1	1	1
Middle Atlantic	87	8	3	1	1
South Atlantic	83	11	4	1	1
East North Central	93	4	2	0	1
West North Central	95	4	1	0	0
East South Central	88	8	3	0	0
West South Central	87	9	3	1	1
Mountain	90	5	4	1	0
Pacific	86	9	4	0	1

OTHER

	Almost None	Few	Some	Most	Almost All
United States	88%	7%	3%	1%	1%
New England	86	10	3	0	1
Middle Atlantic	87	8	4	1	0
South Atlantic	90	6	3	1	0
East North Central	90	6	3	1	0
West North Central	91	7	2	0	0
East South Central	95	3	2	0	0
West South Central	92	5	2	1	0
Mountain	69	9	8	7	7
Pacific	70	16	8	6	0

THE TOTAL FUNERAL IN AMERICAN SOCIETY

The Percentage Of Respondents Which Report The Proportion
Of Their Funerals Which Include Public Viewing With A
Public Service And A Public Committal Service.

	Some or None	Most	Almost All
United States	2%	20%	78%
New England	3	29	68
Middle Atlantic	2	28	70
South Atlantic	1	19	80
East North Central	2	13	85
West North Central	1	11	88
East South Central	1	11	88
West South Central	2	13	85
Mountain	0	23	77
Pacific	5	52	43

THE LESS-THAN-TOTAL FUNERAL IN AMERICAN SOCIETY

	Almost None	Few	Some or Most
United States	78%	16%	6%
New England	75	16	9
Middle Atlantic	68	23	8
South Atlantic	85	11	4
East North Central	83	14	3
West North Central	88	9	2
East South Central	91	5	3
West South Central	88	9	2
Mountain	82	13	29
Pacific	36	35	29

THE LESS-THAN-TOTAL FUNERAL IN AMERICAN SOCIETY

The Percentage of Respondents Which Report The Proportion
Of Their Funerals Which Include Private Viewing With a Public Funeral.

	Almost None	Few	Some or Most
United States	74%	19%	7%
New England	62	27	11
Middle Atlantic	73	19	7
South Atlantic	68	23	9
East North Central	85	11	3
West North Central	83	13	4
East South Central	80	14	5
West South Central	65	24	10
Mountain	69	21	9
Pacific	46	39	14

THE LESS-THAN-TOTAL FUNERAL IN AMERICAN SOCIETY

The Percentage of Respondents Which Report The Proportion
Of Their Funerals Which Include Private Viewing With A Private Funeral.

	Almost None	Few	Some or Most
United States	82%	16%	2%
New England	63	32	5
Middle Atlantic	74	23	3
South Atlantic	86	12	2
East North Central	88	11	1
West North Central	93	t6	1
East South Central	94	5	1
West South Central	93	6	1
Mountain	79	19	2
Pacific	60	33	7

THE LESS-THAN-TOTAL FUNERAL IN AMERICAN SOCIETY

The Percentage of Respondents Which Report The Proportion
Of Their Funerals Which Include No Viewing But A Public Service.

	Almost None	Few	Some or Most
United States	71%	22%	7%
New England	63	25	11
Middle Atlantic	69	22	9
South Atlantic	62	28	1u
East North Central	82	15	3
West North Central	81	17	2
East South Central	77	19	4
West South Central	65	27	8
Mountain	58	34	8
Pacific	44	40	16

THE LESS-THAN-TOTAL FUNERAL IN AMERICAN SOCIETY

The Percentage of Respondents Which Report The Proportion
Of Their Funerals Which Include No Viewing And A Private Funeral.

	Almost None	Few	Some or Most
United States	88%	11%	1%
New England	76	21	3
Middle Atlantic	81	17	2
South Atlantic	89	9	2
East North Central	93	7	0
West North Central	96	3	1
East South Central	97	2	1
West South Central	96	3	1
Moutntain	87	13	0
Pacific	70	24	6

THE LESS-THAN-TOTAL FUNERAL IN AMERICAN SOCIETY

The Percentage Of Respondents Which Report The Proportion
Of Their Funerals Which Include A Graveside Service Only.

	Almost None	Few	Some or Most
United States	69%	26%	5%
New England	83	16	1
Middle Atlantic	85	13	2
South Atlantic	44	44	12
East North Central	78	21	1
West North Central	70	27	3
East South Central	60	34	6
West South Central	57	35	8
Mountain	44	47	9
Pacific	32	51	17

THE LESS THAN TOTAL FUNERAL IN AMERICAN SOCIETY

The Percentage Of Respondents Which Report The Proportion
Of Their Funerals Which Involve Immediate Dispostion
With A Memorial Service.

	Almost None	Few	Some or Most
United States	89%	9%	2%
New England	86	12	2
Middle Atlantic	88	10	2
South Atlantic	89	10	1
East North Central	93	6	1
West North Central	96	3	1
East South Central	97	3	0
West South Central	97	2	1
Mountain	84	14	2
Pacific	60	29	11

THE LESS-THAN-TOTAL FUNERAL IN AMERICAN SOCIETY

The Percentage Of Respondents Which Report The Proportion
Of Their Funerals Which Include Immediate Disposition
Without Any Service.

	Almost None	Few	Some or Most
United States	93%	5%	2%
New England	94	5	1
Middle Atlantic	93	6	1
South Atlantic	92	6	2
East North Central	97	3	0
West North Central	98	2	0
East South Central	99	1	0
West South Central	99	1	0
Mountain	92	7	1
Pacific	60	29	11

THE LESS-THAN-TOTAL FUNERAL IN AMERICAN SOCIETY

The Percentage Of Respondents Which REport The Proportion
Of Their Funerals Which Involve Some Other
Kind Of Service

	Almost None	Few	Some or More
United States	99%	1%	0%
New England	99	1	0
Middle Atlantic	98	1	1
South Atlantic	98	1	1
East North Central	100	0	0
West North Central	99	1	0
East South Central	100	0	0
West South Central	99	0	1
Mountain	98	1	1
Pacific	99	0	1

37. How many funeral homes does your firm operate? (Check one.)

```
1 [] One              5 [] Five
2 [] Two              6 [] Six
3 [] Three            7 [] Seven
4 [] Four             8 [] Eight or More
```

	1	2-3	4 or more
United States	80%	18%	2%
New England	79	20	1
Middle Atlantic	88	11	1
South Atlantic	82	16	2
East North Central	81	16	3
West North Central	72	25	3
East South Central	78	18	4
West South Central	72	21	7
Mountain	76	23	1
Pacific	80	18	2

38. Does your funeral home primarily serve a specific
    nationality, e.g., Irish. Polish, Italian, etc?

    1 [] Yes (Please write in which one(s).)_____
    _____

    2 [] No_____

	Yes	No
United States	13%	87%
New England	34	66
Middle Atlantic	18	82
South Atlantic	5	95
East North Central	13	87
West North Central	14	86
East South Central	4	96
West South Central	7	93
Mountain	4	96
Pacific	7	93

39. Which of the following statements most accurately des-
     cribes your firm's motor equipment?   (Check one.)

     1 [ ] We own all our motor equipment.
     2 [ ] We own part and rent part of our motor equipment.
     3 [ ] We rent all of our motor equipment except our
           passenger car(s).
     4 [ ] We rent all our motor equipment.
     5 [ ] We pool our motor equipment with other funeral directors.
     6 [ ] Other, please describe_____.

	Own All	Rent All	Own Part and Rent Part	Pool and Others
United States	63%	10%	25%	2%
New England	33	24	40	3
Middle Atlantic	42	17	38	3
South Atlantic	81	2	16	1
East North Central	64	11	23	2
West North Central	80	5	14	1
East South Central	83	3	12	2
West South Central	75	.3	19	3
Mountain	77	3	18	2
Pacific	65	7	26	2

40. What is the form of ownership of your firm? (Check one.)

    1 [ ] Individual Proprietorship
    2 [ ] Partnership
    3 [ ] Private Corporation
         How long incorporated?_____
    4 [ ] Public Corporation
         How long a public corporation?_____

	Individual Proprietorship	Partnership	Private Corporation	Public Corporation
United States	46%	15%	38%	1%
New England	38	8	54	0
Middle Atlantic	61	12	26	1
South Atlantic	34	16	48	2
East North Central	51	16	32	1
West North Central	50	15	34	1
East South Central	32	20	47	1
West South Central	31	19	48	2
Mountain	33	11	19	2
Pacific	30	15	53	2

41. How would you describe the organization of your firm?
    (Check one.)

    1 [ ] Tasks are done or supervised personally by one person.
    2 [ ] Tasks are shared or supervised equally by a few
          people.
    3 [ ] Tasks are done by a few separate specialists re-
          sponsible to a manager.
    4 [ ] Tasks are done by many separate specialists re-
          sponsible to a manager.

Tasks Done By

	One Person	A Few People	Separate Specialists
United States	45%	47%	8%
New England	47	47	6
Middle Atlantic	55	38	7
South Atlantic	32	54	14
East North Central	46	48	6
West North Central	48	48	4
East South Central	34	52	14
West South Central	34	47	19
Mountain	40	46	14
Pacific	36	49	15

42. What method of pricing does your firm use? (Check one.)

    1 [ ] Single unit (Price of service includes casket)
    2 [ ] Bi-unit (Services and facilities one figure-casket a
          separate item)
    3 [ ] Multi-unit (Functional, semi-itemized)
    4 [ ] Itemized
    5 [ ] Other, please specify_____

	Single Unit	Bi-Unit	Multi Unit	Itemized	Other
United States	64%	10%	13%	11%	2%
New England	47	18	23	10	2
Middle Atlantic	42	7	14	35	2
South Atlantic	70	8	16	6	1
East North Central	79	5	10	4	2
West North Central	79	8	10	2	1
East South Central	72	4	12	10	2
West South Central	81	8	8	1	2
Mountain	45	33	15	5	2
Pacific	43	34	17	3	3

43. Does your firm maintain its own selection room? (Check one.)

    1 [ ] Yes   2 [ ] No

	Yes	No
United States	91%	9%
New England	87	13
Middle Atlantic	77	23
South Atlantic	97	3
East North Central	91	9
West North Central	98	2
East South Central	97	3
West South Central	99	1
Mountain	99	1
Pacific	99	1

Bibliography

Abt, L.E. and S.L. Weisman, (eds.). *Acting Out: Theoretical and Clinical Aspects*. New York: Grune and Stratton, 1965.

American Blue Book of Funeral Directors. New York: Boylston Publications, 1972.

Back, Kurt and Hans W. Baade. "The Social Meaning of Death and the Law," in John C. McKinney and Frank T. DeVyver, (eds.). *Aging and Social Policy*. New York: Irvington Publishers, 1966, pp. 302-29.

Becker, Howard S. *Outsiders, Studies in the Sociology of Deviance*. New York: The Free Press, 1963.

———. "Problems of Inference and Proof in Participant Observation." *American Sociological Review*, 23 (1958), pp. 656-66.

Berger, Peter L. and Thomas Luckmann. *The Social Construction of Reality*. Garden City, New York: Doubleday and Company, Inc., Anchor Books, 1967.

Blau, Peter M. *The Dynamics of Bureaucracy*. Chicago: The University of Chicago Press, 1955.

Blau, Peter M. and W. Richard Scott. *Formal Organizations: A Comparative Approach*. San Francisco: Chandler Publishing Company, 1962.

Blauner, Robert. "Death and Social Structure." *Psychiatry*, 29 (November, 1966), pp. 378-94.

Bowman, LeRoy. *The American Funeral*. Washington, D.C.: Public Affairs Press, 1959.

Brim, Orville, G., Jr., Howard E. Freeman, Sol Levine, and Norman A. Scotch, (eds.). *The Dying Patient*. New York: Russell Sage Foundation, 1970.

Dahl, Robert A., *Who Governs?* New Haven: Yale University Press, 1961.

Durkheim, Emile. *Suicide*. New York: The Free Press, 1966.

Farberow, Norman L. (ed.). *Taboo Topics*. New York: Atherton Press, 1966.

Faunce, William A. and Robert Fulton. "The Sociology of Death: A Neglected Area of Research," *Social Forces*, **36** (March, 1958), pp. 205-209.

Feifel, Herman (ed.). *The Meaning of Death*. New York: McGraw-Hill, 1959.

Freidson, Eliot. "Client Control and Medical Practice." *American Journal of Sociology*, LXV (January, 1960), pp. 374-82.

———. *Profession of Medicine*. New York: Dodd, Mead and Co., 1970.

Firth, Raymond. *Elements of Social Organization*. Boston: Beacon Press, 1964.

Fox, Renee. *Experiment Perilous*. Glencoe, Ill.: The Free Press, 1959.

Fulton, Robert. "The Clergyman and the Funeral Director: A Study in Role Conflict." *Social Forces*, **39** (May, 1961), pp. 317-23.

———. "Death and the Self." *Journal of Religion and Health*, 3 (July 1964), pp. 359-68.

———. *The Sacred and the Secular: Attitudes of the American Public Toward Death*. Milwaukee: Bulfin Printing, 1963.

———. *Death and Identity*. New York: John Wiley & Sons, Inc., 1965.

———. *A Compilation of Studies of Attitudes Toward Death, Funerals, Funeral Directors*. Privately printed, 1967 and 1971.

Fulton, Robert and Julie Fulton. "A Psychosocial Aspect of Terminal Care: Anticipatory Grief," *Omega*, **2** (May, 1971), pp. 91-100.

Glaser, Barney G. and Anselm L. Strauss. *Awareness of Dying*. Chicago: Aldine Publishing Co., 1965.

Gerth, H.H. and C. Wright Mills. *From Max Weber: Essays in Sociology*. New York: Oxford University Press, 1946.

Goffman, Erving. *Asylums*. Garden City, New York: Doubleday & Co., Anchor Books, 1961.

———. *The Presentation of Self in Everyday Life*. Garden City, New York: Doubleday & Co., Anchor Books, 1959.

Gold, Raymond. "Roles in Sociological Field Observations." *Social Forces*, **36** (1958), pp. 217-23.

Goody, Jack. *Death, Property and the Ancestors*. Stanford: Stanford University Press, 1962.

Gorer, Geoffrey. *Death, Grief, and Mourning*. New York: Doubleday, Inc., 1965.

Gouldner, Alvin W. *Patterns of Industrial Bureaucracy*. Glencoe, Ill.: The Free Press, 1954.

Greenwood, Ernest. "The Elements of Professionalization," in Howard M. Vollman and Donald L. Mills, (eds.), *Professionalization*. Englewood Cliffs, N.J.: Prentice-Hall, 1966, pp. 9-19.

Grollman, Earl A. *Concerning Death: A Practical Guide for the Living*. Boston: Beacon Press, 1974.

Haberstein, Robert W. and William M. Lamers. *The History of American Funeral Directing*. Milwaukee: Bulfin Printers, 1955.

———. *Funeral Customs the World Over*. Milwaukee: Bulfin Printers, 1960.

Hammond, Phillip E. (ed.). *Sociologists At Work*. New York: Basic Books, Inc., 1964.

Harmer, Ruth M. *The High Cost of Dying*. New York: Crowell-Collier, 1963.

Henderson, A.M. and Talcott Parsons. *Max Weber: The Theory of Social and*

Economic Organization. New York: The Free Press, 1964.

Hendin, David. *Death as a Fact of Life.* New York: W.W. Norton & Company, Inc., 1973.

Hertz, Robert. *Death and the Right Hand.* Glencoe, Ill.: The Free Press, 1960.

Hall, Richard H. "Professionalization and Bureaucratization in Large Professional Organization." *American Sociological Review,* **74** (1968), pp. 92-104.

Holzner, Burkart. *Reality Construction in Society.* Cambridge, Mass.: Schenkman Publishing Co., Inc., 1968.

Hughes, Everett C. *Men and Their Work.* Glencoe, Ill.: The Free Press, 1958.

————. *The Sociological Eye: Book 2.* Chicago: Aldine-Atherton, 1971.

Irion, Paul E. *The Funeral and the Mourners.* New York: Abingdon Press, 1954.

Jackson, Edgar N. *Understanding Grief.* New York: Abingdon Press, 1957.

Jennings, George. "Funeral Service is Making Rapid Progress in Great Britain." *The American Funeral Director,* **87,** No. 2 (1964), p. 40.

Kastenbaum, Robert and Ruth Aisenberg. *The Psychology of Death.* New York: Springer Publishing Company, Inc., 1972.

Kephart, William M. "Status After Death." *American Sociological Review,* **15** (October, 1950), pp. 635-43.

Kubler-Ross, Elisabeth, M.D. *On Death and Dying.* London: The Macmillan Company, 1969.

Lifton, Robert Jay. *Home from the War.* New York: Simon & Schuster, 1973.

Malinowski, Bronislaw. *Magic, Science and Religion.* Garden City, New York: Doubleday and Company, Anchor Books, 1948.

Manning, John. "Soviet Funeral Service." *The American Funeral Director,* **89,** No. 1 (1966), p. 30.

Mead, Goerge H. *Mind, Self and Society from the Standpoint of a Social Behaviorist.* Chicago: University of Chicago Press, 1934.

Merton, Robert K. *Social Theory and Social Structure.* New York: The Free Press, 1949.

McCall, George J. and J.L. Simmons, (eds.). *Issues in Participant Observation: A Text and Reader.* Reading, Mass.: Addison-Wesley Publishing Co., 1969.

Miller, George A. "Professionals in Bureaucracy: Alienation Among Industrial Scientists and Engineers." *American Sociological Review,* **32** (October, 1967), pp. 755-68.

Mitford, Jessica. *The American Way of Death.* New York: Simon & Schuster, 1963.

Morgan, Ernest. *A Manual of Death Education and Simple Burial.* Burnsville, N.C.: The Celo Press, 1973.

Mori, Koji. "The Increased Cost of Dying in Japan." *The American Funeral Director,* **87,** No. 9 (1964), pp. 35 and 36.

National Funeral Directors Association. *1972-1973 Directory.* Milwaukee: National Funeral Directors Association, 1972.

Park, Robert E. "Human Migration and the Marginal Man." *American Journal of Sociology,* **33** (May, 1928), pp. 881-93.

Parkes, Colin Murray. *Bereavement: Studies of Grief in Adult Life.* New York: International Universities Press, Inc., 1972.

Parsons, Talcott. *Essays in Sociological Theory Pure and Applied.* Glencoe, Ill.: The Free Press, 1949.

———. "Death in American Society—A Brief Working Paper." *The American Behavioral Scientist*, 6 (May, 1963), pp. 61-65.

———. *The Social System*. New York: The Free Press, 1951.

Pine, Vanderlyn R. "The Effectiveness of Embalming on Microbes Isolated from the Mouth." *The Director*, 38 (January, 1968a), pp. 12-24.

———. "Comparative Studies of the Anti-Microbial Effects of Selected Antibiotics Against Micro-organisms of Embalmed and Unembalmed Human Bodies." *The Director*, 38 (September 1968b), pp. 15-17.

———. "Comparative Funeral Practices." *Practical Anthropology*, (March-April, 1969a), pp. 49-62.

———. "The Sociology of Death." *The American Funeral Director*, 92 (June, 1969b), pp. 29-30, 44.

———. "The Multi-Professional Dimensions of a Funeral Service Practice." Given at the annual meeting of the National Funeral Directors Association, Portland, Oregon, Octorber 9, 1969c.

———. "Grief Work and Dirty Work: The Aftermath of an Aircrash." Given at the annual meeting of the Eastern Sociological Society, New York, New York, April 18, 1970, and in *Omega*, 5 (Winter, 1974).

———. *Findings of the Professional Census*. Milwaukee: National Funeral Directors Association, 1971.

———. "Social Organization and Death." *Omega*, 3 (February, 1972a), pp. 149-53.

———. "Dying, Death, and Social Behavior," Position paper given at the 5th Symposium of the *Foundation of Thanatology on Anticipatory Grief*, Columbia University, New York, New York, April 14, 1972b, and in Bernard Schoenberg, *et al.*, *Anticipatory Grief*. New York: Columbia University Press, 1974, pp. 31-47.

———. "Patterns of Information Dissemination in the Dynamics of Death-Related Communication." Position paper given at the 6th Symposium of the *Foundation of Thanatology on Commuications and Thanatology*, Columbia University, New York, New York, November 17-18, 1972c.

———. *Facts and Figures of the United States: 1972 Edition*. Milwaukee: National Funeral Directors association, 1972d.

———. "Institutionalized Communication About Dying and Death." *Journal of Thanatology*, (forthcoming 1973).

Pine, Vanderlyn R. and Derek Phillips. "The Cost of Dying: A Sociological Analysis of Funeral Expenditure." *Social Problems*, (Winter 1970), pp. 405-17.

Raether, Howard C. *Successful Funeral Service Practice*. Englewood Cliffs, N.J.: Prentice-Hall, Inc., 1971.

Rose, Gordon W., and Alice Bicknell, "The In Vitro Effect of Certain Antibiotics on Cultures Isolated From the Unembalmed Body." Antibiotics and Chemotherapy, 3 (September, 1953), pp. 896-98.

Salomone, Jerome J., Ph. D. "The Status of Funerals and Funeral Directors." *The American Funeral Director*, XC (October, 1967), pp. 69-74.

Selznick, Philip. *TVA and the Grass Roots*. New York: Harper and Row, Publishers, Harper Torchbooks, 1966.

Simmons, Roberta G., Julie Fulton and Robert Fulton. "The Prospective Organ Transplant Donor: Problems and Prospects of Medical Innovation." *Omega*, **3** (November, 1972), pp. 319-39.

Simpson, R.L. and J. Simpson. "The Psychiatric Attendant: Development of an Occupational Self-Image in a Low-Status Occupation." *American Sociological Review*, **24** (1959), pp. 389-92.

Smigel, Erwin, O. *The Wall Street Lawyer*. Bloomington: Indiana University Press, 1969.

Stonequist, Everett V. "The Problem of the Marginal Man." *American Journal of Sociology*, **41** (July, 1935), pp. 1-12.

Sudnow, David. *Passing On*. Englewood Cliffs, N.J.: Prentice-Hall, Inc., 1967.

Sullivan, Walter. "The Neanderthal Man Liked Flowers." *New York Times* (June 13, 1968), pp. 1 and 43.

van Gennep, Arnold. *The Rites of Passage*. Chicago: University of Chicago Press, Phoenix Books, 1960.

Vollmer, Howard M. and Donald L. Mills, (eds.). *Professionalization*. Englewood Cliffs, N.J.: Prentice-Hall, Inc., 1966.

Warner, W. Lloyd. *The Living and the Dead*. New Haven: Yale University Press, 1959.

Webb, Eugene J., Donald T. Campbell, Richard D. Schwartz, and Lee Sechrest. *Unobtrusive Measures: Nonreactive Research in the Social Sciences*. Chicago: Rand McNally & Company, 1966.

Weisman, Avery D. *On Dying and Denying: A Psychiatric Study of Terminality*. New York: Behavioral Publications, Inc., 1972.

Index